BEST PICK

A Journey through Film History and the Academy Awards

John Dorney, Jessica Regan, and Tom Salinsky

ROWMAN & LITTLEFIELD
Lanham • Boulder • New York • London

Published by Rowman & Littlefield
An imprint of The Rowman & Littlefield Publishing Group, Inc.
4501 Forbes Boulevard, Suite 200, Lanham, Maryland 20706
www.rowman.com

86-90 Paul Street, London EC2A 4NE, United Kingdom

British Library Cataloguing in Publication Information Available

Library of Congress Cataloging-in-Publication Data Available

Names: Dorney, John, 1976– author. | Regan, Jessica, 1982– author. | Salinsky, Tom, author.
Title: Best pick : a journey through film history and the Academy Awards / John Dorney, Jessica Regan, Tom Salinsky.
Description: Lanham : Rowman & Littlefield, [2022] | Includes index. | Summary: "A fascinating history of motion pictures through the lens of the Academy Awards, Best Pick provides a decade-by-decade look at the Oscars by examining the Best Picture winners, highest-grossing films, and biggest misses alongside a discussion of the trends, innovations, and stories that defined the decade"—Provided by publisher.
Identifiers: LCCN 2021033738 (print) | LCCN 2021033739 (ebook) | ISBN 9781538163108 (cloth) | ISBN 9781538163115 (epub)
Subjects: LCSH: Academy Awards (Motion pictures)—History. | Motion pictures—Awards— United States—History.
Classification: LCC PN1993.92 .D67 2022 (print) | LCC PN1993.92 (ebook) | DDC 791.43079— dc23
LC record available at https://lccn.loc.gov/2021033738
LC ebook record available at https://lccn.loc.gov/2021033739

John Dorney: *For Mum and Dad for encouraging a love of story and letting me see all the films I shouldn't have.*

Jessica Regan: *For my parents, Maria and Seán, who gave me everything. You are in every line I write. And for the late Kevin Boyle, brother of Fiona, who gave his little sister and her pals access to his VHS library of wonders.*
We thank you, and we miss you.

Tom Salinsky: *For all the people who have introduced me to films I would otherwise never have watched: my parents, Deborah Frances-White, Alex MacLaren, Jamie de Courcey, Robert Khan, and Jason Smith, among many others. And Joe Adamson, Alexander Walker, and David Thomson—only three out of dozens—who showed me that writing about films can be as much of an art as creating them.*

CONTENTS

FOREWORD

Helen O'Hara

The Academy Awards often (some would say usually) get the Best Picture winner wrong. Anyone who's ever seen *Driving Miss Daisy* can tell you that. But how and why they get it wrong has changed over time, and one of the things this book does brilliantly is to explain that. Jessica, John, and Tom have boiled down the years of research that went into their expert podcast and produced an entertaining guide to the whole awards picture, and the social and cinematic context that birthed it.

This is therefore a fascinating snapshot of what Hollywood considers "good" filmmaking. In the early days, with a very small voting body drawn solely from among the most powerful people in the industry, it clearly reflected the values of Tinseltown itself. Now, with a more diverse votership in terms of age, race, sex, and nationality, it shows an awards body that is trying to become more pluralistic and more representative of filmmaking as a whole—albeit still, largely, American Anglophone filmmaking.

Unless you're Martin Scorsese and have already seen everything, you're also going to come out of this with a list of films to seek out so you can catch up with Tom, Jessica, and John. Thanks to them you'll know which Oscar winners to prioritise and which you can maybe skip entirely. They've done the hard work of assessing the worthy winners and embarrassing misses so you don't have to sit through all the Oscar winning films of the 1980s, and for that alone these heroes deserve our undying respect. They even watched *Crash*. On purpose.

The sheer depth of knowledge, passion and research that the Best Pick team have means that you're going to come out the other side armed with a better understanding of film history—and, not for nothing, the knowledge to win any pub quiz going.

I was delighted to guest on the podcast (1942, *Mrs Miniver*) not just because it was a pleasure to talk to the team but because I learned so much from their analysis over the length of the show's run. The Oscars may get it wrong, but this trio is generally right on the money. How do we put them in charge of the little gold guys?

Helen O'Hara is a prominent film critic and editor at large at *Empire Magazine*, Sky Oscars commentator and author of *Women vs Hollywood: The Fall and Rise of Women in Film*.

INTRODUCTION

What do the Oscars mean to you? In the 1930s and 1940s, the ceremony itself was a banquet dinner in a hotel. In the 1950s, it became a lavish televised production. By the 1960s, it was starting to look dated. And yet, that doesn't even get us halfway through its life. Today, many people see it as an irrelevance, a fossil of a bygone age, mired in prejudice, unable to find a tone that connects with a younger audience, and *always* picking the wrong movies. Respectfully, we disagree.

Around the world, especially the English-speaking world, movies mean Hollywood, and Hollywood means Oscars. If you love film, then the Oscars still matter. Winning an Oscar can transform a career. And the upside of the Oscars reserving its highest awards for films that never even dent the top twenty at the box office is that there are other rewards apart from the purely financial, which help filmmakers like Barry Jenkins, Ava DuVernay, Alfonso Cuarón, Yorgos Lanthimos, Greta Gerwig, and Steve McQueen get their films made. Even if that same Academy of Motion Picture Arts and Sciences sometimes gives its top prize to *Green Book*.

So, we don't pretend that the ninety-two Best Picture winners are the ninety-two best films ever made. In fact, we only sometimes find that the Academy has picked what we think is the best film of the year. But that list of ninety-two films is a finite list that permits no arguments. And that's what inspired us.

The three of us had always been keen Oscar watchers. For a number of consecutive Marches, we'd gathered around the television together near midnight with bowls of popcorn and glasses of wine (followed several hours later by mugs of coffee) to watch lavish production numbers, awkward comedy bits, parades of anonymous technicians winning for sound mixing or visual effects, stalwart campaigners denied their prize yet again, first-timers reduced to tears, people unthanked, names mispronounced, and finally—at the end of the night—a new film added to this very specific list.

Gradually, the idea took hold. Ninety-two Best Picture winners. Ninety-two podcast episodes. For each instalment, we researched what happened at that year's awards, looked more widely at the world of film, dug into the making of the winner—and sometimes took detours into other films, filmmakers, trends, and genres. Then we watched the film together and gave our verdict—did the Academy (in our opinion) get it right?

It's been a labor of love. And now, it's done. The project is complete. But we're proud to have amassed a following, and so we're carrying on, interviewing more film fans, recording our own audio commentaries, comparing different versions of the same material, and digging out more stories from the world of movies.

When we recorded the podcast, to keep things interesting, we put all ninety-two Best Picture winners in a hat and drew them out in a random order. For this book, we've taken all that research and rearranged and rewritten it in a more streamlined form. Rather than go movie-by-movie in a random order, we go chronologically through the decades, from the 1920s (albeit there weren't many Oscars in those years) to the 2010s.

Each chapter starts with a reminder of what won Best Picture and what was top of the North American (or worldwide) box office. Then Tom Salinsky talks you through the Oscars. Who was in the running and then fell by the wayside? Whose over-the-top publicity campaign nauseated the voters? Which film was eliminated because of an arcane change in the rules? Whose acceptance speech created waves in the days to come?

Following that, Jessica Regan surveys the decade in film. What new innovations were created to solve particular filmmaking problems? What political forces hemmed in creative minds? What was seen for the first time? And the last?

And then John Dorney picks the film whose backstory is most typical, most extraordinary, most unlikely, or just most interesting, before we give our views in detail about, first, the Best Picture that for us represents the very best that the decade's winners have to offer, and then the one that comes, as some film inevitably must, tenth out of ten. In some cases, this isn't a particularly bad film, but as we made our way through Best Picture history, there were some real surprises, and not all of them were pleasant.

And that brings us to what in many ways was the thought that inspired the whole project—did the Academy get it right? Each of us has our say on every winner from that decade, either endorsing the choice made by the Oscar voters or giving you our own pick instead. You probably won't agree with all our choices. In fact, you certainly won't, as we don't always agree with each other. But maybe there will be some films we single out that you haven't seen. And what a glorious thing that is. To settle down and watch a film—maybe a film made before even your parents were born—for the very first time.

We've had a wonderful time making this podcast and a splendid time writing this book. We hope when we offer criticism that we do so fairly and cogently, and above all, we hope our love of cinema shines through these pages.

A PEDANTIC NOTE ABOUT YEARS

Most Academy Awards shows take place in the spring following the eligibility year. This creates an ambiguity, because the phrase *1975 Oscars* could refer to the forty-seventh ceremony, which took place in the spring of 1975, or the forty-eighth ceremony, which celebrated films made in 1975. Throughout this book, we consistently use the second formulation, and—when talking about the Oscars—the shorthand *in 1975* means "at the forty-eighth Academy Awards, which celebrated films made in 1975." For ceremonies whose eligibility period includes two calendar years, we've used the latter of the two years (because using the earlier of the two years would mean there wasn't a 1933 Oscars).

I

THE 1920s

THE OSCARS IN THE 1920s

It all began because Louis B. Mayer wanted to build a beach house.

The year was 1926. Moviemaking had already become a mature industry—the fourth-largest in the United States. Hollywood made around 500 films a year and showed them to a weekly audience of around 100 million people in 23,000 cinemas. And although it had only been around since 1924, MGM was already the biggest and most successful studio of them all. In their first full year, they released *Ben-Hur* starring Ramon Novarro. This film cost an incredible $4 million, but it made back more than $10 million, and MGM boss Louis B. Mayer became one of the highest paid executives in the country. He had a wife and teenaged daughters, and he wanted a house on the beach in Santa Monica.

Because he had any number of architects, carpenters, painters, and set designers already on staff, he asked MGM's head of design, Cedric Gibbons, to draw up the plans and his production manager to come up with a schedule and an estimate. But when these were delivered, Mayer

	Best Picture	Biggest Earner
1927/1928	Wings	The Jazz Singer (1927)
		The Singing Fool (1928)
1928/1929	The Broadway Melody	The Broadway Melody (1929)
1929/1930	All Quiet on the Western Front	Whoopee! (1930)

got a nasty shock. It was actually going to be far quicker and cheaper to hire outside labor. This was all thanks to something called the Studio Basic Agreement, a contract made between nine film companies and five trade unions. It was signed following almost ten years of unrest, and it set minimum rates of pay for the first time. Now installed in his palatial beach house, Mayer started wondering what on earth would happen if writers, directors, and—God help us all—actors started asking for similar protection. Something had to be done.

On New Year's Day 1927, Mayer invited three close colleagues to lunch to discuss the matter. His guests were actor Conrad Nagel, director Fred Niall, and producer Fred Beeston, and they were all sympathetic to Mayer's plight. What if, Mayer proposed, Hollywood's talent already had a body that could look after their best interests? The other three started chipping in with their own ideas. They could form an elite filmmaking club that would be open only to the best of the best. They could have different branches for different professions. Maybe an annual dinner? Awards were never mentioned.

Mayer loved the idea, and less than two weeks later, he was holding a formal dinner at the Ambassador Hotel, where thirty-six founder members of the International Academy of Motion Picture Arts and Sciences listened as the MGM boss unveiled his plans. He got an enthusiastic reception, and before long, two MGM lawyers were hard at work creating a charter for the new body. Awards were never mentioned.

A launch banquet for three hundred people was held on 11 May 1927, hosted by newly installed Academy president Douglas Fairbanks Sr. At its close, the Academy's membership had increased by 230 people—all of whom had paid the one-hundred-dollar joining fee. A few weeks later, the new organization (now shorn of the *International* part of its name) published a statement of aims. Among these, for the first time, there was a brief reference to awards of merit for distinctive achievements, but nothing was done at this stage to bring them into existence.

Before very long, the Academy was called upon to referee a dispute between studios and talent groups. Maybe not surprisingly for a body created by a producer and half of whose founder members were producers, it sided with the studios, proposing an across-the-board pay cut that would have been near meaningless for top executives but crippling for bit-part players. The debacle hurt the newly formed Academy's hoped-for reputation as an impartial mediating body. Mayer had to do something to keep his new organization relevant, so thoughts turned back to those awards of merit. In theory, a committee to establish these had been set up in May 1927, but it wasn't until June 1928 that this group had anything to show for itself.

Gradually, the structure of the awards began to emerge. Members would vote for their preferred people or films in different categories. Counting the votes would generate short lists of nominees. The winners would then be decided by a Central Board of Judges—one from each of the Academy's five branches—actors, writers, producers, directors, and technicians. Cedric Gibbons had sketched out a possible look for the awards during one of those early committee meetings. The design was refined by his assistant, Frederic Hope, who added the five slots in the reel of film that forms the base of the statuette—one for each of the Academy's branches. Modern awards have twelve slots. The California Bronze Foundry won the job of producing them. Nominees (or "Honorable Mentions" as they were called) were to receive scrolls.

Ballots were sent out, filled, and returned. Finally, in February 1929, the Central Board of Judges was ready to decide the winners. Charlie Chaplin's *The Circus* was eligible, and it had been a huge hit, but late in the day, the Academy decided to revoke all four of Chaplin's nominations and instead grant him an honorary award. In a letter to Chaplin, the Academy attempted to explain that this was not a slight but an indication that he was in a class all his own. Charlie Chaplin's response is not recorded. The Academy had also decided that *The Jazz Singer* should not be eligible for Best Picture, as its gimmick of synchronized dialogue gave it an unfair advantage.

With the nominations now down to two in four categories, the judges began to deliberate. The five people who were supposed to be picking the winners had selected the MGM film *The Crowd* for the Best Unique and Artistic Picture award. But Louis B. Mayer announced that he was going to "supervise" the process, and he argued passionately against a film from his own studio. He privately disliked King Vidor's domestic drama, which hadn't made much money, but more importantly he wanted the Academy Awards to maintain the appearance of impartiality. *Sunrise*, released by Fox and directed by a foreigner who was not a member of the Academy, suited his purpose far better, and he eventually prevailed.

In the end, *Sunrise* received three awards, while the World War I aerial combat drama *Wings* won Outstanding Picture and Best Engineering Effects. The following year, various categories were scrapped, including Best Unique and Artistic Picture. It seems fairly clear that the original intent was to create two equal Best Picture categories, but several years later, it was decided that Outstanding Picture was the same as Best Picture and that *Sunrise* had won some other award. Ironically, it is *Sunrise* whose reputation has endured. It came in seventh in the 2002 *Sight and Sound* poll and fifth in 2012.

The results of all this voting and wrangling were printed on the back page of the *Academy Bulletin* a few days later. A full *three months* after that, a ceremony was staged at the Roosevelt Hotel. It took barely fifteen minutes to hand out the awards, followed by dinner and dancing. How on earth did this modest-sounding event become the most prestigious in the entire show business calendar?

Well, one person we have to thank is press baron William Randolph Hearst, famously parodied by Orson Welles in *Citizen Kane*. Hearst took note of the first Academy Awards and realized that if these were to become tremendously important, then he might be able to arrange matters so that his mistress, movie actor Marion Davies, could win one. Accordingly, he instructed columnist Louella Parsons to lavish every superlative she could muster in her write-up of the ceremony. Accordingly, when the second event rolled around, expectations had been raised.

Another person who had her eye on matters transpiring at the Roosevelt Hotel was silent star Mary Pickford. Pickford's career was in trouble. In 1916, she had been one of the biggest box-office stars in the world and had full authority over the pictures she appeared in. In 1919, she formed United Artists with Charlie Chaplin; D. W. Griffith; and her husband, Douglas Fairbanks. However, she struggled with the transition to sound. Her first talkie, *Coquette*, while not a complete flop, failed to make much of an impact. Her second sound film, *The Taming of the Shrew* with Fairbanks as Petruchio, was a disaster. But Pickford saw a way out.

According to the newspapers—the Hearst papers anyway—these new Academy Awards were a big deal. She invited the Central Board of

Judges to Pickfair Mansions and wined and dined them. *Taming of the Shrew* was outside the eligibility period for the second Academy Awards (maybe for the best), but Pickford nevertheless won Best Actress for *Coquette*, a film very few people saw and hardly anybody liked.

Sadly for Pickford, the strategy didn't work. She'd appeared in more than two hundred silent films, but she only made two more talkies before retiring from acting in 1933. She remained active as a producer until 1949 and was given an honorary Academy Award in 1975, four years before her death. Marion Davies, an accomplished comic actor, was forced into unsuitable dramatic roles by Hearst, and she retired from film acting in 1937 without a single Academy Award nomination to her name.

Mary Pickford's method of steering the voting in her direction cast significant doubt on the integrity of the Academy, so for the third awards, the now six-hundred-odd members of the Academy voted within their branches to decide nominations, and the entire Academy voted on the winners—essentially the same procedure in use today. But this didn't stop Norma Shearer—married at the time to MGM's Head of Production Irving G. Thalberg—from triumphing over hot favorite Greta Garbo to pinch Best Actress. Joan Crawford—who would have to wait until 1946 for her first nomination—commented drily, "What do you expect? She sleeps with the boss."

Adding to the incestuous feel was the fact that the new award for Sound Recording went to Douglas Shearer, brother of Norma, for the MGM production *The Big House*, which also scored a win for Frances Marion, who wrote the screenplay. And it was Louis B. Mayer himself who presented producer Carl Laemmle with his Best Picture Award for *All Quiet on the Western Front*, telling him he thought it might win a Nobel Peace Prize. Laemmle described the event as the proudest moment of his life, next to the "thrill of becoming a grandfather."

It would be decades before the Academy Awards were televised, but portions of these awards were reenacted for movie cameras at some later point. History doesn't record exactly when this happened or whose idea it was, but the footage was spliced into newsreels, and it features Carl Laemmle, Norma Shearer, and Frances Marion accepting their awards. The entire film runs for seven-and-a-half minutes, and you can see the whole thing on YouTube.

Not included in this footage are the two guests of honor. Once the dancing and banqueting was over, Hollywood's censor in chief Will Hays rose to his feet and lectured those present for almost an hour about how important it was for the movie industry's financial fortunes for them also to be guardians of public taste and morality. And Thomas Edison was given an honorary award for his pioneering efforts in early film technology. He did not appear in person, but he did provide a short film in which he offered his thanks—something that you can bet Steven Soderbergh would never have allowed.

THE MOVIES IN THE 1920s

Cinema was but a few decades young and rapidly developing. Since its beginnings as a sideshow novelty, it had gone from capturing snippets of reality to longer narrative features with large casts, elaborate sets, "trick photography," and detailed story lines. This flourishing of the medium was greatly facilitated by the establishment of two simple but transformational practices: having a production schedule and preparing a continuity script.

The center of activity for moviemaking had shifted from New York to California. Hollywood's combination of near-constant sunshine and varied topography made for very favorable shooting conditions. All that was needed now was a commercial structure that could take advantage of these golden opportunities. Enter the studio system.

Theater owners Adolph Zukor; Louis B. Mayer; and Jack, Harry, and Sam Warner came to Hollywood from America's Northeast. In running their theaters, they realized that showing films was more lucrative than hiring live acts. But there wasn't enough product being generated to satisfy the demand, so these five men went west and founded studios that are still in existence today. Together with Darryl F. Zanuck—who began by working with the brothers Warner—they founded Paramount Pictures (Zukor), Metro-Goldwyn-Mayer (Mayer), Warner Bros. Pictures, and 20th Century Fox (Zanuck). RKO was founded by David Sarnoff in 1928, completing the quintet known as the "Big Five." The heads of these studios were responsible for every aspect of the moviemaking process and all the steps in the supply chain—they chose the script, approved the budget, hired the actors, supervised the edit, and finally distributed the finished film to the movie theaters, many of which they owned either partly or outright.

Key to the success of these films was the emphasis on star actors, and nobody did more to develop and commercialize the audience's relationships with star actors than MGM's head of production Irving Thalberg. A precocious talent, he began at Universal, still a teenager, and he was only twenty when studio chief Carl Laemmle left him to negotiate a new bank loan to keep the struggling studio afloat. Thalberg got the loan—but was unable to legally sign the paperwork, as he was still technically underage.

His ability with story and character was amazing, and his understanding of stars' personas was years ahead of his contemporaries. At Universal, he realized that Lon Chaney was a major talent but that his gallery of grotesques weren't winning him an audience. He mandated that future films had to include a moment of redemption for Chaney's character, and in so doing, he turned a character actor into a star. Was it a formula? Yes, if you like, but a hugely successful one.

At twenty-four, he became co-owner of MGM, essentially running the studio alongside Louis B. Mayer. He was hugely influential in shaping how movies were being made. He organized story conferences, held sneak previews for films, and had scenes reshot if the audience feedback wasn't good enough. In 1929, MGM released fifty films. Forty-five of them were profitable. However, he was born with a congenital heart condition, and doctors had warned him he wouldn't live past thirty. He died in September 1936 at the age of thirty-seven.

One reason you might not have heard his name before is that it doesn't appear on any of the dozens of movies he produced. Louis B. Mayer always had his name in the titles, but Thalberg felt that "credit you give yourself is not worth having." His final film, released after he died, was *The Good Earth*, which won numerous Academy Awards. Its opening screen credit was a dedication to Thalberg.

What the movies that made Thalberg's early career didn't have, of course, was synchronized sound. Not because the idea had never occurred to anyone; in fact, Thomas Edison had been showing minute-long films with sound to audiences in New York as early as 1894. But these were viewed by customers who peered into individual booths, and by the mid-1920s, the big money was in projection systems and large auditoriums. The technology already existed to record sound on records (that same Thomas Edison had patented the phonograph in 1878), but many feature films ran more than an hour, and records could only hold three or so minutes of audio. And even if you solved that problem, how could you amplify the recording to the point where it could fill a large theater? And how could you keep the spinning record synchronized with the film projector?

It took decades for these issues to be tackled, and even then, the studios were slow to react. By 1925, at least two separate systems for making sound films had been developed and were being used to show newsreels and other shorts in a small number of American cities. But the Big Five saw no reason to massively disrupt their current highly profitable industry. Adding sound would mean reinventing their business model from scratch, new equipment both on set and in theaters, new approaches to filmmaking and storytelling, a much bigger problem with overseas sales, difficulties for popular stars who weren't used to dialogue, and so on.

Finally, in 1926, Warner Bros. broke ranks. They invested heavily in the Vitaphone sound-on-disc system, envisaging a world in which their silent pictures could be shipped to movie theaters, with records containing music and sound effects, thus saving the cost of a piano player or orchestra. In August 1926, Warner Bros. released the first ever feature-length film with synchronized sound—*Don Juan* starring John Barrymore. At the lavish premiere, they also showed a handful of shorts, all of them with synchronized music and sound effects, and one film that captured a speech by censor-in-chief Will Hays. This was the only item in the running order to include any dialogue.

After the huge financial success of *Don Juan*, Warner Bros. announced that all their productions from now on were going to include sound. Still using the sound-on-disc process—although by now there were around a half-dozen competing systems to choose from—they pumped out four more Vitaphone films in the next twelve months, all with synchronized music and sound effects. And then, in October 1927, they released *The Jazz Singer*, starring Al Jolson as Jakie Rabinowitz, the cantor's son who becomes a singing star under the name Jack Robin. And audiences went crazy.

This was conceived as another silent film with Vitaphone synchronized music, but it contains Al Jolson singing six songs and about two minutes of dialogue, including the famous line "Wait a minute! You ain't heard nothing yet!" which was already a Jolson catchphrase. Watching the film today, it seems very odd that it keeps switching from synchronized singing to silent movie title cards, but if anything, this only seemed to increase the audience's appetite for talkies. The very presence of the silent scenes made them miss the talking scenes all the more. Suddenly, the silent era was over.

During the next two years, Hollywood moviemaking was reinvented from the ground up, at a total cost of around $300 million—almost four times the value of the entire industry. But the studios had no option. The market for silent pictures had entirely dried up. Almost nobody who released a silent movie in the whole of 1927 made a profit from it. It was sound or nothing. Bigger companies invested from their own profits or borrowed the money they needed from Wall Street. Smaller companies were forced to close. It didn't matter that these early talkies were very crude and clumsy compared to their silent counterparts. Silent film was dead and buried.

And it wasn't just in America that change swept the industry. The following year in the United Kingdom, Alfred Hitchcock directed the first British talkie, *Blackmail*, which was another huge hit. The enormous profits from sound films enabled the big Hollywood studios to pay back their investors and ride out the Great Depression. At the first Academy Awards, twenty-five films received nominations. Twenty-four of them were silent. At the second Academy Awards, twenty-eight films received nominations. Only seven were silent, and another six were partially silent. By the third ceremony, one documentary film had only music and sound effects, and every other nominated film was a talkie.

Fairly quickly, the Vitaphone sound-on-disc system, which had been the choice of the Big Five, was abandoned. Although Vitaphone offered excellent audio quality compared to sound-on-film systems, the system was fiddly to say the least, with a new disc for each ten-minute reel of film, each of which had to be carefully cued up in the time it took the previous reel to play through—and *The Jazz Singer*, for example, was fifteen reels. Discs also wore out fast and could easily be damaged in transit. As the audio quality improved, sound-on-film systems—with either optical or magnetic sound strips on the edge of the celluloid—became the norm.

This also meant that motion picture film became standardized at twenty-four frames per second. Cameras used to be hand-cranked, and the frame rate could vary wildly. While acceptable for silent films with improvised live music, this couldn't work with recorded sound. Film stock wasn't cheap, and the rate of twenty-four was deemed to be the best compromise between creating a satisfactory level of realistic motion without burning through miles of expensive celluloid. Modern cinema had arrived.

Some stars managed the transition to sound without issue. Familiar names who began their careers in the silent era include William Powell, Janet Gaynor, Greta Garbo, John Barrymore, Joan Crawford, and Laurel and Hardy. The trio of silent clowns who today are the best-remembered aspect of silent cinema all struggled in different ways. Harold Lloyd was a comfortable public speaker, and he had some hits in the sound era, but remaking his thrill pictures like *Safety Last* (in which he clambers up the outside of a skyscraper) was a disaster. What was a brilliantly comical depiction of high-stakes jeopardy with only piano accompaniment turned out to be horrifying when the hero's cries of distress regularly punctuated the action.

The box-office failure of *The General* (now seen as a masterpiece) forced Buster Keaton to take a contract at MGM, who had no idea what to do with him, and so he faded from view. Although his output slowed, Charlie Chaplin continued to be a major force in American movies, stubbornly making dialogue-free films throughout the 1930s, but he eventually retired his Little Tramp character and never again achieved the level of success he had enjoyed in his heyday.

A lot of movies in this period are hybrids of one kind or another. *All Quiet on the Western Front* was released in both sound and silent versions. *Blackmail*, mentioned earlier, began as a silent film and was hastily converted to sound. And plenty of major stars weren't able to sustain their careers, for a variety of reasons. The likes of Clara Bow, Emil Jannings, Ramon Novarro, John Gilbert, and Mary Pickford, who had once ruled the box office, were no longer able to draw crowds. Pretty much the only star in Hollywood who didn't worry about what this new technology would mean was Rin-Tin-Tin. Provided the microphones could pick up his barking, he was happy.

THE MAKING OF *WINGS*

Writers: Hope Loring, Louis D. Lighton, John Monk Saunders, Julian Johnson
Director: William A. Wellman
Producers: B. P. Schulberg, Adolph Zukor for Famous Players-Lasky/Paramount
Cast: Clara Bow, Charles "Buddy" Rogers, Richard Arlen, Gary Cooper
Won: Outstanding Picture, Best Engineering Effects (Roy Pomeroy)
Length: 111 minutes
Budget: $2 million
Box office: $3.6 million
Rotten Tomatoes: 93%

Wings starts off with John Monk Saunders, a man born in 1897 in Minnesota. A gifted student, he went to Oxford as a Rhodes scholar, where he hung out with John Masefield and Rudyard Kipling, before joining the Air Force during World War I and serving as a flight instructor in Florida. He was desperate to be involved in the fighting in France, but he was never sent and was bitterly disappointed, weeping on the wing of his plane on the night of the Armistice. This frustration lingered with him for the rest of his life.

While working as a reporter in New York, he started to sell short stories to magazines and began to crave literary fame and the wealth that came with it. In 1924, he sold the rights for one short story to Famous Players-Lasky Pictures (later Paramount) and so was introduced to Hollywood. Then, in 1926, they also bought his unfinished novel about World War I pilots, *Wings*, for $39,000. This was highest sum paid for film rights at that time—well over a half-million dollars in 2021 money.

The production was equally huge. Most films in those days took a month to shoot. *Wings* took nine. It had a budget of $2 million and was shot between 7 September 1926 and 8 April 1927. The director selected for the film was William A. Wellman. Wellman had started in the business as an actor but hated it and soon moved to directing, mainly making B pictures. He was an unlikely choice for the film, but he was the only director in Hollywood at the time with combat pilot experience. He'd flown in France during the war; won the Croix de Guerre; had three recorded "kills" of enemy craft; and had once been shot down, leading to a lifelong limp. Despite all this, his lack of experience making big movies did lead to a reduced fee. Major directors would usually get $175,000 for a film, but he got a mere $250 a week.

Authenticity was the watchword. Leading men Richard Arlen and Buddy Rogers both flew their own planes. Arlen had flown in World War I, and Rogers underwent flight training (logging more than eight hundred hours of flying time) so that he, like Arlen, could be filmed in close-up in the air. Most of the time, they not only assumed the flying duties but also operated the camera themselves, as the cockpits were only big enough for one person. The actors would get the plane in the air, fly it, film themselves, and then land—acting all the time. Getting used to this took time, and they needed more pilots and more planes. Seeing it as great recruiting tool, the US military was happy to help, sending in thousands of soldiers and almost all of their pursuit planes.

This drive for authenticity didn't always make for efficient filmmaking. Wellman needed clouds in the sky to give the planes scale, so he couldn't film on clear days—leading to a four-week delay. But the studio's loss was a gain for the cast, who thoroughly enjoyed their downtime staying together at the Saint Anthony Hotel. By the time of their departure, after nine months, all the elevator girls were reportedly pregnant. According to Wellman, leading lady Clara Bow (the original It Girl after her success in the movie *It*) had relationships of some kind with actors Arlen and Rogers, three pilots, and a writer and began an affair with the then-unknown Gary Cooper. She certainly had a better time at the hotel than in the film, where she felt her part was only set dressing.

Eventually, Wellman got everything in the can, taking six weeks to finish the editing and dedicating the film "To those young warriors of the sky whose wings are folded about them forever." It was a huge hit when it premiered in August 1927, running for more than a year. This didn't, however, lead to lasting success for John Monk Saunders. After the triumph of *Wings*, he became a full-time screenwriter and married *King Kong* star Fay Wray—but it turns out that the giant ape wasn't the biggest monster in her life. He had multiple affairs, was accused of plagiarism, got addicted to drink and drugs, and was involved in fistfights at Hollywood parties. It's perhaps not a surprise that he was partially blacklisted—at which point his behavior got worse.

He became vehemently pro-Nazi, was sometimes heard being anti-Semitic, and once surreptitiously injected Wray with a drug, as well as sold off their home and contents and absconded with their child. After their divorce in 1940, it seemed as if he might be turning his life around and kicking his alcohol habit—but he hanged himself at the age of forty-one. Screenwriter Adela St. Rogers said she thought he was "staging his own unhappy ending to a strange, not entirely self-imposed exile from the one place he most wanted to be—which was Hollywood."

Wings had a happier ending. The film was thought to be lost completely for many years, with no copies known to exist, until 1992, when a print was found in the Cinémathèque Française film archive in Paris and a spare negative was found in the Paramount vaults. For the film's restoration, the original score was unearthed from the Library of Congress and recreated, meaning we can still enjoy the very first Best Picture winner today.

BEST OF THE BEST: *ALL QUIET ON THE WESTERN FRONT*

Writers: Maxwell Anderson, George Abbott, Del Andrews, C.
   Gardner Sullivan; based on the novel by Erich Maria Remarque
Director: Lewis Milestone
Producer: Carl Laemmle Jr. for Universal
Cast: Lew Ayres, Louis Wolheim, John Wray, Arnold Lucy, Ben
   Alexander
Won: Best Picture, Best Director
Nominated: Best Writing, Best Cinematography (Arthur Edeson)
Length: 133 minutes
Budget: $1.2 million
Box office: $3 million
Rotten Tomatoes: 98%

Jessica Regan: This was a book that had been circulated, serialized, and translated to worldwide acclaim—it was one of the first texts to be burned by the Nazis, so you know you're onto a good thing. Its impact meant it was ripe for adaptation, and Hollywood laid claim to it within two years of its publication. It certainly rattled some cages; screenings of the film in Germany were disrupted by the Nazi followers, "brown-shirts," escalating to attacks on Jewish members of the audience.

As noted above, the filmmakers shot it simultaneously as a silent film and as a sound film. This gave it a global reach that it otherwise might not have had; language wouldn't be a barrier to it being received internationally, as title cards could easily be translated whereas dubbing was an audio bridge too far.

The story follows young Paul Bäumer and his contemporaries as they are inspired to join the army by their jingoistic professor, who urges the defending of the "Fatherland." But they do not find glory or heroism in the trenches, only disease and degradation, and while they can physically come home from the battlefields, their minds never leave the war. The loneliness of knowing you will forevermore be out of place and time, as only your fellow soldiers can begin to know what is in your heart and on your mind, is communicated painfully well in the stilted exchanges and misunderstandings upon his return. Trauma is granular, and it is present in every frame of this film. The loss of the lead protagonist's innocence and idealism becomes a microcosm for what the war did for the world.

The technical achievement of this film cannot be overstated. Sound, for all its great leap forward in storytelling possibilities, presented enormous technical difficulties and seemed to set moviemaking back considerably, particularly in terms of cinematography. This film illustrates how quickly it all got back on track—quite literally, as tracking shots create a marvelous fluidity with an almost Fincher-esque flourish near the beginning. The brilliantly staged battle sequences are initially impressive but truthfully transmute into something a great deal more harrowing and relentless. The sounds of shelling and bombardment become interminable, jangling the nerves of the viewer. It is a superb use of this new technology, using audio to engage empathy with the soldiers' pitiful situation as much as any character could. The constraints the production was working under are hard to fathom by our modern-day standards—there was no CGI, barely any postproduction, and yet shot after shot is mesmeric, and nothing feels awkward or strained.

Spielberg has stated that this film was a major influence on *Saving Private Ryan*, but where Spielberg cannot help but go for the bravura shot and other war films can seem to revel in the gore (*Hacksaw Ridge*, I'm looking at you), director Lewis Milestone shows a somber restraint, particularly with the ending. It is stark and earned, and as the sound-track cuts completely, we are alone in the silence left by the absence of life. This is a film that is a great deal more visceral and technically dazzling than it has any need to be, considering it is almost a century old. It is emotively edited and sincerely acted, with a production design that recreates tiny hovels as faithfully as battlefields or a rustic boudoir. Every department triumphs in the telling of this tragedy.

The author of the book, Erich Maria Remarque, prefaces it with, "This book is to be neither an accusation nor a confession, and least of all an adventure, for death is not an adventure to those who stand face to face with it. It will try simply to tell of a generation of men who, even though they may have escaped (its) shells, were destroyed by the war." I cannot imagine a film made at this time—or at any time, in fact—that could have realized that simple intention better.

WORST OF THE BEST: *THE BROADWAY MELODY*

> **Writers:** Edmund Goulding, Sarah Y. Mason, Norman Houston, James Gleason; songs by Nacio Herb Brown and Arthur Freed, Willard Robison
> **Director:** Harry Beaumont
> **Producers:** Irving Thalberg, Lawrence Weingarten for MGM
> **Cast:** Charles King, Anita Page, Bessie Love, Jed Prouty
> **Won:** Best Picture
> **Nominated:** Best Director, Best Actress (Love)
> **Length:** 100 minutes
> **Budget:** $379,000
> **Box office:** $4.4 million
> **Rotten Tomatoes:** 35%

Tom Salinsky: Like anything else, the Hollywood musical took a while to perfect. On Broadway, in 1927, Oscar Hammerstein and Jerome Kern had revolutionized the form with *Showboat*, in which all of the songs developed characters or advanced the plot rather than just being standalone showcases, but it wasn't until the early 1930s that movies began to take full advantage of the new medium.

One often-overlooked film is the charming *Love Me Tonight* from 1932 starring Maurice Chevalier and directed by Rouben Mamoulian.

As the film opens, young Parisian tailor Chevalier begins singing the film's signature song, "Isn't It Romantic," to one of his clients. As the song develops, it is picked up by the client, who strolls out of the shop singing it. He passes it on to a taxi driver until eventually half of Paris is joining in. This was revolutionary—constructing a musical sequence *in the edit* and across multiple locations in a way that could never be replicated on the stage. Suddenly, all those earlier movie musicals looked confined, old-fashioned, and limited.

So, *The Broadway Melody* finds itself trapped between two innovations. Synchronized sound has come to the movies, and for a year or two at least, just the fact that popular stars can talk and sing and live in an aural world is enough for many movie fans. But the coming of sound brings endless technical challenges, and so the years 1928–1930 are virtually a nadir in terms of visual sophistication. *Wings* has cinematic flair to burn. *The Broadway Melody* looks like it was made in 1900, as directors and crew struggle just trying to capture moving images and live sound at the same time.

It doesn't help that this effort is saddled with a story that barely qualifies as anything other than a series of set pieces, most of which involve renditions of the title song. Backstage musicals live or die by their ability to instill in the audience the sense of urgency that stars, dancers, backers, producers, and their loved ones feel about the success of the production they are all involved in. But the characters here are so thinly drawn that it's hard to get terribly invested in their petty concerns. In the best movie musicals, the song-and-dance numbers emerge organically from the emotions of the characters, creating heart-stopping moments simply not available to nonmusical stories. In plenty of merely very good musicals, a few excellent showstopping numbers make up for deficiencies in the plotting and characterization. Here, it's frustrating when the poorly staged numbers stop the plot dead in its tracks, but the plot is so banal that very quickly I start longing for another song to break it up.

There are some standout routines, but none of them are from the stars. Bessie Love was an accomplished dancer, but costar Anita Page, rather less so, and it's painfully obvious in many sections that the choreography was designed around this constraint. However, some of the specialty acts in the last third are genuinely eye popping, including a tap dance en pointe that would put Cyd Charisse or Leslie Caron to shame.

It feels churlish to blame Harry Beaumont, Irving Thalberg, and company for failing to innovate sooner or for laboring under the weight of unprecedented technical challenges, but the fact remains that there are a great many other films from this period that are more charming, make better use of the resources available, and generally make for a more engaging viewing experience. It helps to view movies from this era kindly and with expectations tempered. What's disappointing about *The Broadway Melody* is that even through this lens, it's a bit of a letdown. Worth seeing as a protoversion of all those backstage musicals to come—it's easy to see the roots of far better films like *42nd Street* here—but even compared to other musical films made the same year, this seems both flimsy and creaky.

DID THE ACADEMY GET IT RIGHT?

1927/1928: *Wings*

John Dorney: The Oscars are born as the silent era dies—but this means that the awarded movies are the pinnacle of this style of film-making. The sheer technical achievement of **Wings** is not to be over-stated, with its dizzying, vertiginous dogfights the obvious star turn. But the movie still manages to tell a strong, surprising story that's all the more tense for key set pieces being shot for real. It's not a film you can just sit down and watch, sure, but if you put in the effort, it rewards you emphatically. The first winner of Best Picture is a thoroughly deserving recipient.

Jessica Regan: Unquestionably. Every single choice in this film is made in the pursuit of artistic excellence, from the sage, characterful title cards to the bravura tracking shot that traverses several tables in a Parisian café, telling us in seconds the situations of several of its patrons. It is staggering to consider that this film is nearly one hundred years old. But the true star of **Wings** is the camerawork. Swooping and soaring, it catches every thrilling beat of the air battles. It is an extraordinary feeling to watch an epic action sequence and realize nearly a century later that it could hardly be improved on. Even Fritz Lang's visionary and highly influential *Metropolis* doesn't give me pause. The Academy got it right the first time.

Tom Salinsky: The Academy begins as it means to go on—for the next fifty or so years at least. *Wings* is real blockbuster entertainment—rarely subtle but powerful, bombastic, brilliantly staged, and even moving at times. This is a year when the great silent clowns were all a little under par: Chaplin's *The Circus* is vastly overshadowed by the masterpieces either side of it, Harold Lloyd's *Speedy* is a bit undisciplined following the excellent *The Kid Brother* the year before, and Keaton's *Steamboat Bill Jr.* takes forever to get going before an admittedly crackerjack climax. So, it's the dramas I'm drawn to, especially the heartbreaking *The Last Command*—probably my favorite film from this twelve-month span. But if I were an Academy voter in 1928, I would have given *The Last Command* Best Unique and Artistic Picture, and I would have given Outstanding Picture to **Wings**.

1928/1929: The Broadway Melody

John Dorney: It's the first talkie to win Best Picture and is pretty much the first movie musical and so has a reasonable claim to being the Best Picture of its year, even if it's more than slightly dull when watched over ninety years after it was made. But one of this year's films that isn't dull in the least is **The Passion of Joan of Arc**. It's a difficult watch in every sense, with the inherent problems of watching a silent movie to overcome before you even get to the brutal content. But it is completely mesmerizing, and—if you can stomach it—it's a true work of art.

Jessica Regan: Ah, the awkward but necessary transitional winner between the pinnacle of silent film and the new adventures in sound. Throw in some off-color "jokes" (even allowing for the time) and a deeply sleazy leading man who is not much better than his Jack Warner surrogate nemesis, and as a viewing experience, it is an uphill slog. I will admit that Bessie Love breaking down in her dressing room as her life falls apart in a matter of minutes is an island of truth in a sea of artifice. But this year, my heart belongs to **The Fall of the House of Usher**, an exquisitely gothic, haunting visual poem that is as impressive as it is transportive.

Tom Salinsky: As noted earlier, the rush to create talkies in the wake of *The Jazz Singer* meant that very little Hollywood product was of a super-high caliber around this time. A few European filmmakers blended silent and sound techniques with more skill, and there were one or two silent-era holdouts. Buster Keaton's last silent film, and his first for MGM, is one of his finest. Given a lavish MGM budget, Keaton goes to town, but after this, the studio reined him in, and soon he was reduced to bit parts and gag writing for other comedy stars. Nevertheless, for years afterward, MGM bosses would show new writers, directors, and stars this film as an object lesson in how to make a comedy. *The Cameraman* is my pick from a rather creaky collection.

1929/1930: All Quiet on the Western Front

John Dorney: *All Quiet on the Western Front* is a brutal watch, the great-grandfather of later war films like *Saving Private Ryan*. A movie made between the wars, with the Germans as the heroes, it left me feeling shell-shocked like no other, with an ambition and power far ahead of its time. A very worthy winner indeed.

Jessica Regan: It is notable for being a story of war told from a German soldier's perspective. It is precious for being made a little more than a decade from the time of the events it depicts. But its importance as a historical document is not the reason it should have won. It is simply an excellent film, a devastating watch, and a truthful, moving portrait of the young men of World War I who came back dead or not really alive from the atrocities they witnessed. *All Quiet on the Western Front* sets the bar for Best Picture winners and war films—and cinema in general—commendably high.

Tom Salinsky: It's an old story—war is hell—that filmmakers keep on telling. There's a clear artistic line that connects this film to Sam Mendes's *1917*, via *Paths of Glory*, *Apocalypse Now*, *Platoon*, and countless others. But there are a few elements which have never been captured quite as clearly as they are here. A compassionate and detailed evocation of a haunting book, *All Quiet on the Western Front* comprehensively proves that early talkies have much more to offer than overhead shots of dozens of anonymous dancers and bloodless gangster slayings.

2

THE 1930s

THE OSCARS IN THE 1930s

Throughout the 1930s, the Academy Awards as we know them gradually emerged, while the Academy itself fought for its identity and existence. One of the first things to change was that someone eventually decided that having the awards straddle two calendar years was cumbersome and confusing. To regularize this, the sixth Academy Awards were held a full sixteen months after the previous event, making 1933 the only calendar year since the Academy Awards were created that no ceremony was held. It was at this ceremony that Walt Disney, accepting the award for Best Short Subject (Cartoon), became the first person on the Academy stage to refer to the statuette as an "Oscar." The origins of

	Best Picture	Biggest Earner
1930/1931	Cimarron	City Lights
1931/1932	Grand Hotel	The Kid from Spain
1932/1933	Cavalcade	Roman Scandals
1934	It Happened One Night	Cleopatra
1935	Mutiny on the Bounty	Mutiny on the Bounty
1936	The Great Ziegfeld	The Great Ziegfeld
1937	The Life of Emile Zola	Saratoga
1938	You Can't Take It with You	Snow White and the Seven Dwarfs
1939	Gone with the Wind	Gone with the Wind

this nickname are the subject of much debate, but it was obviously already in common use by this time.

During the sixteen-month gap between ceremonies, the Academy had been intervening in Hollywood labor disputes, generally without much success, and it had faced accusations of a monopoly as Roosevelt tried to lift America out of the Great Depression. Uncertain that the Academy had their best interests at heart, a group of actors quit to form the Screen Actors Guild in July 1933—the one thing that Academy founder Louis B. Mayer had been hoping to prevent. They joined forces with the Screen Writers Guild to publish a monthly magazine, and by August, their membership was more than one thousand, while membership of the Academy was severely reduced as a consequence.

The other change during this long gap was that Prohibition had been repealed. The ban on alcohol in the United States had been in force since 1920, and it ended on 5 December 1933, making the sixth Oscars the first where you could have a drink. One person who might have needed to take advantage of this new freedom was Columbia's star director Frank Capra. Capra had become consumed with thoughts of Oscar success and was convinced that *Lady for a Day* would win all four Oscars for which it was nominated—which would set a record. It didn't win for its writing or Best Actress, but it was still in the running for Best Picture and Capra for Best Director. Emcee Will Rogers opened the Best Director envelope and said the following words: "Well, well, well, what do you know. I've watched this young man for a long time. Saw him come up from the bottom, and I mean the bottom. It couldn't happen to a nicer guy. Come on up and get it, Frank."

Capra leaped out of his seat and began to make his way to the front, as the audience erupted in delighted applause. His long journey to the stage was hampered by the fact that the spotlight seemed to have trouble finding him. "Over here!" he yelled jubilantly, waving his arms. Finally, the spotlight found its target. On the other side of the room, Frank Lloyd, the director of *Cavalcade*, was bathed in light as he bounded onto the platform, and Rogers handed him the Oscar. Capra returned to his seat, taking what he described in his autobiography as the "longest, saddest, most shattering walk in my life. I wished I could have crawled under the rug like a miserable worm."

Capra's humiliation didn't last very long. At the 1934 awards, his film *It Happened One Night* made a clean sweep of Best Picture, Best Director, Best Screenplay, Best Actor, and Best Actress—but that wasn't the way the evening was supposed to go. Bette Davis was widely expected to be nominated for her role in *Of Human Bondage*, which *Life* magazine called "probably the best performance ever recorded on screen by a US actress." So, there was outrage when the nominations were announced and Davis had been overlooked completely.

Part of the issue for Davis was that she was under contract at Warner Bros. but had been loaned out to RKO for this movie. RKO didn't want to campaign for her to win Best Actress because they wouldn't benefit from her increased profile, and Warner Bros. didn't want to give free publicity to a film made by a rival studio. The whole debacle probably did end up benefiting Davis at least as much as winning would have—maybe even more—but also started to raise questions about how the Academy functioned, who its members were, and whether it still had a future. Something had to be done.

To quell the unrest, the Academy decided to allow write-in votes for the final ballot. If you didn't like how the nominations turned out, you could write in whichever name you thought was missing. So, many sources list Davis as a nominee this year, but it was only as a result of write-in votes, and in the end, it was Claudette Colbert who won anyway ("in a walk" according to emcee Irwin S. Cobb, who revealed how the voting had gone at the end of the evening).

Davis continued to fume and stew, but following his triumphant win, Frank Capra became not just the darling of the Academy but also its president. And he was the one who had to figure out how to keep the show on the road, as the Writers and Directors Guilds tried to organize a boycott of the next awards. His task was made even harder when the studios, scenting blood, decided that the Academy was finished, so they withdrew their financial support, as well.

With some cunning, Capra announced that 1935 awards would be a tribute to legendary director D. W. Griffith. Griffith had only made two talkies and then retired in 1931, but Capra persuaded him to personally attend the ceremony to accept an honorary award. Armed with this news, he began calling the stars and directors of the year's biggest movies to secure their attendance, and then he got Academy staff to give out tickets to assistants, secretaries, interns, and family members to fill any remaining empty seats. It worked. The Oscars went ahead, and even Bette Davis was pleased, managing to win her first Oscar for

Dangerous, although she still grumbled to friends that this was a consolation prize and that *Of Human Bondage* was both a better film and a
better performance from her.

Also grumbling about his Oscar was Dudley Nichols, who won Best
Adapted Screenplay for *The Informer*. Nichols was not just a screenwriter. He was president of the Screen Writers Guild—the very body
attempting to put the Academy out of business. After some tense communications between Nichols and Capra—including the Academy mailing Nichols his statuette and Nichols mailing it right back again—Nichols opted to refuse his award. He thus became the first person ever to
decline an Oscar. A couple years later, when Capra had brokered a
peace between the Academy and the guilds, Nichols publicly collected
his statuette as a token of the understanding between the two groups.

In 1935, three men were nominated as Best Actor for *Mutiny on the
Bounty*—Clark Gable, Charles Laughton, and Franchot Tone. None of
them won, and partly in response to this, Capra introduced two new
awards categories—Best Supporting Actor and Best Supporting Actress. However, for the first seven years of their existence, people who
won in these categories didn't get statuettes; they received only plaques.
This may have been connected to another problem that Capra was
trying to solve. No longer able to depend on the studios to fund lavish
banquet dinners, the Academy was in serious need of extra cash. Guest
tickets for the ceremony usually went for about $5, but for the 1936
awards, Capra jacked it up to $10 for guests and a whopping $25 for the
best seats—that's around $450 today. This was widely criticized, but in
the end, all 1,150 seats were sold.

Yet another Capra innovation was to have the ballots counted in
secret. Previously, the Academy board had known the results of the
voting ahead of time, but now, nobody would know who had won what
until the press was briefed about an hour before the ceremony started.
This press briefing enabled them to meet their morning print deadlines.
And surely, the Academy could trust the press to keep their secrets for a
few hours?

At the 1937 awards, the first to be staged under this new system,
Best Supporting Actress went to Alice Brady for *In Old Chicago*. Nurs-
ing a broken ankle, Brady couldn't have attended the ceremony even if
she had known in advance she had won, and so her representative
accepted the statuette on her behalf and offered a few dignified words

of thanks before leaving the stage with her award. To this day, nobody knows who this man was, where he went, or what became of Alice Brady's Oscar. She was given a replacement a couple weeks later.

Or so the legend goes. For a while, this was my favorite story about the Oscars, and it is recounted in numerous authoritative-sounding texts. But in 2013, an enterprising graduate student named Olivia Rutigliano took it upon herself to try to track down the whereabouts of various missing Oscars, and Alice Brady's was at the top of her list. Among the people she contacted was Academy librarian Libby Wertin—who it turns out had solved the mystery almost a decade earlier.

According to contemporary news reports collated by Wertin, it was *In Old Chicago* director Henry King who accepted Alice Brady's award. It was presented to her by her costars that same night, and the only reason it wasn't in her possession a few days later was that she had returned it to the Academy for engraving—as was the practice in those days. It was never lost and never had to be replaced. Quite where and how this legend arose is not clear. Its earliest appearance in print seems to be in the amazingly comprehensive doorstop of a book *Inside Oscar*, first published in 1986, but there is no clear citation given there, and both authors died horrifyingly young and are not available to discuss where they got the story from.

Also at the 1937 awards, Luise Rainer became the first performer to win back-to-back Oscars for *The Great Ziegfeld* and *The Good Earth*, a feat duplicated the following year by Spencer Tracy for *Captain's Courageous* and *Boys Town*. However, when his second Oscar was delivered to him, he was incensed to see that the inscription read "Dick Tracy." A sheepish Academy had a replacement quickly made. Tracy would go on to be nominated six more times, but this was his last win.

Frank Capra had successfully fended off the guilds, got the studios back onboard bankrolling the annual banquet, and had become the first person to win three Best Director Oscars. Now he stood down as Academy president and—almost on his way out the door—made a deal with Warner Bros. for the rights to bring movie cameras into the 1939 ceremony to make a short subject about what previously had been a private affair. It was called *Cavalcade of the Academy Awards*, and you can see the whole thing on YouTube. It manages to be both pompous and twee, but it's a fascinating glimpse of the early Oscars, years before regular television coverage.

The decade ended with what is widely considered to be Hollywood's annus mirabilis. Of the ten Best Picture nominees, almost any would be considered a worthy winner, which makes the fact that this was pretty much a sweep for *Gone with the Wind* all the more impressive. And it really was a sweep. It started the night with a record-breaking thirteen nominations, and it won an equally record-breaking eight competitive awards, plus a special award for its production designer, William Cameron Menzies, and the Irving G. Thalberg Award for producer David O. Selznick. It's the longest film ever to win, and it's the first color film to win. *A Star Is Born*, another Selznick production, had been the first color film nominated for Best Picture in 1937.

Best Supporting Actress broke barriers, as well. Legend has it that Hattie McDaniel marched into Selznick's office and dumped a stack of reviews of *Gone with the Wind* on his desk. She called particular attention to the *Los Angeles Times*, which—among many publications printing praise for her work—described her performance as "worthy of an Academy Award." Selznick got the message and submitted her name to the Academy.

When the nominations were announced, both McDaniel and her costar Olivia de Havilland were included in the Best Supporting Actress category, meaning that McDaniel was the first Black person to be nominated for an Academy Award. Typically, at Academy Awards dinners, guests sat at tables, grouped by movies. Selznick had already organized a *Gone with the Wind* table, where he would sit with Clark Gable, Vivien Leigh, Olivia de Havilland, and so on. However, the Ambassador Hotel in Los Angeles was segregated, a polite way of saying that Black people weren't allowed in. This policy was eventually overturned by law, almost *twenty years later*.

So when Hattie McDaniel, her escort, and her white agent were shown into the Coconut Grove, they were not sitting with Selznick and the white actors. They were shown to a small table at the side, toward the back, and had only been allowed that because Selznick had asked the hotel to admit them as a special favor to him. If she felt slighted, McDaniel did not let this show in her dignified and heartfelt acceptance speech.

Best Actor was widely expected to go to Clark Gable because *Gone with the Wind* was winning everything else. At one point, emcee Bob Hope cracked, "What a wonderful thing, this benefit for David Selznick." But actually, it was British actor Robert Donat who won for *Goodbye Mr. Chips*. This one loss reportedly meant that Selznick was unable to fully enjoy his success, feeling that the publicity department had managed to drop the ball with Best Actor. Gable himself was also gloomy. Mrs. Gable, Carole Lombard, tried to cheer him up, saying, "I just know we'll bring one home next year." Gable didn't smile. "No we won't," he replied, "This was my last chance." Lombard was furious. "Not you, you self-centered bastard. I meant me."

THE MOVIES IN THE 1930s

At the start of the 1930s, cinema as we know it—feature-length films with synchronized sound—was still a child, and like the development of a child's brain, its learning was exponential, its development in spurts. The evolution of this nebulous medium is thrillingly nonlinear. To overlook the films of this period in favor of the smoky chiaroscuro and cleaner craft of the 1940s is to miss out on perhaps the most dynamic decade of cinema in terms of pioneering innovation.

The early years of the talkies include some wonderfully bold forays into genre. Considering the technical limitations of the time, it would have been tempting for Hollywood to stick to farces, melodramas, and pretty people talking in rooms—screwball comedies originated in this period, after all. But very early on, audiences could enjoy the incredible spectacle of people playing God and giving us monsters. James Whale's *Frankenstein*, released in 1931, features an iconic physical performance from Boris Karloff and incredible makeup artistry from Jack Pierce (who also contributed to the look of Bela Lugosi's Dracula). Rounding out this hat trick of literary-sourced nightmarish creatures is *Dr. Jekyll and Mr. Hyde*. This time, legendary makeup artist Wally Westmore was responsible for actor Frederic March's astonishing transformation. But what is perhaps more shocking than any of these creations is that it would be a half-century before the Academy would honor the craft of makeup.

Technical achievements did not stop there. RKO's *King Kong* employed rear projection, miniature models, and the best stop-motion ever filmed hitherto thanks to the efforts of chief technician Willis O'Brien. As groundbreaking as these visual effects were, maybe even more so was its musical score by Max Steiner. It was the first feature-length score composed for an American sound film, and it was performed by an unprecedented forty-six-piece orchestra. The dialogue (including Fay Wray's iconic screams), the music, and the phenomenal sound design by Murray Spivak were all recorded on separate tracks, another first.

The big ape saved RKO's fortunes (along with Astaire and Rogers), but it was a diminutive star who came to the rescue of 20th Century Fox. In 1934, Shirley Temple found her breakthrough role in *Stand Up and Cheer*. Despite playing a fairly minor part, she steals the show, and this preternaturally talented six-year-old went on to such hits as *Baby Take a Bow*, *Bright Eyes*, and *Poor Little Rich Girl*.

And it wasn't just RKO that was struggling. Although cinema provided much succor and escapism during the Great Depression, audience attendance was down 40 percent. The moguls had spent enormous sums on sound conversion and acquiring movie theaters, and some found themselves on the brink of bankruptcy, just as another enemy loomed on the horizon.

The Legion of Decency had been established in 1933 by the Catholic Church in response to films exploring adult themes (and just Mae West in general). Now, they urged a nationwide boycott of films they considered indecent, and the studios responded swiftly. Unable to withstand any further catastrophes and unwilling to submit to government censorship, the industry itself beefed up the powers of the Motion Picture Producers and Distributors of America (MPPDA), which had been headed by Will Hays since 1922. A new set of rules was drawn up, and Hays was given the ability to fine studios and refuse seals of approval to movies that didn't abide by those rules, set out in a document called "The Motion Picture Production Code" (also known as the Hays Code or sometimes the Breen Code, after Hays's enforcer, Joseph Breen).

The exhaustive list of rules that Breen was to enforce were in some cases understandable—a ban on "apparent cruelty to children and animals" seems fair enough. But many of them badly restricted the stories that Hollywood could tell and the characters they could portray. One rule might be seen to be promoting respect and tolerance—no film was to show "willful offense to any nation, race or creed"—but another entrenched racism and exclusion in films by banning depictions of "miscegenation"—interracial sexual relationships. One Best Picture winner—Frank Capra's *You Can't Take It with You*—was even criticized by Breen for showing an equal, almost collegiate, relationship, between the central white family and the Black servants who worked for them.

Sometimes a film didn't even make it into the country to be censored. In 1935, the US Treasury Department upheld a Commissioner of Customs decision to prohibit the import of the notorious Czechoslovakian film *Ecstasy*, with a young Hedy Lamar as Eva, because it contained nudity and was the first nonpornographic film to exhibit sexual intercourse and depict a female orgasm. This was the first time that customs laws were used to prevent a film from entering America.

The Code's strictures had an incalculable artistic and cultural impact but what followed is widely regarded as Hollywood's golden age. Were we better off having the Code as cinema found its way in the early decades? Did it force filmmakers to be inventive and resourceful in ways they perhaps might not have been had they been allowed to put all and anything up on the big screen? Conversely, if we had had positive representations of female sexuality, would sexism behind and in front of the camera have been able to thrive so unchecked? Or were we saved a body of exploitative work that would have hastened the "pornification" of mainstream tastes? We'll never know, but whatever gains were made in terms of taste and restraint were surely outweighed by the vision, storytelling, representation, and progress that the Code thwarted or erased outright.

One vision that was unfettered by the Code and realized to neat perfection was Walt Disney's. On a soundstage on Hyperion Avenue in the mid-1930s, Walt Disney performed the story of Snow White as he saw it in his head—complete with gestures, voices, and movement—to a presumably captive audience of creatives. The budget was originally $250,000, but the cost of the first full-length cell-animated feature in the history of motion pictures ballooned to $1.5 million. To Walt and his banker's relief, animation's quantum leap forward went on to gross $8 million on its initial release and many millions more during its various rereleases. Understandably so, for it is exquisitely wrought, with memorable songs, dashes of humor, and chilling peril—an honest-to-goodness fairy tale brought to colorful, kinetic life.

The 1930s was an astonishing decade for female roles. The ladies dominated the screen—Bette Davis, Maureen O'Sullivan, Jean Harlow,

Joan Crawford, Barbara Stanwyck, Greta Garbo, and Claudette Colbert dazzled and delighted audiences. You couldn't move for luminous, crackling performances in this era. In 1932, there was a 50–50 gender split between the top ten grossing movie stars. Contrast this, depressingly, with 2018, when there are more men called Chris than there are women in the year's list of top ten grossers.

As cinemas struggled, many of these stars were blamed for the box office's ever-diminishing returns. On 3 May 1938, an ad in a trade paper taken out by the Independent Theatre Owners Association branded a number of film stars, including Marlene Dietrich, Fred Astaire, and Greta Garbo, "box-office poison." The accuracy of this label is debatable, and it does seem that the ad's author, Harry Brandt, was out for blood, frustrated by years of disappointing ticket sales and the block-booking practices of movie studios, which forced him and others to accept packages of films rather than picking and choosing what they could show.

One actor who did not take this ignoble moniker lying down was Katharine Hepburn. She left RKO when she began to receive salary offers lower than what she had been paid at the start of her career. She turned to theater for salvation, and it delivered. She put her own money into *The Philadelphia Story*, written for her by playwright Philip Barry. It opened on Broadway on 28 March 1939 to rave reviews and ended up grossing more than $1.5 million during its year-long run.

Hepburn controlled the movie rights and eventually sold them to MGM for $250,000. She likely could have negotiated a higher amount up front from another studio considering the success of the play, but at MGM, Hepburn was given what she desired more than money: control. At a time when many stars were at the mercy of the studio system, she personally selected the cast and crew for the film. Her instincts proved correct when the movie version opened to widespread critical acclaim and commercial success, garnering multiple Oscar nominations.

Production companies created by women because they aren't getting good roles isn't a modern solution to an age-old problem. Neither is financial risk in favor of creative freedom. Harry Brandt's advert was destabilizing and unwelcome, but perhaps, like the Code, it was its own dark gift.

There is one female director of some note—or rather notoriety—who emerged in the 1930s: Nazi propagandist Leni Riefenstahl. Her documentary *Triumph of the Will* changed propaganda forever. She deployed moving cameras, aerial photography, and long-focus lenses to create a brilliantly executed but inaccurate and dangerously false depiction of the Nazi Party. Charlie Chaplin's satire *The Great Dictator* was inspired in large part by Riefenstahl's film, and Frank Capra used significant footage from it, overlayed with a mocking narration, in the first installment of his propagandistic film produced by the US Army, *Why We Fight*.

After an unpredictable decade of creative highs and financial lows, the 1930s went out with a big bang of Technicolor, epic storytelling, and iconic characters. Amid a prodigious number of now-classic films, both *Gone with the Wind* and *The Wizard of Oz* were released this year. *Oz* cemented Judy Garland's status in the firmament, no matter what came after. 1939 became the jewel in the crown of a decade when the movies would see off the Depression, sabotaging distributors, censors, and even its own existential crisis to thrive artistically and establish itself beyond any doubt as an industry of necessity and Hollywood as a hub of world-class creativity.

But twisted through this dream-weaving were dark threads of exploitation, addiction, unchecked mental health deterioration, and rank hypocrisy. They won't *show* sexual exploitation or drug pushing, but they'll practice it in offices and on sets, in rooms without windows and spaces without safety. There would be many casualties in the years to come, not least of all Miss Judy Garland and Miss Vivien Leigh, the two female stars who made this decade's finale so fantastic.

THE MAKING OF *GONE WITH THE WIND*

Writer: Sidney Howard, based on the novel by Margaret Mitchell
Director: Victor Fleming
Producer: David O. Selznick for Selznick International/MGM
Cast: Vivien Leigh, Clark Gable, Olivia de Havilland, Leslie Howard, Hattie McDaniel, Oscar Polk, Butterfly McQueen, Thomas Mitchell, Barbara O'Neill, Evelyn Keyes, Ann Rutherford
Won: Best Picture, Best Director, Best Actress (Leigh), Best Supporting Actress (McDaniel), Best Adapted Screenplay, Best Color Cinematography (Ernest Haller, Ray Rennahan), Best Film

Editing (Hal C. Kern, James E. Newcom), Best Art Direction
(Lyle Wheeler)
Nominated: Best Actor (Gable), Best Supporting Actress (de Havil-
land), Best Visual Effects (Jack Cosgrove, Fred Albin, Arthur
Jones), Best Original Score (Max Steiner), Best Sound Recording
(Thomas T. Moulton)
Length: 221 minutes
Budget: $3.85 million
Box office: $390 million
Rotten Tomatoes: 90%

Margaret "Peggy" Mitchell had quite the life. Born in Atlanta, Georgia,
in 1900, she was raised on stories of the Civil War and the gallantry of
the South, before becoming a tomboy, a flapper, and a journalist in the
1920s. She married an athlete, but he drank rather too much, so she
divorced him and married the best man instead. She was an active rider
but was invalided by a fall, so while she recuperated, she began to write
a novel about survival, following a young woman named Pansy O'Hara.
After ten years' work, she finally let a publisher see the book. Macmillan
was keen to publish it, with one alteration. The heroine's name became
Scarlett.

The novel, entitled *Gone with the Wind*, was published in the middle of the Depression in 1936. Katherine Brown, from the literary department of Selznick International Pictures, got passed a copy of the
book from Macmillan's rights department. She recommended it to
Selznick, but he was reluctant to commit to a movie version, as there
was no one under contract who was an obvious choice for the lead. He
wrote apologetically back to Brown, rejecting the proposal, but Brown
was so enthused by the material that she nonetheless approached Selznick's business partner, Jock Whitney. When Whitney shared her excitement, Selznick eventually relented, and the deal was closed in the
week of publication, with the rights purchased for $50,000. Selznick
took a copy with him on holiday to Hawaii—and it was only at this point
that he *actually read the book*.

Selznick asked Sidney Howard to write the screenplay, as he was
good but not tied to a studio. Howard agreed, as long as he could work
from home at his farm, three thousand miles away in Massachusetts. By
Christmas, he had a fifty-page treatment, in which he very consciously
didn't correct what he considered faults of construction. By this point,

the book had become a runaway best-seller, and Margaret Mitchell had become a big celebrity, so Howard felt he didn't want to try to improve on success. It certainly wasn't because Mitchell would have objected. She had no interest in the film and was happy to let Selznick and company do whatever they wanted with it.

She was possibly the only person in America who had no interest in the film, however. Everyone was wondering who would play Scarlett. Katharine Hepburn, Miriam Hopkins, Joan Crawford, and Margaret Sullavan were all possibilities for the role. A national radio poll selected Bette Davis as the ideal choice. And the studio was inundated with mail-in suggestions, covering a total of 121 potential actors. Only one person—a man from New Zealand—suggested Vivien Leigh. Selznick at this point had neither a finished script nor the money he needed to turn such a document into a movie, but he fully understood that whipping up a storm of intrigue in the casting was a great way of keeping up interest in the project. He announced a nationwide search and sent talent scouts across the country to audition people, including testing practically every Miss Atlanta from the previous twenty-five years.

In contrast, the country pretty much considered only one person to be their ideal Rhett Butler—and that person was Clark Gable. But he wasn't going to be easy to get, as he was the biggest star at MGM, and they weren't happy to loan him out. Approaching MGM to discuss using Gable created two different problems. First, the actor was likely going to come with a very high price tag, frustrating Selznick's ambitions to bring the project in cheaply. Second, he was going to have go cap in hand to the man who ran Hollywood's biggest studio, Louis B. Mayer, who also happened to be his father-in-law.

However, when negotiations began with MGM, it turned out that they were interested in more than just loaning out an actor. Eventually, a deal was struck where they would provide not just Clark Gable but also half the budget. In exchange, they would gain distribution rights and half the profits for seven years. Suddenly the film was back in business—except that Gable didn't want to do it. He felt the novel was too well known and that everyone had a preconceived idea of who Butler was, an idea he wouldn't be able to compete with. Gable at the time was in the midst of divorcing his second wife, Maria Langham. The deal he eventually signed paid him a bonus, which he was able to pass on to Langham as part of the settlement, and gave him a weekend off to marry wife number three, Carole Lombard. He was contracted in August 1938, with the stipulation that filming had to start in January 1939. There was still no finished script and no Scarlett.

That's not to say that no script existed. It's just that the screenplay that Sidney Howard had delivered would have resulted in a movie something like five hours long. Despite his agreement that he could write on his farm, Howard reluctantly came to Hollywood to try to trim it down. But Selznick was busy working on *The Prisoner of Zenda*, so Howard helped write some of that, feeling his time was a little bit wasted. After a month, they got back to the main event and worked hard on it—and ended up with a draft that was fifteen pages longer.

Selznick thanked Howard for his time and hired playwright Oliver Garrett to take over. He then took a month out in Bermuda to try to achieve something filmable. Meanwhile, a clear front-runner had emerged for Scarlett O'Hara—Paulette Goddard. Other people tested include Katharine Hepburn—who was still carrying the slogan "box-office poison" and who Selznick felt wasn't sexy enough—and Lana Turner—who looked too young. But there was one person who didn't favor Goddard because she thought she should play the part—Vivien Leigh.

Like countless others, Leigh had read the book when it was first published. Now she had become convinced the part was made for her, and she began to pursue it. She was recommended by a talent scout in 1937, and Selznick watched her in the film *Fire over England*, but he wasn't convinced. By this stage, Leigh was having an affair with Laurence Olivier. The two had met backstage after Leigh's performance in *The Mask of Virtue* in London in 1936, and although both were married to other people, she reportedly told a friend, "That's the man I'm going to marry," after this first encounter.

In 1938, Olivier traveled to America to film *Wuthering Heights* for Sam Goldwyn. Vivien Leigh accompanied him, at least partially to try to secure the part of Scarlett. She reread the novel on the journey and was taken on by Olivier's American agent, one Myram Selznick (brother of David). When they met, Myram asked them to accompany him . . . to a fire.

At this point, the backlot of Selznick International Studios had been filled with old sets going back many years, including the set of *King Kong*. Needing to clear it for fresh construction, the studio opted to incinerate it all, but knowing that they needed footage for *Gone with the Wind*'s burning of Atlanta, they filmed it, too. So, on 10 December 1938, seven Technicolor cameras recorded the conflagration, with stunt doubles doing a lot of the work, including an as-yet-uncast Scarlett hiding her face. Myram, Olivier, and Leigh arrived on set, at which point Myram went up to his brother and introduced the young actress with the words, "Meet your Scarlett O'Hara."

The subsequent screen test went incredibly well, and she was told she had the part on Christmas Day. But that was just the start for Leigh, who had to take many hours of accent classes alongside multiple make-up tests and fittings. She was not allowed to live with Olivier while the film was being made and was under twenty-four-hour guard to keep the press away in case he swung by. Gable had an easier time of it, refusing to play the role with anything other than his own accent. He and Leigh displayed what was described as a "cool friendliness," never being the best of friends but never being enemies either.

During this time, the screenplay kept developing. New writers were constantly brought in and then replaced, including a quickly fired F. Scott Fitzgerald. The script was a mess, with Selznick basically writing it himself by this point, but they still had to hit their locked-in deadline, so eventually shooting began. Early on, the producer had decided he wanted Selznick International's first contract employee and his personal friend George Cukor to direct. Now, finally, Cukor had something to point his cameras at besides Hollywood's largest-ever bonfire.

After ten days of production, they had managed to capture about twenty-five minutes of footage, at least ten of which had to be reshot. The first shot for Leigh was Scarlett's intro, but this isn't the version we see in the film, as they reshot this material five times over the course of a month before everyone was satisfied that everything was perfect, that her hair wasn't too red, and that the dress was just right. Cukor was too slow-paced for Selznick, but the director thought the script was the problem and refused to work without a better one. There were big arguments, and Cukor quit, much to the sadness of Leigh, who adored him and felt that her last hope of enjoying the shoot went with him.

The top choice to replace Cukor was Victor Fleming, a big-name director and friend of Gable's who was then working on *The Wizard of Oz*. Louis B. Mayer allowed him to be taken off *Oz* before it was completed (he ended up being one of at least three directors on that project) so he could move on to *Gone with the Wind*. He read the screenplay, immediately turned to Selznick, and said, "You haven't got a script." Production was shut down for seventeen days, and Ben Hecht was called in to do rewrites—using Howard's original treatment as the basis. Two weeks later, Selznick was popping pills, and Hecht was a wreck, running and hiding when they tried to get him for another week, fleeing halfway across the country on a train, and refusing to answer the phone.

Filming eventually resumed in March with the blokey Victor Fleming getting on well with Gable but less so with Leigh, whom he kept trying to push in unexpected directions. But now Selznick began to run into new problems. They only had enough money for another three weeks, and MGM was unwilling to stump up more cash, so Jock Whitney and his sister supplied further funds to keep the studio going—Selznick also had *Intermezzo* with Ingrid Bergman in production and was beginning work on Alfred Hitchcock's *Rebecca*.

And one particular line in the script was proving problematic. Margaret Mitchell's book includes Rhett telling Scarlett, "My dear, I don't give a damn," which Selznick hoped to retain some version of. But the Hays Office forbade any such profanity, despite Selznick arguing that "this word as used in the picture is not an oath or a curse. The worst that could be said of it is that it's a vulgarism." With the censor not budging, Selznick tried various alternatives, including, "I don't give a Continental," "My indifference is boundless," "The whole thing is a stench in my nostrils," and around a dozen others. Finally, he returned to the Hays Office and secured special dispensation to use the awful word—but on condition (according to some sources) that Gable misstress the line, putting the emphasis on *give* instead of *damn*.

By now, the stress was beginning to show on everyone. Victor Fleming was physically exhausted, taking pills to keep going, until he eventually reached a breaking point. Selznick was always arguing with him and telling him he was doing it wrong. After a big altercation with Leigh, he walked off the set and had a nervous breakdown. By this stage, there was too much momentum to stop, so MGM brought in a temporary replacement—Sam Wood—and Fleming eventually returned after two weeks off. But Wood didn't actually leave, shooting more material in parallel. Selznick must have realized that this was the only way he was ever going to get the movie finished, so at one point, six units were simultaneously filming different scenes for *Gone with the Wind*. A disorganized Selznick was taking Benzedrine and getting ready for his own breakdown, with everything in such a mess that they ended up having a wrap party, followed by more reshoots.

After five months and almost $4 million, filming was at last completed. Finally, Selznick was in his happy place—editing the material without any interference from directors or writers or stars or fathers-in-law. Now, he could put together the film he wanted. An initial sneak preview of a 265-minute rough cut was greeted with ecstatic cheering by the California crowd who had paid to see an unrelated double feature. When the screening ended, the same crowd gave it a standing ovation. It went on to break box-office records everywhere. Within four years, it is estimated that half of all Americans had bought tickets to see it. By that stage, it had earned its makers $32 million, making it not just one of the most successful but also one of the most profitable enterprises in all of movie history.

BEST OF THE BEST: *IT HAPPENED ONE NIGHT*

Writer: Robert Riskin, based on *Night Bus* by Samuel Hopkins Adams
Director: Frank Capra
Producer: Frank Capra for Columbia Pictures
Cast: Clark Gable, Claudette Colbert, Walter Connolly, Roscoe Karns, Jameson Thomas
Won: Best Picture, Best Director, Best Adapted Screenplay, Best Actor (Gable), Best Actress (Colbert)
Length: 105 minutes
Budget: $325,000
Box office: $2.5 million
Rotten Tomatoes: 98%

Jessica Regan: A comedy winning Best Picture is an incredibly rare occurrence, and this was the first instance of such a black-swan event. The country was clawing its way out of the Great Depression, and audiences were understandably seduced by the well-intentioned America presented by Frank Capra.

Claudette Colbert and Clark Gable are simply dynamite together. Their dynamic is not one of lazy antagonism that vanishes when someone stands in some good light halfway through the film. It is complex, surprising, and for all the screwball elements, it rarely feels dated. She needs his protection and street smarts; he needs her story. But what she has an abundance of, he has no interest in: money. Her access to financial resources usually gives her power over others. Here it holds no sway. Gable's Peter Warne is not just immune to the allure but rather contemptuous of wealth. It's an interesting reversal of the aspirational values usually associated with the American dream—the thinking being: the more you have, the better you are doing. Here the goal is to be the kind of person who cannot be bought. Integrity is the ultimate prize.

Gable is cast against type, having played all manner of tough guys, from cowboys to gangsters, in his previous work. Here we get to see another side of him: vulnerability breaks through, and so does the light. Five short years later, he would forever be associated with the man who throws Scarlett over his shoulder, doesn't take no for an answer, and in the end couldn't "give a damn." But it is in this earlier performance that we see other, arguably more sophisticated strings to Gable's bow—his gentle, goofy chatter, reassuring a woman enough that she's safe spending the night in the same room as him. His walls, as well as the "walls of Jericho," come down. A real man can make you eggs, procure you a toothbrush, and get your dress laundered and pressed, and it ain't even noon. I mean damn, that's attractive.

Colbert's Ellie Andrews feels fresh and contemporary, full of wit and invention. From the outset, we get a sense of her acuity. She has the good sense not to buy her own bus ticket to avoid being traced. She may be out of her comfort zone, but she is capable. Clueless but fearless, she can improvise on a dime and deploys her charms to winning effect when necessary. Serious credit must go to Colbert for playing such an unlikeable figure—the rich, superficial, pampered brat—with such heart and chutzpah that we root for her all the way.

Capra does a marvelous job of populating his film with intriguing peripheral characters. There are moments reminiscent of the best of the Coen brothers films—*Raising Arizona* and *O Brother, Where Art Thou?* spring to mind. Capra has been accused of oversentimentality and outright mawkishness in other works. This always manages to stay on the right side of the line, with all emotional gratification feeling heartfelt and hard won.

As we traverse the highways and byways of this nation of immigrants, diversity is represented and celebrated by a mosaic of accents in one memorable bus sing-a-along. There is a sense of the scale and breadth of America that is sorely lacking in other Best Picture winners that are on the road, such as *Rain Man* and *Green Book*.

True, we lose some momentum when the journey portion of this film is concluded. The absence of the chemistry we had so enjoyed until now is suddenly glaring, and for the first time, I can hear the plot gears grinding as we approach the climax. There is also some casual violence in language and actions toward Ellie from Peter Warne and her father, respectively. This lets the experience of the film down a little, as the gender politics feel so progressive in other ways. Even allowing for the intervening almost ninety years, these moments still jar.

But this is a minor complaint, easily forgiven, and the rest of this confection is delightfully light and charming—words you don't always associate with a Best Picture winner. Despite being a small story concerning a handful of protagonists, it still manages to touch on the heart and soul of America. This is achieved through the level of detail that enriches every aspect of it, from scene composition to plot devices and ruses to the gorgeous, swoony lighting. These actors look like the stars they are in every shot, and every shot is interesting. *It Happened One Night* is a precious film of care and craft that feels light but never flimsy. That is an exceptionally fine achievement of the kind that the Academy would do well to recognize more often.

WORST OF THE BEST: *THE GREAT ZIEGFELD*

Writer: William Anthony McGuire; songs by Walter Donaldson, Harold Adamson
Director: Robert Z. Leonard
Producer: Hunt Stromberg for MGM
Cast: William Powell, Myrna Loy, Luise Rainer, Frank Morgan, Virginia Bruce, Reginald Owen
Won: Best Picture, Best Actress (Rainer), Best Dance Direction (Seymour Felix)

Nominated: Best Director, Best Original Story, Best Art Direction
(Cedric Gibbons, Eddie Imazu, Edwin B. Willis), Best Film Edit-
ing (William S. Gray)
Length: 177 minutes
Budget: $2.2 million
Box office: $4.6 million
Rotten Tomatoes: 64%

John Dorney: Calling your story "The Great" anything is perhaps a
hostage to fortune. If your final word is *Gatsby* or *Escape*, then the
implicit promise is fulfilled. If it is, instead, *Ziegfeld*, then it most emphatically isn't—which is a cheap way of saying that this three-hour
movie is something of a slog. And that's not just because of its overall
length—individual scenes are interminably long, too. The whole thing is
overly ponderous and pointless. Hitchcock said that drama is life with
all the dull bits cut out. This film is life with all the exciting bits removed instead.

If you can reach it, the second half certainly picks up, roughly with
the surprisingly late arrival of second-billed Myrna Loy, utilizing her
already-established chemistry with William Powell. But you have to get
through two hours of story first. Not that there is much. The film as a
whole feels like an apology for bastards, suggesting that real love is
letting men do whatever they want. Florenz Ziegfeld as a person comes
across incredibly poorly, unable to stop telling people what to do and
how to dress and just generally behaving pretty rudely.

That we're willing to spend any time with him at all, let alone three
hours, is because of a winning central performance from the ever-
charming Powell. However, even he struggles—his glib insouciance is
enjoyable, but other than a couple of beats of emotion, he never quite
gets below the surface. In a film of about half the length of this one, you
might be able to get away with that, but when it's the length of an epic,
it'd be good to see a little bit of development.

The film has no curiosity about who this man is, what makes him
tick. We only learn about when his shows fail through newspaper headlines rather than seeing how it affects Ziegfeld himself. And because he
just breezes through everything, still living in luxury, still being waited
on, it's impossible to care for him. The character never really changes,
other than gaining a faint dusting of talcum powder to his hair every
twenty minutes or so to suggest he's getting older. Ziegfeld's a shyster

who always just about scrapes things together—for his entire life. This may be true to history, but a biographical picture needs to do more than just blandly relate real events. It still needs to have form and shape; otherwise, why is it worth telling at all?

The reason, in this case, is likely the opportunity for spectacle. The film is filmed to the rafters with glorious costumes and some delightful restaging of genuine performances from the time. These sequences are often fun and sometimes realized in astonishingly avant-garde ways, though they're not really worth wading through the rest—certainly not when the first, positioned just before the interval, takes so long to arrive. And they suffer slightly from diminishing returns. There's only so many lavishly staged musical sequences a person can watch out of context.

But the variable joy of these numbers is also the key to another of the film's problems. For a long time, the movie feels like it can't decide whether it wants to be the story of Ziegfeld or a documentary about his Follies. Rather than narrowing in on one or the other, it dissipates, if anything, the longer it continues, breaking into another five or six mini-plots, seemingly determined to follow every single person involved, from Fanny Brice playing herself to Luise Rainer breaking our hearts brilliantly—quite some time after her character seems to have departed the story.

It is at times well shot and has some impressive visuals. But they're largely swept away by vast waves of nothing. Which pretty much sums up the whole piece. Sadly, this potentially interesting film is ultimately only "Great" in terms of its length.

DID THE ACADEMY GET IT RIGHT?

1930/1931: *Cimarron*

John Dorney: *Cimarron*, a film that seemingly can't decide whether it's racist or not, is problematic as hell and has a couple performances that are left over from the silent era, which means that while it's ambitious in a way that appeals to me, it simply doesn't deserve the top spot. *City Lights* defies all stereotypes of Charlie Chaplin as a mawkish sentimentalist (though elements of that still hang on in there). But I'm going to go for *M*, the terrific, chilling story from Fritz Lang of child murder and kangaroo courts that will linger forever in your mind.

Jessica Regan: This is early cinema that has creaky moments and some cringeworthy acting but shows true innovation, possesses some great flourish, and imparts vision. What I find most interesting is how the lead—in a nonshaming way—encourages his wife to be an advocate and ally for oppressed groups and not to allow her compassion to be stunted by her own situation. But even our hero's benevolent form of othering is critiqued by the filmmaker's gaze. In one scene, he does not notice the lethal distress of a seemingly beloved Black character. Is the movie saying, "If you don't take care of vulnerable minorities, they'll die when you're not looking?" Is this Hollywood's first woke Oscar winner? It is certainly pioneering on many fronts, not just technical. And that makes *Cimarron* a very worthy, if not outstanding, winner.

Tom Salinsky: *Cimarron* has its clunky moments, but the sweep of the story and the way it documents the evolution of the West from wilderness to frontier to thriving economy is genuinely fascinating, if a little arid. What's frustrating is that the early promise of screwball fireworks between Richard Dix and Irene Dunne never really materializes. However, this detailed account of America's pioneers collides with one of Hollywood's pioneers who unveiled his masterpiece this year. *City Lights* is Charlie Chaplin at his funniest, most inventive, and most affecting, and I have to admire his stubborn perversity in refusing to be bullied into making a talkie.

1931/1932: *Grand Hotel*

John Dorney: I like it but not quite as much as Jack Lemmon seems to in *The Apartment*. Other films from this year have proved longer lasting and more influential. The most notable amongst them is Universal's *Frankenstein*, a film that infected our collective minds and has probably defined what that story is to a modern audience more than the original book itself.

Jessica Regan: It's glossy, it's starry, it's gorgeous. It features a scandalously alluring Joan Crawford. But it takes discomfiting, dark turns. It is a film preoccupied with death, which sits a bit awkwardly with this nascent device of the great ensemble. I found it luxuriated in emotion rather than story—secrets aren't revealed, setups aren't paid off. Condiments do not a meal make, and for all the lashings of chemistry and oodles of charm, it looks tasty but doesn't nourish completely. James Whale's monster movie is no beauty, but it is **Frankenstein** that touches the soul and deserved the Oscar—an enduring meditation on our humanity wrapped up in a thrillingly executed genre film.

Tom Salinsky: Although blessed with some wonderful performers at the peak of their powers, this feels rather like wandering in and out of a 1932 multiplex (if such a thing existed), just catching bits of different films—some better than others. There are lots of better choices for Best Picture, if you can put aside the snobbery that often infects the Academy. *Scarface*, *Shanghai Express*, and especially *Frankenstein* are all wonderful entertainment, but just nosing ahead I think is **Dr. Jekyll and Mr. Hyde**, which combines a bravura performance, amazing camerawork, and what was then called trick photography, and it ultimately does have something to say about repression, society, and the need for self-expression.

1932/1933: *Cavalcade*

John Dorney: *Cavalcade* is impressively made but never quite comes together, despite an at-times-sparkling script from Noël Coward. So we have to deal with the elephant—or rather giant ape—in the room. While *King Kong* is obviously iconic, it's nonetheless a slightly grubby, rather nasty film that leaves a bit of a sour taste in the mouth and is really a B picture in its dark heart, so it's not going to be my pick either. Instead, while I'm tempted by the utterly charming Capra comedy *Lady for a Day*, I'm going to go for the even more charming **Trouble in Paradise**, the story of two funny and sexy criminals falling for each other in an incredibly inventive and witty movie that still manages to push the cinematic envelope from time to time.

Jessica Regan: I find this film a fascinating time capsule full of heart and sophisticated storytelling. It is lean and brisk, despite being a saga spanning decades, and it is told through the personal rather than the political. At the forefront of this film is a loving marriage that is never twee or saccharine—the focus is often on the mental anguish of the women left behind as their sons, brothers, fathers, and husbands go off to war. The use of montages not just to show the passage of time but also to critique the machine of war and its hollow promise is extremely affecting, not to mention impressive. Ignore Rotten Tomatoes on this occasion; actors in training especially seek it out . . . it's *Cavalcade*.

Tom Salinsky: It might be as racist as anything, show a total disregard for human (or giant simian) life, and be generally bonkers, but there's nothing quite like *King Kong*. It takes a little while to get going, but as soon as our heroes set foot on that island, it's a roller-coaster ride of entertainment, with a commitment to special effects work that is unbelievable. It easily has the biggest cultural footprint of any film this year, and as much as I love the sophisticated comedies of Lubitsch and Capra (and the Marx Brothers), *Kong* is undeniable.

1934: *It Happened One Night*

John Dorney: I'm going to throw out a recommendation for the lovely comic whodunnit *The Thin Man*, but *It Happened One Night* is so obviously delightful that I really can't give the Oscar to anything else.

Jessica Regan: This is a fish-out-of-water, odd-couple romantic comedy all wrapped up in a road movie that entertains, excites, and still manages to have real emotional heft. It's doing so many things and doing them all brilliantly. I adore this film, and I applaud the Academy's choice heartily. The Oscar rightly went to *It Happened One Night*.

Tom Salinsky: The film you're supposed to pick from 1934, if you're a real cineaste, is *L'Atalante* (although it wasn't released in the United States until 1947), and it is gorgeously romantic, but I'm a total sucker for this combination of farce plotting, snappy dialogue, love against all odds between brash fellas and spunky dames. Gable and Colbert have charisma to spare, and it even makes me well up at the end. Just don't ask why on earth it's called *It Happened One Night*.

1935: *Mutiny on the Bounty*

John Dorney: This film is never quite as thrilling or morally complex as I wanted it to be, bar a few interesting beats where it seems to switch protagonists in the second half—although it's by no means bad. But in cinema history, it's easily overshadowed by *Top Hat* and James Whale's follow-up to his 1931 classic *Frankenstein*. They're both perhaps a little ripe by modern standards, performance wise, but it really has to be one

THE 1930s

of them, and I'm going for **The Bride of Frankenstein**, largely for the magnificent Elsa Lanchester, who creates an instant icon.

Jessica Regan: This got me from the beginning. With superb editing and brisk and brutal exposition, it gets straight down to business. Three very different but equally excellent central performances, as well as tremendous support from the rest of the cast, showcase some of the best ensemble acting of the period. It is viciously violent at turns but not gratuitously so. It asks important questions about leadership that never cease to be relevant. Films can take you to places you've never been to, more than any other art form, and **Mutiny on the Bounty** certainly does that for me.

Tom Salinsky: The staging is quite staggering and not just "for the time"—you can taste the brine in shot after shot. Laughton and Gable are both having a ball, and there's strong support from the rest of the cast. But the middle of the film fatally overlooks the motivations of the mutineers, and we have to piece together the cost of their rebellion for ourselves. Equally well mounted and generating a pace and daring that would leave a modern audience breathless is Alfred Hitchcock's peerless adventure romp **The 39 Steps**, which is even more fun than *Mutiny* and absolutely iconic.

1936: *The Great Ziegfeld*

John Dorney: Perhaps surprisingly, I am a little tempted by a yes, as I think as a piece, it has insane ambition—even if the execution fails to match it. But I'll go for Fred and Ginger in **Swing Time**. It's not a perfect film, not least for having an embarrassing blackface sequence in the middle, but it's half the length of *Ziegfeld* and has a lot of charm.

Jessica Regan: It is worth investigating for the costuming, choreography, and cameos, but this is meat with no bones, so—to use the parlance of the time—a lot of baloney. Special mention must be given to Virginia Bruce for some truly excellent drunk acting and to the production design for many glorious avant-garde visuals. If the Oscar were for Best Bastard, I would give it to this film in a New York minute, but I would not give Best Picture to this bloated, indulgent, incurious march through the life of the titular chauvinist impresario. I can happily give Best Picture to Charlie Chaplin's **Modern Times**, whose visuals are not only transportive but also memorable, with a substantive message that has continued to resonate through our twentieth and twenty-first centuries.

Tom Salinsky: You can't blame *The Great Ziegfeld* for being made in 1936 and thus being a bit slow and creaky, but seven years on from *The Broadway Melody*, I feel we're entitled to something with a bit more charisma than this ill-shapen old warhorse. Compared to this lumpen monstrosity, Capra's lightness of touch and surefooted storytelling seems almost magical. And you can very nearly watch **Mr. Deeds Goes to Town** twice in the time it takes to watch *Ziegfeld* once.

1937: The Life of Emile Zola

John Dorney: For about the first thirty minutes, when it's actually telling the story its title promises, this movie struggles to take off. A whistle-stop tour through the life of a literary icon isn't the most thrilling prospect, and so it proves. But the film begins to hit home when it becomes clear that it's really the story of the Dreyfus affair and the horrors of anti-Semitism (despite not saying the *J* word out loud). As an all-too-currently relevant study in racism, this film still packs enough power that I'm happy to give **The Life of Emile Zola** the prize, even with those first thirty minutes.

Jessica Regan: This film stirred up a cauldron of thought within me: the lengths institutions will go to avoid reform, how the Dreyfus affair was a harbinger of the evil that was to roll out across Europe, human capacity not just for transgression but also indifference, and so on. It is a straight story simply told but not without moments of cinematic flourish—including a progenitor courtroom speech and an acting moment for the ages when Alfred Dreyfus, played by Joseph Schildkraut, gets his freedom. I think **The Life of Emile Zola** succeeds in its intentions. It is solid, thought-provoking cinema, and more than that, it is a warning that we would do well to continuously heed: "These things are closer than you think."

Tom Salinsky: *Zola* doesn't do very much wrong—the story is told clearly and concisely, the performances are strong, and William Dieterle keeps the whole thing moving. But I want more from a Best Picture winner than a competent retelling of a fascinating historical episode. I'd have been very happy to see either of the brilliant screwball comedies *The Awful Truth* or *Nothing Sacred* win Best Picture or

Frank Capra's ludicrously ambitious *Lost Horizon*, but **Snow White and the Seven Dwarfs** is a landmark film, with almost unparalleled aspirations, and it still holds up today.

1938: You Can't Take It with You

John Dorney: *You Can't Take it with You* is fine, but it's utterly unmemorable, particularly when it's up against a number of classics, most notably *The Adventures of Robin Hood*, still to this day the definitive cinematic take on the enduring legend. But the best film of the year is easily **Bringing Up Baby**, the epitome of the screwball comedy, which remains an absolute pleasure from beginning to end.

　Jessica Regan: This is so diverting and entertaining with its Coen-brothers-style characters and Wes Anderson-esque production design. But I have to give it to the film that had me exclaim aloud on more than one occasion. **La Grande Illusion** is a film that made films better. It is a lesson in artistic authenticity and integrity. If you haven't already, do see what all the fuss is about. You won't be disappointed. Maybe watch *You Can't Take It with You* afterward, though!

　Tom Salinsky: Capra's film is full of his trademark wit and heart and deserves to be better known. It seems almost absurd to compare it to Jean Renoir's masterpiece *La Grande Illusion*, which began the slow infiltration of foreign language films into the Oscars, finally culminating in *Parasite*'s Best Picture win more than eight decades later. Luckily for me, I end up comparing like with like. For all its bonkers charm, *You Can't Take It with You* can't quite eclipse Howard Hawks's lightning-fast **Bringing Up Baby**, which posterity has dubbed the archetypal screwball comedy for good reason. It's sublime.

1939: Gone with the Wind

John Dorney: It probably is the biggest film of all time, adjusting for inflation, and the fact that something this old and riddled with such potentially awkward racial politics can still hold my attention for its vast running time says something for its quality. It's up against *The Wizard of Oz*, which is obviously another timeless classic, but for sheer sumptuous indulgence and the sexiest couple in movie history, there's very little that can top **Gone with the Wind**.

Jessica Regan: The first half is breathtaking—bathed in gloriously expressive lighting and studded with Technicolor sunsets. Vivien Leigh is just spectacular. Neither a Madonna nor a whore, she is a wonderful antiheroine, compelling in her caprice, mercurial and evolving, but always utterly herself. Her fall from grace and dignity becomes a fascinating study in what war does to you and how these wonderful female characters survive with and for each other. But it becomes almost claustrophobically unpleasant in the second half, as Rhett and Scarlett take lumps out of each other and tragedy upon tragedy feels heaped on to give heft. So, it has to be *The Wizard of Oz*—a dream of a film in every sense, full of wonderment and some of the best songs ever sung on the silver screen.

Tom Salinsky: Early portions of this film are very engrossing, with Vivien Leigh creating one of the most complex character studies of any woman in cinema history. Scarlett's rise, fall, and rise again are fascinating, and the epic scope of the burning of Atlanta helps the story to feel cinematic. But the structure begins to creak in the last quarter, as arbitrary misfortunes pile up and the film becomes more about incident and less about character development. So, while I'm pleased to have seen *Gone with the Wind* for the first time, at the age of forty-seven, I would have been even more pleased to have watched *The Wizard of Oz* for the twentieth. This remarkable film burrowed into my imagination when I was about eight years old, and I've loved it every time I've seen it. Judy Garland's sheer conviction anchors every bonkers moment, but nobody puts a single foot wrong. It's perfection.

3

THE 1940s

THE OSCARS IN THE 1940s

The decade began with secrecy at the top of the agenda. For the first Oscars, the winners had been published months before the actual presentation dinner, but for the second to the twelfth awards, although no one else was told, the full list of winners was given to the press a few hours before the ceremony began so the papers could meet their print deadlines. This worked well until the 1939 awards, when the *LA Times* jumped the gun and printed the results in full before the ceremony had even started.

So, from the 1940 ceremony onward, only the accountants at Price Waterhouse would know the results of the voting, and presenters would

	Best Picture	Biggest Earner
1940	Rebecca	Boom Town
1941	How Green Was My Valley	Sergeant York
1942	Mrs. Miniver	Mrs. Miniver
1943	Casablanca	This Is the Army
1944	Going My Way	Going My Way
1945	The Lost Weekend	The Bells of St. Mary's
1946	The Best Years of Our Lives	The Best Years of Our Lives
1947	Gentleman's Agreement	Welcome Stranger
1948	Hamlet	The Red Shoes
1949	All the King's Men	Jolson Sings Again

have to open a sealed envelope to learn the winners of the awards they were giving out. This suddenly made the Oscars exciting again, although it drove the papers crazy. But Americans were shortly to get more excitement than they could handle. The attack on Pearl Harbor in December 1941 had dragged the United States into World War II, and the effects were already being felt.

Under the circumstances, the usual lavish banquet dinner seemed out of step, and newly installed Academy president Bette Davis thought things had to change. At the time, Davis was a four-time nominee and had won two Oscars, and she had big ideas about how she was going to carry out her new office. Her idea was to make the presentation of the Academy Awards a public event for the first time. She wanted it to be a show rather than a private dinner. She argued that it should be staged in a theater or a cinema and recommended her friend Rosalind Russell to produce it. She even suggested that the money raised in ticket sales be donated to the British war relief.

The Academy clearly wasn't ready for changes this sweeping. With his head in his hands, then vice president Walter Wanger asked her, "You already have two Oscars. What do you have against the Academy?" Davis quickly realized that her appointment was only meant to generate good PR and that she was expected to be a good girl and let the board continue running things. Despite Darryl F. Zanuck threatening that if she resigned, she would never work in Hollywood again, she quit, and outgoing president Walter Wanger was forced to step into the breech. Most of Davis's suggestions were in fact implemented over the next few years, particularly after the overcrowded 1942 awards, at the end of which, many impatient guests were still standing at 1:00 a.m., listening to Greer Garson's six-minute-long acceptance speech when she won Best Actress for *Mrs. Miniver*.

The other big story of the early 1940s was of course Orson Welles's controversial movie debut, *Citizen Kane*. Despite losing money—in part due to opposition from newspaper magnate William Randolph Hearst, who recognized himself in Charles Foster Kane—RKO's film earned nine nominations, including an astounding four for Welles himself as producer, director, star, and cowriter of the film. *The Little Foxes* had the same number of nominations but won nothing, which also set a record. But *Kane*'s only win was for its screenplay. Neither Welles nor his cowriter, Herman J. Mankiewicz, were present, and when their win was announced, some of the audience were said to boo and hiss, such was the negative publicity whipped up against the film. Best Picture that year went to John Ford's bucolic Welsh family drama *How Green Was My Valley* (with a single Welsh actor in the cast).

Once World War II started, patriotic films ruled the awards. As well as Best Actress, *Mrs. Miniver* also won Best Picture and four other Oscars, and then in 1943, *Casablanca* won Best Picture, Best Director, and Best Adapted Screenplay. But in 1944, the tide turned, as Leo McCarey's feel-good bit of fluff *Going My Way* managed to beat several more "important" films, including Selznick's American riff on *Miniver*, *Since You Went Away*; Darryl F. Zanuck's 154-minute epic *Wilson*, starring Alexander Knox as the twenty-eighth American president; and Billy Wilder's proto-noir masterpiece *Double Indemnity*.

Wilder got his revenge the following year when his alcoholism drama *The Lost Weekend* triumphed over McCarey's sequel *The Bells of St. Mary's*, but Zanuck never got his closure. For years afterward, he would complain to friends and colleagues that the Academy were philistines and idiots for not giving Best Picture to *Wilson*. He even brought it up when *accepting* his Best Picture Oscar for *Gentleman's Agreement* in 1947! Seemingly devoted to self-sabotage, a few years later, he passionately argued to the Academy board of governors that the Irving G. Thalberg Memorial Award was so important that it should only be given to a producer who can win a two-thirds majority from the voting board members. At the 1949 awards, this procedure was adopted, and it was Zanuck himself who became the first producer to be considered under the new rules. He fell short by one vote.

Bing Crosby's costar in *Going My Way* was veteran Irish actor Barry Fitzgerald, who was nominated both as Best Actor and Best Supporting Actor, as there was no rule preventing the same performance from appearing in two categories—although one was hastily added after this double nomination. Maybe not surprisingly, Fitzgerald did win Best Supporting Actor and, despite having the chance to win two Oscars, only went home with one. However, due to wartime metal rationing, his statuette was made of gold-painted plaster, and while celebrating at home, Fitzgerald managed to smash it to pieces with a golf club. The Academy replaced it—the first time it had had to do so—and so, in a way, Barry Fitzgerald did manage to get two Oscars for one performance. After the war, anyone else who had a plaster statuette was invited to exchange it for a gold-plated bronze one.

Then in 1947, Harold Russell was nominated as Best Supporting Actor, despite not being a professional actor but a serviceman who had lost both hands in an explosives accident while working as an instructor in the US Army. William Wyler had cast him in *The Best Years of Our Lives* to give the story a bit of extra verisimilitude. Because his nomination obviously wasn't going to turn into a win but they wanted to honor this brave man in some way, the Academy voted him an Honorary Award, which he gladly accepted. However, later in the evening, when Anne Revere opened the envelope, she discovered that Best Supporting Actor had in fact gone to the same Harold Russell, making him the only person in Oscar history to *actually* win two awards for one performance. Although the audience gave him warm applause, Cary Grant (who had been nominated twice and never won) is said to have whispered to the person sitting next to him, "Do you know where I could get a stick of dynamite?"

Joan Crawford's career had stalled in the early 1940s, but *Mildred Pierce* was her comeback vehicle, and she desperately wanted the box-office returns and glowing reviews to turn into a gold statuette (or even a plaster one). She hired publicist Henry Rogers, who—together with the producer of *Mildred Pierce*, Jerry Wald—began an Oscars campaign that was unlike anything Hollywood had ever seen before. While the film was still in production, Wald told Rogers to call gossip columnist Hedda Hopper and claim that he had been privately raving about Crawford's performance. Wald knew Hopper would call him to confirm the story, and he was happy to oblige. Hopper printed the story, and Rogers planted dozens more like it over the next few months. Amazed at the apparently spontaneous groundswell of support for Crawford, the studio began taking out ads in the trade papers and arranging special screenings of the film for Academy members.

When the nominations came out, Greer Garson got her fifth successive nomination, but Crawford was the hot favorite. However, on the big night, she got a sudden attack of nerves and told Rogers that she couldn't go to the ceremony. She persuaded a doctor to record her as having a temperature of 104 and retired to bed to listen to the show over the radio. When Charles Boyer read out her name, her health took a dramatic turn for the better. She bounded out of bed, showered, brushed her hair, and then returned to her bedroom in a satin bed jacket.

Director Michael Curtiz, who'd collected the award on her behalf, arrived with her Oscar in his hands and an entourage of photographers. She received her statuette sitting up in bed, perfumed, resplendent, radiant. "Usually I'm ready with the wisecracks," she said, "but my tears speak for me. This is the greatest moment of my life." She also claimed to have voted for Ingrid Bergman. In the next morning's newspapers, there were so many pictures of Crawford in bed that a casual reader could have been forgiven for assuming that the entire ceremony had taken place in her boudoir. Crawford was the only woman in her forties to win Best Actress during the 1940s (she was forty-two). She was nominated two further times, but this was her only win.

The very next year, Rosalind Russell had got the part of her life with the film version of Eugene O'Neill's play *Mourning Becomes Electra*. She'd been nominated in 1942 and 1946 and lost both times, but this time she, too, called for Henry Rogers. Russell's husband, producer Fred Brisson, promised Rogers a small bonus for a nomination and a large bonus for a win. Despite the fact that Russell herself was unwilling to leave the East Coast to give interviews to LA papers or appear on any radio shows to promote the movie, Rogers outdid himself to secure his client an Oscar. He managed to persuade a Las Vegas casino to publicly offer odds on the year's Best Actress race—these naturally made Russell the favorite. He got local Rosalind Russell fan clubs formed across the country. He secured an "Actress of the Year" accolade from a local PTA. And then the pieces started falling into place when Russell won Best Actress at the fifth Golden Globes.

At the Oscars, Best Actress was the last award to be given out, and Rosalind Russell's win was thought to be such a forgone conclusion that the audience was already filing out of the theater when Fredric March opened the envelope—to reveal that the actual winner was Loretta Young for *The Farmer's Daughter*. This was a kick in the teeth for Rosalind Russell for a number of reasons. First, this was another RKO production but one that newly installed head of production Dore Schary had brought with him from Selznick International. *Mourning Becomes Electra* had begun under the previous regime, and Schary thought it was boring. Second, *The Farmer's Daughter* was a fluffy comedy well within Loretta Young's comfort zone, whereas Russell had poured her heart and soul into *Mourning Becomes Electra*. Third, Russell had been offered Loretta Young's part after Ingrid Bergman had turned it down. Henry Rogers had been so confident of victory that he had already told his wife to start spending his win bonus on furnishing their new home. When the award went to Loretta Young, Mrs. Rogers ran to the ladies' room to throw up.

As the 1940s came to an end, Oscar's outlook became notably more international. In 1947, Vittorio de Sica's *Shoeshine* was given a special award for the year's best foreign-language film. Nine years and seven special awards later, the category of Best Foreign Language Film was introduced at the twenty-ninth Academy Awards. Also at the 1947 awards, Best Black-and-White Art Direction went to David Lean's *Great Expectations* and Best Color Art Direction went to Powell and Pressburger's *Black Narcissus*—both British films. Next, it was time for the cinematography awards, where Best Black-and-White Cinematography went to *Great Expectations* and Best Color Cinematography went to *Black Narcissus*. All four awards were accepted by nineteen-year-old Jean Simmons—who surely must be the only person ever to collect four consecutive Academy Awards!

THE MOVIES IN THE 1940s

After the upheaval of 1930s, the 1940s should have been a time for consolidation, but war put paid to that. Disney didn't make a full-length animated feature between *Bambi* in 1942 and *Cinderella* in 1950— instead releasing six "package" films made up of unrelated or vaguely related shorts, many of them with explicit propaganda messages. In fact, American cinema was positively eager to include political messages in support of the war effort. To pick just one example out of countless, Hitchcock had completed his second American film, *Foreign Correspondent*, but before its release he learned of the imminent bombing of London and quickly added a final scene in which Joel McCrea's character, speaking from Britain, delivers a radio broadcast to America, imploring them, "Hang on to your lights! They're the only lights left in the world!"

But the government wasn't going to wait around for enterprising expat directors to take matters into their own hands. Following the bombing of Pearl Harbor, the Office of War Information was formed by President Roosevelt, and very quickly it looked to Hollywood to help them get the public on its side. Its director, Elmer Davis, observed, "The easiest way to inject a propaganda idea into people's minds is to let it go through the medium of an entertainment picture when they do not realize they are being propagandized." A Bureau of Motion Pictures was formed, which published a manual for the motion picture industry, emphasizing that this was a common man's war and that the four freedoms (freedom of speech and religion and freedom from want and fear) were at stake for the whole world.

This body analyzed scripts and even story treatments to ensure that Hollywood's entire output was all speaking with one voice. If you think that sounds less than democratic, then you may not be surprised to learn that before long, President Truman was in the White House; Republicans made gains in Congress; and the Office of War Information was defunded, with many of its leading lights hounded as suspected communists. More on that story later.

War also meant that money was hard to come by. This is one reason color didn't sweep through the industry the way that sound had in the late 1920s. Color was vastly more expensive, and most moviegoers were happy with black-and-white. As well as the cost of film stock, processing, and licensing, Technicolor cameras were huge and bulky, requiring enormous lamps to blast the set with light. Directors had to suffer Technicolor consultants telling them how to shoot their films, and there was a sense also that color was vulgar and brash, whereas black-and-white was classy and restrained. So despite the conspicuous success of *Gone with the Wind* and *The Wizard of Oz*, many studios continued releasing monochrome movies well into the 1950s and even the early 1960s.

As the war continued, a young director named Vincente Minnelli made his first feature. He would go on to marry Judy Garland in 1945 and direct her in a number of her best-remembered roles, but his first film was *Cabin in the Sky*, a musical based on the successful Broadway play. Despite the fact that the United States was still in the grip of racial segregation, Minnelli began his career directing a film with an all-Black cast, including Ethel Waters, Louis Armstrong, and Lena Horne. Horne was the first African American woman to sign a long-term contract with a major studio (MGM), but the Minnelli film aside, they generally had her appear only in self-contained musical numbers that could be removed from the final film for distribution in southern states.

The war also led to an influx of European directors into Hollywood, including Billy Wilder, Fritz Lang, Edward Dmytryk, and Otto Preminger, and they brought new ideas and new techniques with them. German expressionism had already started to have an impact on the work of directors like Hitchcock and Orson Welles. At the same time, popular novelists were altering their approach, as the drawing-room poisonings of Agatha Christie and Conan Doyle were replaced by the much more brutal worlds created by Dashiell Hammett, Raymond Chandler, and James M. Cain. Combined, these new trends in verbal and visual storytelling gave birth to what is arguably the first genre of cinema—the film noir. Slapstick is a film version of clowning. Western movies are film versions of western novels. Musicals are film versions of Broadway shows. But film noir couldn't have existed before the movies.

Neither *Rebecca* from 1940 nor *Citizen Kane* from 1941 are generally seen as classic noir films, but they both bear some of the hallmarks. The 1941 version of *The Maltese Falcon* is probably the first movie where all the pieces come together. Humphrey Bogart plays Sam Spade, the cynical hero of Dashiell Hammett's convoluted novel. John Huston wrote the script, and it was his first film as director. It also cemented Bogart's star status after twelve years in the business. Whereas the gangster films of the early 1930s had been straightforward, good-guys-versus-bad-guys thrillers, in these newer films, even the heroic detectives were flawed and prone to moral weakness.

In fact, a general distrust of authority was in the air, and some long-standing norms were being questioned. Olivia de Havilland had signed with Warner Bros. in 1936 and starred as Maid Marion opposite Errol Flynn's Robin, was seen in the western *Dodge City*, got loaned out to Selznick for *Gone with the Wind*, and had a big hit with *Hold Back the Dawn* from a screenplay by Billy Wilder and others. But she'd also turned down several projects that hadn't appealed to her, leading to her being suspended and a general cooling of relations between her and the studio. In 1943, her seven-year contract was up, and she was preparing to start offering her services elsewhere. However, Warner Bros. took the position that her time on suspension should "stop the clock" and that her contract still had six months to run.

This was an old trick, and she wasn't the first to object to it—Bette Davis had taken the same studio to court over a similar situation in 1936—but de Havilland was the first to win. Although the case lumbered on for several years of judgments, rulings, appeals, and counterappeals, in 1945, the California Court of Appeal finally ruled in her favor, creating a legal precedent still known as the De Havilland Law. She went on to create complex and dramatic characters in such movies as *The Heiress*, *The Dark Mirror*, and *The Snake Pit*, for which she won the Oscar for Best Actress.

And more trouble was to come for the studio system. All the big Hollywood studios were, in the modern parlance, vertically integrated. They owned the stars, they owned the land the movies were filmed on, they owned the intellectual property, and they controlled the means of distribution—owning many cinemas outright and block-booking films into those they didn't. (This was the practice that had so displeased Harry Brandt of "box-office poison" fame.) And for years, the American Justice Department had been attempting to break up their effective monopoly.

In 1948, the antitrust case found its way to the Supreme Court, and it ruled against the studios, forcing them to sell their interests, either in making films or showing them. Paramount Pictures was the company whose name was on the docket, but the ruling affected every studio in Hollywood. This new status quo remained in place for almost seventy years, until 2019 when the Department of Justice under President Donald Trump struck down these laws, once again giving Hollywood studios complete control over when and where their product is shown.

In Britain, legislation was also being brought in that would alter the way the film industry operated. The Nazis had been vanquished, but the United Kingdom's finances were in tatters, and in 1947, the Labour government started looking for ways to cut imports in order to keep as much cash inland as possible. Although imported films from America only made up a tiny percentage of the total spending, they were included, and a 75 percent duty was slapped on Hollywood product entering the country. America responded by boycotting films from the United Kingdom. The intention had never been to give British filmmakers a clear run at the domestic audience, but that was the inevitable outcome.

It didn't hurt that British cinema was flourishing in any event—even supplying films to the United States that did well both at the box office and at the Oscars. British movies like Olivier's *Hamlet*, Noël Coward and David Lean's *In Which We Serve*, and the films of Powell and Pressburger were gaining widespread attention. The cycle of Ealing comedies began in 1947 with *Hue and Cry*, written by T. E. B. Clarke and directed by Charles Crichton. This was followed by such all-time classics as *Whiskey Galore, Kind Hearts and Coronets, Passport to Pimlico, The Lavender Hill Mob, The Man in the White Suit*, and many others. These films made stars of actors like Dennis Price, Stanley Holloway, Joan Greenwood, and especially Alec Guinness.

But UK cinema owners were struggling to find enough product to fill their screens. Before the legislation, around 80 percent of films shown in the United Kingdom were from America. Now, UK studios had to find a way to massively ramp up production—without the financial benefits of being able to export films to the United States, where a far bigger audience existed. After a great deal of wrangling, the mutual bans were lifted in March 1948, but the new wave of British films was somewhat swamped by the backlog of American material that had built up over the preceding six months. Particularly badly hit was the Rank Organisation, which controlled both British movie studios and British cinema chains (no antitrust case here).

Meanwhile, in Italy, the fall of Mussolini's fascist government created a new freedom for filmmakers, who for years had had their output tightly controlled by the state. Once again, funds were limited, but such directors as Luchino Visconti, Roberto Rossellini, Michelangelo Antonioni, and Vittorio de Sica developed a new kind of cinema. Dubbed neorealism, these films used documentary-style camerawork and often nonprofessional actors, and they explored tales of the poor, the working class, and the mundane. When Rossellini's *Rome, Open City* won the Grand Prix at the Cannes Film Festival, the whole world was talking about Italian cinema.

This was, in fact, the first ever Cannes Film Festival, but the idea had come about many years earlier. In 1932, the French minister for national education suggested that France should host an international film festival, but it was hard for him to arrange the necessary funding and organization. Meanwhile, in Venice as part of the Venice Biennale—an annual arts event dating back to 1895—the world's first international film festival had already gotten underway. However, in the late 1930s, fascist groups took control of the Venice festival, and in 1938, the official recipient of the Mussolini Cup was Leni Riefenstahl's Nazi propaganda film *Olympia*. French juror Philippe Erlanger wanted a European film festival that would not be subject to that kind of political pressure. He rekindled the idea with the French government, and the town of Cannes was selected as the venue. The first Cannes Film Festival was set for September 1939. It was officially canceled one month before.

Once the war was over, Philippe Erlanger returned to his project. In September 1946, the first Cannes Film Festival took place, still based on the principles established in 1939. As a welcoming initiative, for this first year only, every participating nation was awarded a Grand Prix. As well as Rossellini's film, other recipients included Billy Wilder for *The Lost Weekend* and David Lean for *Brief Encounter*, as well as films from France, Sweden, Soviet Russia, and more.

The stage was set for a world of filmmaking that was far more international and far more interconnected than ever before. But Hollywood—far from embracing these new opportunities to learn from and be influenced by new ways of thinking—was about to retreat into an insular paranoia that would both create some indelible art and also senselessly wipe out many promising careers.

THE MAKING OF *REBECCA*

Writers: Robert E. Sherwood, Joan Harrison, Philip MacDonald; based on the novel by Daphne du Maurier
Director: Alfred Hitchcock
Producer: David O. Selznick for Selznick International Pictures/ United Artists
Cast: Joan Fontaine, Laurence Olivier, Judith Anderson, George Sanders, Reginald Denny
Won: Best Picture, Best Black-and-White Cinematography (George Barnes)
Nominated: Best Director, Best Actor (Olivier), Best Actress (Fontaine), Best Supporting Actress (Anderson), Best Screenplay, Best Original Score (Franz Waxman), Best Black-and-White Art

Direction (Lyle R. Wheeler), Best Film Editing (Hal C. Kern),
Best Special Effects (Photographic Effects: Jack Cosgrove, Sound
Effects: Arthur Johns)

Length: 130 minutes
Budget: $1.3 million
Box office: $6 million
Rotten Tomatoes: 100%

Daphne du Maurier's 1938 novel *Rebecca* is the story of two women.
But the making of the movie version is the story of two men—two very
independent men: Alfred Hitchcock and David O. Selznick.

Selznick had formed Selznick International Pictures in 1935, and
four years later, he had his biggest success with *Gone with the Wind,* a
film that had been an absolute mess behind the scenes, as detailed in
chapter 2. He'd obsessed over every detail, whether it was the script,
the casting, the scenery, or the director(s). He was a man who only
wanted to see one vision on the screen—his own, the producer's—and
in his mind, the success of the movie vindicated his overcontrolling,
dictatorial style. He was a big deal—but he needed more directors on
his payroll.

On the other side of the pond, in England, was one possibility:
Alfred Hitchcock, a director who claimed he never wanted to be a
director. He'd started off working on title cards and art direction, before ending up assisting British director Graham Cutts in Berlin at the
age of twenty-five, where the work of revolutionary filmmakers like
Murnau and Lang taught him how to tell a film story visually.

So, when his boss, Michael Balcon, persuaded him to start directing,
he was very keen on using pictures over words. And he prepared meticulously, drawing every single camera move in advance, three frames a
page. Very little was left on the cutting-room floor; he used everything
he shot and didn't shoot things he didn't end up needing, saving money
(his movies would come in for around half the usual cost of other films
of the time). His work was so detailed that he would say the most boring
thing about a film was shooting it because he'd already made it in his
mind.

This approach led to him becoming something of a star director in
England, but unfortunately, British cinema at the time was in decline
and wasn't taken terribly seriously. That meant that even given his star
status, he didn't always manage to do things his own way. His produc-

tion of *Jamaica Inn* (based on another du Maurier book) had not been a happy experience. Despite knowing the author due to working with her actor-manager father, he didn't get as much input as he wanted. He had to obey the orders of his star and producer, Charles Laughton, who'd originally been cast in one role before asking to play another one—which then had to be changed from a priest to a squire and was revealed as the villain a lot earlier than planned in order to give Laughton a bigger role.

Feeling a lack of respect, he put out word that he'd like to make movies in Hollywood. He knew that working in America would likely mean losing even more autonomy, but he thought this would be made up for in terms of money and prestige projects. Somewhat to his chagrin, he only got one response—from David Selznick, who put him on a seven-year contract. Initially, they wanted to make a film about the *Titanic* that would have involved sinking a real ship. When this—shockingly—proved too expensive, they moved on to a different project. This project was the recent hit novel *Rebecca*.

It's not entirely clear when *Rebecca* arrived in the conversation. Selznick brought it to the table, but it appears Hitchcock was already keen to work on it, and the producer had dangled it like a carrot to get him to sign on. So, Hitchcock dived in, downplayed the romance to Selznick, and refashioned it according to his own taste, making it more of an action film. His process was to work with a writer doing a detailed outline, scene by scene, beat by beat. Only then would they move onto dialogue. When adapting material, he liked to pull it apart, later saying, "I believe that I owe much of the success I have been lucky enough to achieve to my 'ruthlessness' in adapting stories for the screen."

His treatment began with a scene featuring Maxim de Winter, sailing on the Riviera and smoking a cigar, causing his new wife and fellow passengers to feel nauseous. Hitchcock often used comic beats like this to leaven the suspense in his British films, but it struck Selznick as vulgar, unsophisticated, and tasteless. In fact, he felt this way about the whole treatment. He wanted his *Rebecca* to be a scrupulously faithful adaptation that would satisfy readers of the book and keep its Gothic gloom intact, and Hitchcock's treatment was emphatically not that. Selznick sent a three-thousand-word memo expressing his displeasure, stating that as they spent the money to buy the book, they should make the book.

They argued for nearly a year as the screenplay was developed, and casting was an equally lengthy process. Having considered names like Ronald Colman, David Niven, and William Powell to play Maxim, they eventually settled on Laurence Olivier, who was then hot from his success playing Heathcliff in *Wuthering Heights*. Olivier at least hoped that they might cast his new wife, Vivien Leigh, in the film, as she had also just had huge success with *Gone with the Wind*, but ironically Selznick was less keen because he disliked her screen test (feeling her too famous to be a convincing ingénue), and he was hoping to whip up the same global frenzy as he had when casting her as Scarlett O'Hara. Dozens of actresses auditioned, with Joan Fontaine only slowly emerging as the top choice.

Filming started five days after the declaration of World War II. It was originally supposed to shoot for thirty days at a cost of $750,000, but it eventually became sixty-three days at a cost of $1.28 million. As with his British films, Hitchcock's movie was planned to the last detail, but Selznick wasn't happy with this. Hitchcock shooting only what he needed meant that there was only one way to edit the shots together—Hitchcock's. Selznick wanted more shots and coverage so he could re-cut the scenes if he wanted to. This didn't go down well with Hitchcock, and so there were more fights. Hitchcock felt constrained and compromised. He resented the finished film and later dismissed it as not a proper Hitchcock picture.

With tempers fraying and a seven-year contract to fulfill, Selznick rented him out to other producers and studios at twice the salary he was paying—basically living off Hitchcock for several years. Of the ten films Hitchcock made in this period, only three were for Selznick. The most successful was *Spellbound*, whose commercial triumph made him a major box-office draw for the rest of his life and led to his collaboration with Ben Hecht on *Notorious*. Although a Selznick production, this was made without the producer's interference, as he had by now fallen in love with Jennifer Jones and got bogged down in making the movie *Duel in the Sun*, intended to relaunch her career. This movie flopped, but *Notorious* became a masterpiece—the first in Hitchcock's golden period.

The two men parted ways with *The Paradine Case*, although it wasn't entirely their final connection. For the villain in *Rear Window*, Hitchcock envisaged a tall, sturdy man with a shock of white hair and round spectacles. He cast Raymond Burr and coached the actor on how to walk and how to stand, even when answering a telephone. Half of Hollywood recognized the caricature that Hitchcock fashioned—but Selznick's reaction is not recorded.

BEST OF THE BEST: *CASABLANCA*

> **Writers:** Julius J. Epstein, Philip G. Epstein, Howard Koch; based on the play *Everybody Comes to Rick's* by Murray Burnett, Joan Alison
> **Director:** Michael Curtiz
> **Producer:** Hal B. Wallis for Warner Bros.
> **Cast:** Humphrey Bogart, Ingrid Bergman, Paul Henreid, Claude Rains, Conrad Veidt, Sydney Greenstreet, Peter Lorre
> **Won:** Best Picture, Best Director, Best Screenplay
> **Nominated:** Best Actor (Bogart), Best Supporting Actor (Rains), Best Cinematography (Arthur Edeson), Best Film Editing (Owen Marks), Best Music (Max Steiner)
> **Length:** 102 minutes
> **Budget:** $1 million
> **Box office:** $3.7 million
> **Rotten Tomatoes:** 97%

Tom Salinsky: *Casablanca* is awkwardly constructed and drenched in movie clichés, and very little of what happens on-screen makes any sense at all.

Casablanca is a beloved masterpiece for a reason. Every department is at the top of its game, and the film contains more indelible images, quotable lines, and memorable moments than almost any other.

Both of these accounts are fairly undeniably true. Here, I shall attempt to explain why the truth of the first paragraph is entirely irrelevant and hope to elucidate why amid a glut of similar-feeling gangster/war/one-man-against-the-world pictures of the 1940s (from Warner Bros. and other studios), it's *Casablanca* that stands alone.

As many know, the story began life as an unproduced play entitled *Everybody Comes to Rick's*. Under the careful supervision of producer Hal Wallis, various screenwriters contributed ideas, with the Epstein twins emphasizing the wisecracks, Howard Koch leaning heavily on the political angle, Casey Robinson building up the romance, and dozens of little contributions from other people here and there—including members of the cast: legend has it that "Here's lookin' at you, kid" was Humphrey Bogart's contribution.

Bogart was just emerging as a major star, and this film refined his persona. Early tough-guy roles in films like *Angels with Dirty Faces* and *Dead End* hadn't begun to stretch his acting talents, but with John Huston's film version of *The Maltese Falcon*, he was allowed some dry humor. Now with *Casablanca*, he combined both these elements with a deep, aching vulnerability. It's a truly remarkable piece of movie acting.

It doesn't hurt that he shares the screen with a goddess in human form. Ingrid Bergman is not only captivatingly beautiful in this film, but she is also a remarkably sensitive actor who gives tremendous depth to her character. Ilsa never comes across as a prize to be won or a token female. She's never less than a fully realized human in her own right. With a spectacular supporting cast of wonderful character actors (Claude Rains, Conrad Veidt, Sydney Greenstreet, Dooley Wilson, Peter Lorre), it's hardly surprising that Paul Henreid struggles to register—but if he'd worked harder, that might have upset the delicate balance of the film.

And that's what makes all this work. Despite the fact that the Moroccan locations were thrown together in the studio from sets left over from *The Desert Song* and *Now Voyager*, despite being shot in ten weeks flat, despite Bogart and Bergman working from half-finished scripts, and despite the nonsensical premise of the travel papers that cannot be questioned or canceled, everything is in perfect balance. That's why the structural "mistake" of the Paris flashback works so seamlessly, as well. At the exact point that our curiosity about Rick and Ilsa's relationship eclipses our interest in the political intrigue plotline, we finally get the answers to our questions, without the suspense becoming frustrating. Oh, and that ending, sweated over endlessly by that team of writers, which now seems like absolute perfection. Rick completes his journey from cynical sad sack to self-sacrificing patriot. Still mordant and pragmatic but now with a noble purpose for the first time in his life. The "hill of beans" speech is pure Hollywood hokum, but by God, it works.

Even the music survived a backstage battle of egos. Composer Max Steiner hated "As Time Goes By" and petitioned to have it replaced with a composition of his own. When he lost that fight, rather than dig in his heels and refuse to include it except when Sam plays it, he selflessly incorporated the song's melody into his score, both unifying and strengthening the overall musical structure of the film, as well as emphasizing the tune's key role in the unfolding human drama.

Credit for much of this must go to producer Hal Wallis, who supervised the writing, picked the director (Michael Curtiz, who in response to Wallis's anxiety about the implausible travel papers, told the producer, "Don't worry, I make it go so fast, nobody will notice."), assembled the cast and got lucky when the Allied invasion of North Africa suddenly put the name *Casablanca* on the front page of every newspaper in late 1942. But studio boss Jack Warner failed to give him the credit he felt he was due at the Academy Awards.

When his film was announced as the winner of Best Picture, at Grauman's Chinese Theatre, Wallis was stuck in the middle of the row and watched dumbfounded as Warner bounced out of his seat and collected the award instead of him. Wallis had produced five films for Warner Bros. in 1943, and every single one of them had won at least one Oscar, and he'd been given the Irving Thalberg Memorial Award at the same ceremony. But he regarded Jack Warner's behavior at the awards as a personal affront, and he left the studio as soon as his contract was up.

Meanwhile, *Casablanca* has become one of the most popular Best Picture winners of all time and one of the most beloved films ever made. I still come across people who claim to be cinephiles but also think *Citizen Kane* is boring (it isn't), but you don't have to know the first thing about cinema to enjoy *Casablanca*. You can just sit back and let the story carry you away.

WORST OF THE BEST: *GOING MY WAY*

Writers: Frank Butler, Frank Cavett, Leo McCarey
Director: Leo McCarey
Producer: Leo McCarey for Paramount
Cast: Bing Crosby, Barry Fitzgerald, Frank McHugh, James Brown, Gene Lockhart, Jean Heather, Risë Stevens

Won: Best Picture, Best Director, Best Screenplay, Best Story, Best
   Actor (Crosby), Best Supporting Actor (Fitzgerald), Best Original
   Song ("Swinging on a Star")
Nominated: Best Actor (Fitzgerald), Best Cinematography (Lionel
   Lindon), Best Editing (Leroy Stone)
Length: 126 minutes
Budget: $990,000
Box office: $7.8 million
Rotten Tomatoes: 83%

Jessica Regan: With a title that could be a placeholder or describe a
teen sex comedy from the 1980s, this Best Picture winner would seem
to indicate that the Academy in its entirety lost its mind or a bet or both.
It's hard to know how the pendulum could have swung so egregiously
the other way. It's almost as if some studio bigwig said after *Casablanca*'s win the previous year, "Ya know what? These pictures are getting
too smart, sophisticated, and challenging. Let's do the *opposite*. Now,
stay with me, fellas—let's go for something simpler. And there's nothing simpler than no plot, some kids and priests, and a few ditties. Amir-
ite, fellas?"

I'd like to think there was a copy girl (with enough smarts to run a
studio but enough awareness to know that was unlikely to happen in her
lifetime) inwardly fuming as they broke out the brandy and cigars and
backslapped themselves on not losing their common touch. "How can
they?" she mutters to herself as she types the minutes of the meeting.
"They can make any film, tell any story—and they choose this? After
Kane? We're doing this now?!" The laughter intensifies, as does the
half-remembered nostalgia. These men are not Hollywood elites, no
siree. They remember where they came from. They remember Father
MacIrish and Big Ears O'Crooner and the songs they sang and the fun
they had—oh yes, they remember. Did a church burn down? Maybe.
Do we know why? Nah, stick it in the script. After all, we should have a
bit of plot, particularly toward the end.

It looks and feels the way it was reportedly made—with no great
craft or intention, no purpose beyond having people wander in and out
of rooms singing a song here and there. The camera is unforgivably
static, particularly in the opera scene. Shooting scenes meant to depict a
live performance of an opera on stage level makes it look like a costume
party. Barry Fitzgerald brings pathos that isn't on the page, and I did

find it touching when he is reunited with his mother. I appreciate it must have seemed like a warm hug from across the water to the generations of the Irish diaspora who had been crossing the Atlantic since the 1800s. But this is not a Best Picture winner by any stretch or allowance. It is barely a motion picture.

It is hard to swallow Crosby as a kindhearted singing priest and friend to young boys, considering the horrific abuses alleged by his son Gary in his memoir *Going My Own Way*; his Mafia ties; and the tragic suicides of his two sons, Lindsay and Dennis. I cannot censure a film for what is beyond its purview. But I can condemn Crosby for playing an anticharacter. There are no choices, no discernible traits, no stakes, no change, no journey whatsoever. I would go so far as to say, never has so little been done by a lead in a Best Picture winner—not to mention an actual Best Actor winner! Even when the acting isn't to my taste (hello, *Gladiator*), I can always discern choices, commitment, hard work. Not here. I see a man running out the clock, waiting for someone to yell, "Cut!" so he can get back to what he really cares about—pleasing himself. Acting is not so much about pretending as it is about revealing. A generous person usually makes for a generous actor, a chaotic person can make for an unpredictable one, and so on so forth. Here, Crosby lacks a character on-screen. If his sons' accounts are anything to go by, he lacked character in real life, too.

The romance in the film plays out between two bafflingly unappealing people—sure let's make *that* choice—with a postcoital Code-skirting moment that jars so tonally you are left wondering not for the first time, What were they thinking? What are they doing? And why are they doing it? As our disillusioned copy girl clears the ashtrays away and cleans the glasses, alone in the quiet solitude of that empty office on the Paramount backlot, she is surely left wondering the same.

DID THE ACADEMY GET IT RIGHT?

1940: *Rebecca*

John Dorney: It's a shame that Hitchcock's only winner of the big prize should be such a middling title in his catalogue that fails to capture the claustrophobic atmosphere of the original novel. He did many other far, far better films, and aspects of this one feel dated and silly now. *The Philadelphia Story* is an obvious classic, and *The Great Dictator* may be tonally all over the shop but is a fascinating watch nonetheless. But they're not my pick. I'm going to give the prize instead to the delightful Christmas movie **The Shop around the Corner**, which showcases the "Lubitsch touch" at its most charming. Remade twice (as *In the Good Old Summertime* with Judy Garland and *You've Got Mail* with Tom Hanks and Meg Ryan), the original is still the best.

Jessica Regan: Even allowing for the attitudes of the time, the misogyny threaded through this entire enterprise means it is now only watchable as a camp classic. Olivier is not brooding and mysterious but rather dull and irritable. Joan Fontaine, doing her level best but still playing an infantilized sap, just about holds it together. Judith Anderson's performance as Mrs. Danvers is the flavor that changes the whole dish, elevating the film to a level of silliness that makes it far more tolerable and quite good fun in parts. Far, far better is **The Philadelphia Story**. Sexy, charming, and irresistible, it is as bracing as the sea breeze so longed for by Katharine Hepburn's Tracy Lord. I adored my time spent in the company of these characters, and I cannot say that about the Academy's choice this year.

Tom Salinsky: Sadly, *Rebecca* looks very dated now, while other films from the same year seem fresh and vibrant. I would have been very happy to see either *The Shop around the Corner* or *The Philadelphia Story* win the big prize, but the lethally funny **His Girl Friday** is not only my favorite film from this year, but it's also one of the funniest films ever made and has a shot at being the best remake ever filmed, as well.

1941: *How Green Was My Valley*

John Dorney: Otherwise known as *How Fake Was My Accent*, this film remains in the shadow of this year's obvious winner, **Citizen Kane**, and even nonwinner *The Maltese Falcon*. It's still directed by John Ford, who is an absolute cinematic master, so it does manage to have some striking and memorable visuals lifting its not terribly exciting plot. But not enough to contend with the "greatest film of all time" or even come close.

Jessica Regan: John Ford takes us on a surprisingly spiritual and contemplative journey to a Welsh mining town, exploring what Eckhart Tolle would term the pain-body inheritance of generational trauma through deprivation and subsequent emigration. I do understand why the Academy picked *How Green Was My Valley*. It is a very fine film and perhaps unfairly overlooked considering the cultural impact of its chief competitor. But **Citizen Kane** should have won—and not just because of the benefit of hindsight. It gets you by the throat and doesn't let go, and it continues to inspire anew.

Tom Salinsky: John Ford's film is warm and embracing without being overly sentimental, and it must have resonated strongly with American families sending their boys off to war. But the story never reaches outside the small Welsh village, and the episodic structure grates after a while. In a slightly odd year, when a couple of master filmmakers are noticeably off their game (both Hitchcock's *Suspicion* and Capra's *Meet John Doe* have compromised endings), **Citizen Kane** still manages to lay waste all before it. True, it's very showy—even show-off-y—but as well as dazzling in the manner of its telling, it also expertly manages to balance a big story about power, wealth, and influence and a personal story about loneliness, isolation, and ambition. It also doesn't hurt that it's one of the most thoroughly entertaining movie masterpieces, full of cracking gags and with an enviable lightness of touch.

1942: Mrs. Miniver

John Dorney: It was said at the time that this film pretty much brought America into World War II. And so, for historical significance alone, it probably deserves the Oscar. But it is an excellent film in its own right, subverting expectations and illustrating painfully the human cost of war with a few bitter last-act twists. The subversion of *To Be or Not to Be* is worth mentioning, too, but **Mrs. Miniver** just takes it by a nose for me.

Jessica Regan: There is a tendency for films of this time told from a female perspective to be pejoratively and retroactively described as "melodrama." They tend not to carry as much weight in the minds of cultural curators as films about soldiers and prisoners of war who are men. Unusually for the subject matter, this film and its frames are filled with women. Wyler is a masterful conductor of nuance, and all these slight human moments amount to something really quite profound and affecting. There is so much to be enjoyed, from the game performances to the stiff-upper-lip stoicism punctuated by moments of absurdity, sensuality, and backyard peril, that all play out in that little time-capsule corner of London that is Mrs. Miniver's world. **Mrs. Miniver** feels so progressive for giving us this perspective and a timely, worthy winner of Best Picture.

Tom Salinsky: This year is bonkers. In any normal year, I could have happily given the prize to *Bambi*, *49th Parallel*, *The Man Who Came to Dinner*, *Sullivan's Travels*, or *Now Voyager*, and I think I'd enjoy rewatching any of those more than the necessarily constrained *Mrs. Miniver*. However, this year also gave us Ernst Lubitsch's sublime **To Be or Not to Be**, which is one of my favorite films of all time. To make a film that funny with stakes that high is a triumph indeed. To have made such fun of the Third Reich in 1942 tips this film into all-time-masterpiece territory.

1943: *Casablanca*

John Dorney: *Casablanca* is destined to be one of the immortals, a film that is now almost eighty years old and resolutely of its time yet still able to connect with and move audiences to tears today. It's delightfully funny and heartbreakingly romantic and has a punch-the-air finale. There is literally never a bad time to watch this movie. It's an obvious and easy choice.

Jessica Regan: The ending might have some ambiguity, but I possess none in this instance. I heartily back the Academy's choice of **Casablanca**. For all the treasures contained within this film—flawless performances, every evocative frame filled with storytelling, one of the most quotable scripts of all time—I am struck by what it doesn't have, considering when it was made. There are no grotesques and caricatures, there is no slut-shaming, no judgment of the affair, no toxic competition between Victor Laszlo and Rick. Bergman's Ilsa has wonderful agency and pragmatism as well as blood-rushing chemistry with Bogart. It is but two decades shy of being a century old, and there remain timely lessons to be learned from the storytelling, the acting and style, and the content itself—fight the good fight, and protect refugees.

Tom Salinsky: It's absolute perfection, of course, balancing the needs of an exotic spy caper, a heartbreaking romance, a call to patriotic arms, and a wartime adventure and doing it all with great jokes, wonderful casting, and astoundingly precise pacing. Bogart was never better, and Bergman is sublime. I mourn the overlooking of Powell and Pressburger's *The Life and Death of Colonel Blimp*, possibly not a greater film, certainly a less purely entertaining one, but hugely ambitious and a towering achievement nonetheless. Sadly, it was hardly seen in the United States on its first release. But even that can't distract me from wholeheartedly endorsing the Academy's choice. It has to be ***Casablanca***. It's undeniable.

1944: *Going My Way*

John Dorney: This deeply boring Bing Crosby vehicle would be long confined to the ashes of history were it not for its inexplicable winning of the Academy Award. Practically any other film this year could have won it, and it would have been an improvement. But when one of those films is Billy Wilder's masterful noir ***Double Indemnity***, it becomes practically an obligation.

Jessica Regan: The Academy wasn't alone in its love of this film—it was also number one at the US box office this year. Some critics bridled at it, but it was largely adored—however, not by me, as you will have learned by now. I would give the Oscar to ***To Have and Have Not***. It has refreshingly multicultural moments that aren't about exoticizing or fetishizing but rather showing one of cinema's earliest "safe spaces." If it's music you're after, walk right along past the winner and enjoy the supreme skills on display here. Believe the hype about Lauren Bacall's entrance and her chemistry with Bogart. Unusually for its genre, this film has a happy ending—much like Bogart and Bacall, whose subsequent marriage defied expectations by lasting until his death from cancer in 1957. Bacall said of him, "No one has ever written a romance better than we lived it."

Tom Salinsky: Maybe not the worst but certainly the least interesting Best Picture we had watched to this point, *Going My Way* is generally fairly competent but is never inspired, coasting by on Crosby's affable charm and Fitzgerald's comfort in his character. Other films this year offered a counterpoint to the prevailing mood of doom and foreboding, such as *The Miracle of Morgan's Creek* and the luminous *Meet Me in St. Louis*, but it's a fatalistic masterpiece that obviously should have won in the form of Billy Wilder's intense and thrilling **Double Indemnity**, with its crackerjack screenplay, exemplary cast, and sublime photography.

1945: The Lost Weekend

John Dorney: One of the other contenders this year, *Spellbound*, has a dream sequence that has haunted my sleep for decades, but the rest of it is undeniably mid-tier Hitchcock. *Mildred Pierce* is probably more successful and enjoyable overall, but when **The Lost Weekend** hits, it feels so fresh and modern that it is the natural choice.

Jessica Regan: Ray Milland gives a performance for the ages, genuinely harrowing in this brilliant interrogation of the disease of alcoholism. It is unfortunate some of the supporting characters are thinly drawn and blandly played. It is a hard watch, and all involved deserve credit for not shying away from its awful truth of all-consuming addiction. But when you know the lead is doomed from the start and we have no idea how he came to be in such a lamentable state, it can limit emotional engagement. Best Actor all the way, but for Best Picture I believe the Academy should have honored a deeply satisfying and surprising saga with a character who compelled me utterly. Unlike her brat daughter, I root for **Mildred Pierce**.

Tom Salinsky: It's a huge achievement by all concerned, and if it doesn't represent Wilder at his absolute peak, then it's still more complex, better constructed, more thought-provoking, and just more plain entertaining than just about any other film from 1945. *Mildred Pierce* is delicious, but the compromised ending hurts it. **The Lost Weekend** is exactly the film Wilder wanted it to be.

1946: The Best Years of Our Lives

John Dorney: I went in rather dreading this one—a three-hour movie that's largely faded from the consciousness on this side of the pond. And how wrong that dread proved. This is a corking film, humane and honest, and it's exactly the film the world needed after the war. Even against stone-cold classics like *Les Enfants du Paradis*, *The Big Sleep*, and *It's a Wonderful Life*, **The Best Years of Our Lives** thoroughly deserves the crown.

Jessica Regan: Oh my goodness, what a movie! Brilliantly acted and almost unbearably moving—I was a sobbing mess by the end. William Wyler is a true craftsman, filling the frame with storytelling and drawing out riches from every department. Harold Russell is extraordinary. He couldn't have done more to forge a path for differently-abled actors, and it is a reflection on the limits of studios' imagination, not on his star turn, that casting didn't become more diversified in the wake of his performance. A work of such integrity and completeness, it is the *Citizen Kane* of family-driven narratives. The Academy was completely correct, and if you haven't seen it yet, watch **The Best Years of Our Lives** as soon as you can.

Tom Salinsky: An unfairly neglected masterpiece whose strikingly relaxed and naturalistic acting style might have seemed revolutionary at the time but the impact of which may have been overshadowed by the explosion of Method masculinity that was just around the corner. Wyler directs with his usual impeccable taste. Thank you, Academy voters of 1946, for bringing this to our attention. All that having been said—films like **It's a Wonderful Life**, which burrow into the zeitgeist and which enchant multiple generations of moviegoers, are incredibly rare. As good as Wyler's film is, Capra's crowning achievement is a landmark of cinema, and it should have won.

1947: *Gentleman's Agreement*

John Dorney: *Gentleman's Agreement*'s heart is undeniably in the right place, and it's saying something brave and important for its time. However, bar a few flashes, it doesn't really deal with its subject matter, anti-Semitism, in the strongest way possible and is very much a curate's egg. It probably wouldn't be my winner in many Oscar ceremonies, but this year it's up against the majesty of **Black Narcissus**, one of my favorite films of all time—a rich and heady brew filled with sumptuous visuals and an intense plot that, despite putting Jean Simmons in brownface, is still such an amazing spectacular that it really has to be the winner.

Jessica Regan: As well-intentioned as this film is, a character cosplaying Jewishness is tricky to countenance and becomes an exercise in allyship with mixed results. The female characterizations are refreshing, with both women possessing a dynamism and inner life, particularly a lovely and luminous Celeste Holm. I appreciate how this film challenges the chattering classes as to what anti-Semitism can look like—and it isn't always in jackboots. But the cause gets a little cheapened when it becomes a mere obstacle to his romantic relationship, which was hard to get behind at the best of times. For this reason, I opt instead for **Great Expectations**, a marvel of a movie—enchanting, thrilling, and unsurpassed in the canon of Dickens adaptations for screen.

Tom Salinsky: In a year that includes a peerless literary adaptation in the form of *Great Expectations*, the return of one movie legend with *Monsieur Verdoux*, and the origin story of another with the deeply affecting *Shoeshine*, a movie would have to be pretty special to earn my vote. *Gentleman's Agreement* is not that film—but yet again Powell and Pressburger prove that they were always ahead of the game. **Black Narcissus** is a near miracle of moviemaking that has to be seen to be believed, and it leaves its competition in the dust.

1948: Hamlet

John Dorney: What's surprising about Laurence Olivier's *Hamlet* is how cinematic it is. Often, movie adaptations of stage pieces can find themselves trapped by the proscenium arch, and this emphatically doesn't. It is thrillingly directed and takes the Shakespearean classic into the dark territory of gothic horror. In many other years, it would be a worthy winner. However, this is the year of Powell and Pressburger's magnificent **The Red Shoes**, which is a haunting exploration of sex and repression, where a sequence trapped behind a proscenium arch is, if anything, the highlight. It should have won.

Jessica Regan: Laurence Olivier doesn't merely film this play; he really plays with film. The actor-savant crafts an adaptation that leans into the interiority of all the characters in a way that deepens the experience of this story. Shakespeare's story is a cornerstone of culture now, but this film must have been an entry point for so many people in multiple countries to *Hamlet* and the wider works of Shakespeare. It uses the form audaciously without conceptualizing characters but instead gives lingering examinations of their choices. I expected a dusty, creaking experience of a play I was all too familiar with, and instead, I felt I was being told it anew. Unlike our melancholic protagonist, I face no agonizing choice or insoluble dilemma—it's *Hamlet*.

Tom Salinsky: Olivier's *Hamlet* is a compromise. The text has been cut in half, and the ambition strains the budget. Other noted classics from this year, like *The Treasure of the Sierra Madre*, are the best possible versions of themselves, but although marvelously entertaining, they seem not too dissimilar from other works from the same filmmakers around the same time. Even within the remarkable canon of Powell and Pressburger, though, **The Red Shoes** is something very special. I'm slightly amazed that it got so many nominations, and I can kind of understand why the Academy didn't give it the big prize, but they obviously should have.

1949: All the King's Men

John Dorney: I struggled with this year. The reason for this is that it's the year before *All about Eve*, which, if you look, is part of one of the strongest lineups in awards history. And I kept wanting to see something get close to its level—or indeed that of *Sunset Boulevard* or *The Third Man*—and I never did. So, I probably underrated what I saw instead. On the night I gave top honors to *The Heiress*, a film about mousy Olivia de Havilland opting not to take any more of your shit, but in retrospect, I think I'll move back to **All the King's Men**, which has a massive weight of ambition that the other films don't, even if it doesn't quite stick the landing.

Jessica Regan: This film has some fascinating contemporary resonances, along with a brevity and cynicism that are near revelatory for the period. Mercedes McCambridge gives a dazzlingly sophisticated, sexually ambiguous performance that would feel right at home in any modern-day political drama. I'll allow that this study of the political rise and moral demise of a man lacks the inciting incidents necessary to fully understand the corruption of his moral compass, but for its uncanny prescience and bravery in its bleakness, I give it to **All the King's Men**.

Tom Salinsky: Rossen's film feels stiff and old-fashioned in a way that the best films of this era—*Sunset Boulevard*, *All about Eve*, *The Heiress*, *White Heat*—really don't. And the "right" answer for this year is of course Vittoria de Sica's *Bicycle Thieves*. (Or is it *The Bicycle*

Thief? Discuss.) But I can't overlook my love for ***On the Town***. There may only be snatches of location filming but what snatches! And Gene Kelly and Frank Sinatra are joined by two of the best female dancers on the MGM lot—Vera-Ellen and Ann Miller. With rich comic support from Jules Munchin and Betty Garrett and a perfect blend of Bernstein's more avant-garde melodies and Roger Edens's less-challenging new songs, it's an unqualified joy.

4

THE 1950s

THE OSCARS IN THE 1950s

In 1946, an average of around 90 million Americans went to the movies every week. Ten years later, this number had been cut in half. Something had changed, and that something was television. Television broadcasts had begun in America in 1941, and by the end of 1948, NBC, CBS, ABC, and the DuMont network were all showing a full schedule of programs throughout prime time. In 1946, only six thousand homes had televisions. By 1951, it was twelve million.

The big studios had initially tried to deal with this threat by buying up television stations, but the 1948 antitrust case put paid to that. And the shrinking box office put extra pressure on the symbiotic relationship

	Best Picture	Biggest Earner
1950	All about Eve	Samson and Delilah
1951	An American in Paris	Quo Vadis
1952	The Greatest Show on Earth	The Greatest Show on Earth
1953	From Here to Eternity	The Robe
1954	On the Waterfront	White Christmas
1955	Marty	Cinerama Holiday
1956	Around the World in 80 Days	The Ten Commandments
1957	The Bridge on the River Kwai	The Bridge on the River Kwai
1958	Gigi	South Pacific
1959	Ben-Hur	Ben-Hur

between the studios and the Academy. The Academy, although dreamed up by MGM boss Louis B. Mayer, was an independent body. It didn't make movies, but without them, it had no reason to exist. Movie studios liked having the Academy there because having someone put on a big annual party and generate newspaper headlines about their product helped to drive ticket sales. So, for years they had been happy to fund the awards show (apart from a brief wobble in the 1930s), treating it as a sort of marketing spend.

That changed in 1952. Seeing their profits and audience being eroded by television, Universal, Columbia, Republic, and Warner Bros. issued a joint statement saying that they would not be paying anything toward the Oscars ceremony. Academy president Charles Brackett barely had time to react to this news when he received a phone call offering him $100,000 for the television rights to the show. And so, the twenty-fifth Oscars became the first to be televised.

Bob Hope, who hadn't hosted the show since 1946 when he'd begun working for the enemy (i.e., making television specials), was invited back into the fold, and he emceed the show from California, with Conrad Nagel and Frederic March overseeing cutaways to a different theater in New York. The practice of hiring seat-fillers hadn't yet been devised, and the NBC cameras captured footage of empty seats, which Conrad Nagel assured viewers were being held for actors performing on Broadway who would be occupying them as soon as the curtain came down.

The early black-and-white cameras also struggled with some aspects of the show. Ladies were asked to wear pale colors and gentlemen to tint their white shirts blue to avoid them glaring. Popular actor Ronald Reagan provided a running commentary for the television audience. And in what seems to have been a genuine surprise, an honorary award was presented to Bob Hope, who'd been making jokes all evening about his lack of Oscar success. He'd been given special awards in 1940 and 1944, but this was the first time he'd been given a real full-size Oscar statuette, and he looked genuinely amazed and moved to have been so honored. He even bit its head to make sure it was real.

The 1952 Oscars is best known now for the ponderous circus epic *The Greatest Show on Earth* winning Best Picture, while all-time classic *Singin' in the Rain* was almost completely overlooked. Jean Hagen was nominated as Best Supporting Actress for playing squeaky-voiced Lina

Lamont, and it was nominated for its score, but it won nothing at all. I think it probably didn't seem quite so remarkable then. *An American in Paris*, from essentially the same team, had won six awards the year before, and it had also made a lot more money. Today it's far easier to see *Singin' in the Rain* as the one where everything clicks, everything works. And being a film made in the 1950s but set in the 1920s means that it doesn't look dated even today. But Academy voters in 1952 probably saw it as just another glossy crowd-pleaser rolling off the Freed Unit production line. It wasn't until 1958, when it was rereleased as part of a package of MGM musicals, and critics including Pauline Kael started singling it out, that it was hailed as a masterpiece.

The regular presence of television cameras put more pressure than ever before on having stars for those cameras to be trained on—especially those nominated for acting awards. In 1954, this even extended to an NBC television crew wheeling their equipment into Judy Garland's hospital room. Garland had prematurely given birth to Joey Luft two days before the ceremony, but producers wanted to make sure she could give a speech on TV should she win—and she was thought to be a shoo-in for her role as Esther Blodgett in the (first) remake of *A Star Is Born*. She had been Hollywood's darling for twenty years, and this was her triumphant comeback after four years off-screen.

But it was new kid on the block Grace Kelly, who had taken a much less glamorous role than usual in *The Country Girl*, who pinched the win at her first and only nomination. In fact, she had four films out in 1954, prompting Bob Hope to comment that he thought a special award should be given for producers brave enough to make a film without Grace Kelly in it. Garland sat up in her hospital bed, in full makeup; saw William Holden read out Grace Kelly's name on the television; and then had to watch as the camera crew just packed up all their equipment and left her there alone. Sid Luft told her, "Fuck the Academy Awards, baby. You've got yours in the incubator."

After three previous nominations, Marlon Brando won Best Actor in 1954 for *On the Waterfront*, telling the audience, "I don't think that ever in my life have so many people been so directly responsible for my being so very, very glad. It's a wonderful moment and a rare one, and I'm certainly indebted. Thank you." He even clowned around with emcee Bob Hope, producing one of the most celebrated photographs in

Oscar history. At this stage at least, refusing the award seemed the furthest thing from his mind.

This was only the third year that the awards were televised—but already there were complaints about the show being too long. Producer Jean Negulesco decided that what was slowing things down was all that tedious reading out of the nominees. So, he just had the names superimposed on the screen. These were not always totally legible, however, and as the night wore on, it gradually dawned on all concerned that reading out the nominees was an essential part of the night's drama. In the event, the show was only ten minutes shorter than the previous year's.

Jerry Wald, producing the 1958 awards, was even more determined to keep the running time under control. The previous ceremony had overrun by six minutes, and so this year, he was almost neurotic about ending the show on schedule. When some of the presenters were swapping jokes for slightly longer than he was comfortable with, he started dropping production numbers, in some cases minutes before they were due to begin. But after Ingrid Bergman gave Best Picture to *Gigi*, the producer realized with horror that far from overrunning, he actually had twenty minutes of airtime left. Poor Jerry Lewis attempted to ad-lib to fill the rest of the slot, as viewers started to turn off their televisions, and the audience began to file out of the theater. Eventually, NBC cut to a rerun of a sports documentary.

The 1956 ceremony was the first at which all the films nominated for Best Picture were in color (although black-and-white wasn't dead yet—the following year, two Best Picture nominees were in black-and-white), and Best Picture nominees trended toward huge, widescreen epics. Jerry Lewis's opening monologue had a lot of fun at the expense of the long running times and big budgets of the films nominated. "I didn't see all of *War and Peace* because the kid in front of me grew up," he commented. Then he told the audience "*Giant* cost me $300: $3 to get in and $297 for a babysitter." To be fair, it would take you fourteen-and-a-half hours to watch all five of 1956's Best Picture nominees. Even the shortest, *The King and I*, is well over two hours, and *The Ten Commandments* is nearer to four hours than three. The decade ended with the 212-minute *Ben-Hur* winning Best Picture—the only Best Picture winners with longer running times are *Lawrence of Arabia* and *Gone with the Wind*.

In 1956, Ingrid Bergman won Best Actress for *Anastasia* in what was the final chapter of her rehabilitation in America. Bergman had been a huge Hollywood star in the 1940s, but polite American society couldn't stomach her extramarital affair with Italian director Roberto Rossellini, particularly not when she bore him a son. This might all seem very tame now, but in 1950, questions were being asked on the floor of the US Senate.

Six years later, with Bergman and Rossellini both having divorced their previous spouses and now married to each other with two further children (including Isabella Rossellini), America was ready to welcome her back. Fox took a chance and cast her in a fairly mainstream movie. TV talk show host Ed Sullivan organized a write-in vote to see if Americans thought seven-and-a-half years' penance was enough. The result was 2,500 letters of support for Bergman but also 1,500 votes cast against her. God alone knows what would have happened if the vote had gone the other way! She wasn't present at the awards show, but she did supply a prefilmed announcement for Best Director, shot on a Paris rooftop.

High Society—the musical remake of *The Philadelphia Story* with Frank Sinatra, Bing Crosby, and the ubiquitous Grace Kelly—was one of the biggest hits of 1956, and so it wasn't surprising to see it earn a nomination for its screenplay. But unbelievably, as they tallied the votes for writing, the Academy managed to confuse the opulent MGM all-star musical with a Bowery Boys production-line comedy released the previous year. The Bowery Boys writers, Edward Bernds and Elwood Ullman, gallantly withdrew their names from consideration, and the Oscar went to *The Brave One*, but Bernds and Ullman remain the only people to have been nominated for an Oscar *by mistake*.

And the weirdness doesn't end there. The award for *The Brave One* was collected by Jackie Lasky Jr., vice president of the Writers Guild, on behalf of credited screenwriter Robert Rich, who was unable to attend the ceremony on account of the fact that he did not exist. The film was really written by Dalton Trumbo, who was blacklisted following his refusal to "name names" to the congressional committee trying to weed out Hollywood communists. This is even more ironic when you consider that the Academy, hoping to stop this kind of thing from happening, had just ruled that anyone who had refused to talk to the committee would not be eligible for a nomination.

The following year, Best Adapted Screenplay went to *The Bridge on the River Kwai*, and the statuette was awarded to the credited screenwriter Pierre Boulle, who had also won the BAFTA, where he told the audience that he hadn't actually written the script himself. Director David Lean and producer Sam Spiegel were quick to attribute this to false modesty, but Hollywood insiders already knew that the French-speaking Boulle barely understood English, let alone wrote whole English-language screenplays. The actual writers—Carl Foreman and Michael Wilson—were of course blacklisted, and so at the Oscars, it was Kim Novak who accepted the award on behalf of Pierre Boulle. In 1976, at the Writers Guild, the truth came out, and Carl Foreman jokingly asked if they could work out a custody agreement with Boulle. In 1985, seven years after Wilson's death and one year after Foreman's, the Academy presented their widows with honorary awards.

THE MOVIES IN THE 1950s

As noted previously, Hollywood viewed television as the enemy and was quick to woo audiences back into movie theaters with such innovations as Cinerama, a process of projecting images from three synchronized 35mm projectors at the same time onto a gigantic, curved screen. They also tried 3D and even gimmicks like Smell-O-Vision. Cinerama was only used on a handful of movies, but widescreen was a trend that was here to stay. The first studio to release a mainstream feature film in widescreen was 20th Century Fox, whose anamorphic Cinemascope process was built on Henri Chretien's work from as far back as 1926. This system produced an image twice as wide as those that were being captured with conventional lenses—and it only needed one projector, unlike Cinerama. It was introduced to audiences in 1953 with *The Robe*, and Fox quickly followed it up with *How to Marry a Millionaire* in the same format. Both films were big hits, and before long, Cinemascope was joined by Todd-AO, Panavision, VistaVision, and more widescreen formats besides—and Fox licensed its technology to many other studios, including Disney.

At least Uncle Walt was still running the studio that bore his name. Louis B. Mayer, however, was forced to resign in 1951 after twenty-seven years as the head of MGM. It wasn't his history of ruthless exploitation that was his undoing but a young executive, formerly RKO's production chief, Dore Schary. After repeated clashes over budget and content, Mayer informed Nick Schenck, president of Loew's, which controlled MGM, "It's either me or Schary"—and Schenck chose Schary. Mayer was the head of MGM during the making of some of the greatest films in movie history and ran a studio that could justifiably claim to have "more stars than there are in heaven." He was also alleged to have abused Judy Garland and to have attempted to assault Jean Howard, apparently blacklisting the agent she went on to marry. Not only did he make or break stars, but also, much like his contemporary Jack Warner, his actions authored a playbook of malfeasance that would be co-opted by Hollywood power players for decades to come.

The sci-fi boom was fueled by 3D as the genre came into its own in the 1950s. The "golden age" of 3D commenced in 1952 with the release of *Bwana Devil*, which used the red-green anaglyph process—a relatively cheap system based on a principle dating all way back to 1856. *Robot Monster*, *It Came from Outer Space*, *Columbia's Man*, and *House of Wax* were among the many 3D sci-fi films released the following year. Christian Nyby's *The Thing* (a.k.a., *The Thing from Another World*) was one of the earliest examples of an alien invader film, featuring filmdom's first space monster. Rumors abound that it was ghost-directed by its producer Howard Hawks, but the truth is probably lost to history. Robert Wise's *The Day the Earth Stood Still* features one of the most famous phrases in sci-fi history—"Klaatu barada niktu"—as well as never-before-seen visual effects and an iconic Bernard Herrmann score. The cult classic was also the first of many 1950s Cold War–inspired science-fiction films and features the first modern movie robot, the silver giant Gort.

It is little wonder that Hollywood was in thrall to sci-fi films. The town was steeped in fear and paranoia about unknowable forces and otherworldly menace as one of the darkest chapters in Hollywood history was still unfolding. The House Un-American Activities Committee (HUAC) hearings created a deep schism in the industry. Louis B. Mayer, Ronald Reagan, Walt Disney, Elia Kazan, and Gary Cooper are among those who testified on the existence of communism in Hollywood. Between 1947 and 1952, some three hundred people who worked across the industry—including Orson Welles, Charlie Chaplin, Myrna Loy, Katharine Hepburn, Joseph Losey, and Judy Holliday—

found themselves and their careers under a cloud, either falsely accused of being a communist or alleged to have Bolshevik sympathies for not testifying. The fallout was swift and devastating. Alvah Bessie, Herbert Biberman, Lester Cole, Edward Dmytryk, Ring Lardner Jr., John Howard Lawson, Albert Maltz, Samuel Ornitz, Adrian Scott, and most famously Dalton Trumbo were actually fined and imprisoned for refusing to cooperate. They were known as the Hollywood Ten.

Not only were blacklisted writers deemed unemployable pariahs, but also, their names were taken off existing credits. Charlie Chaplin and Joseph Losey decamped to Europe, and actor John Garfield died at the age of thirty-nine from a heart attack, alleged to have been brought on by the stress of being blacklisted. The hearings concluded in the mid-1950s but not before afflicting many creative people and their families with erasure, exile, and tragedy. The HUAC continued to exist for a further two decades.

The studio system was still in place, but the cracks were beginning to show. Universal wanted James Stewart to appear in two films—*Winchester 73* and *Harvey*—but would not agree to his proposed fee of $200,000. Hollywood superagent Lew Wasserman negotiated an alternative first-of-its-kind deal: Stewart would receive no upfront payment for appearing in both films but would instead get paid a percentage of the profits. And he would also have a say in casting and choice of director. It was bonanza payday for Stewart, who earned some $600,000 just for *Winchester 73*, and this was the first step toward stars dictating terms to studios instead of the other way around.

The Production Code was also in decline. Roberto Rossellini's controversial anthology film *L'Amore* features Anna Magnani as an intellectually disabled woman who believes herself to be the Virgin Mary after becoming unwittingly pregnant. It was imported into the United States by Joseph Burstyn and played at the Paris Theatre in Manhattan in 1950. Under pressure from the Roman Catholic archdiocese, who deemed the film blasphemous, it was banned by the New York State Board of Regents under thirty-year-old censorship regulations barring "sacrilegious" films. The film lost its license, and Burstyn duly appealed the decision. The New York Appeals Court upheld the Board of Regents decision—but the following year, the Supreme Court, in a unanimous ruling, determined that the New York Board of Regents could not ban the film, stating, "It is not the business of government . . . to suppress real or imagined attacks upon a religious doctrine, whether they appear in publications, speeches or motion pictures." In a crushing blow to the Code, film was no longer subject to federal law and could enjoy the same First Amendment protections as free speech (although local censorship boards could still take action if they saw fit).

United Artists withdrew from the Motion Picture Association of America when it refused to issue a Production Code seal to director Otto Preminger's drug addiction drama *The Man with the Golden Arm*, starring Frank Sinatra. The success of the film helped to lift some of the Code's embargoes. Struggling to keep up with the times, the regulations were amended to permit portrayals of prostitution and abortion as well as light profanity (the use of the words *hell* and *damn*). Also, the miscegenation clause was looking increasingly untenable. The Caribbean romance film *Island in the Sun* had not one but two interracial romances, although a scripted kiss between Dorothy Dandridge and Denis Archer was not filmed, on orders of Fox chief Darryl F. Zanuck.

By 1954, RKO Studios had incurred losses amounting to $20 million. Howard Hughes (its owner since 1948) began to sell off the studio's film library to television and laid off hundreds of employees. RKO was the first studio to sell its film library of 740 films for $15.2 million to the C&C Television Corporation, which then distributed the films to TV stations for broadcast. RKO's *King Kong* was first broadcast on US television in 1956, and other classics of the pre-1948 period could now be seen on TV, such as Orson Welles's *Citizen Kane* and *The Magnificent Ambersons*, as well as the Astaire-Rogers musicals. MGM followed suit and made 770 films released prior to 1949 available to TV stations. Some $20 million changed hands, and it is considered still to be the biggest single day's business in the history of the industry. Howard Hughes pressed on with selling RKO to the General Tire and Rubber Corporation for $25 million, and by 1957 all film production had ceased.

Russia was taking root in one part of Hollywood: acting took a great leap forward with the Method, a revolutionary acting style founded by Moscow native Konstantin Stanislavski that prized truthfulness above confection. Lee Strasberg and Stella Adler, students of Stanislavski, brought his teachings to America—although their interpretations of Stanislavski's "system" varied. Early proponents included Montgomery

Clift, Paul Newman, James Dean, and Marlon Brando. As actors, they did not so much light up the screen but immolated it.

Lesser known perhaps is that Marilyn Monroe was also a student of Strasberg's. It felt at times as if her outrageous beauty obscured the sensitive, nuanced, and thoroughly modern performer who struggled to be seen amid the two-way glare of photographers' flashbulbs and her own luminosity. A similar fate befell Dean, although he worked against his preternatural symmetry wherever he could. We were robbed of Dean when he was twenty-four by a fatal road accident and Monroe when she was thirty-six by barbiturates—or perhaps by the mental illness that precipitated her need for them. As painful as it is to contemplate the roles we never got to see them play, we can take solace in the incomparable bodies of work they left behind.

There were more than one thousand theaters in America that screened Black-audience films either exclusively or on a preferential basis by 1921. This system lasted until the mid-1950s and went into decline as the civil rights movement gathered momentum. While no one would argue against the elimination of segregation, the late actor and director Ossie Davis explains, "Integration dislocate[d] many of the structures we had in our community by which we expressed ourselves economically, culturally, religiously, and otherwise." There was a terrible subsequent neglect of talent, of voices, of points of view as Hollywood continued to perpetuate white narratives. Studios clearly had neither the will nor the inclination to support Black voices in cinema. The financial success of *Carmen Jones* (it made more money than even the year's Best Picture winner *On the Waterfront*) was dismissed as an outlier—despite its clear crossover appeal.

The 1950s drew to a close swathed in glorious Technicolor, as lavish biblical epics and Douglas Sirk melodramas had fully unseated the smoky noirs of the 1940s. Partly because of the phenomenon of the drive-in movie theater, the teen market was being courted by Hollywood as never before. The tent poles of the old ways—the Studio System and the Production Code—were irrevocably eroded, and the touchpaper was lit; the cultural revolution of the coming decade was imminent. Cinema would be right there along with it, not only to capture it on camera, but also to blow the bloody doors off.

THE MAKING OF ON THE WATERFRONT

Writer: Budd Schulberg; based on *Crime on the Waterfront* by
  Malcolm Johnson
Director: Elia Kazan
Producer: Sam Spiegel for Horizon Pictures/Columbia
Cast: Marlon Brando, Karl Malden, Lee J. Cobb, Rod Steiger, Pat
  Henning, Eva Marie Saint
Won: Best Picture, Best Director, Best Screenplay, Best Actor
  (Brando), Best Supporting Actress (Saint), Best Art Direction
  (Richard Day), Best Cinematography (Boris Kaufman), Best
  Film Editing (Gene Milford)
Nominated: Best Supporting Actor (Cobb, Malden, Steiger), Best
  Score (Leonard Bernstein)
Length: 108 minutes
Budget: $910,000
Box office: $9.6 million
Rotten Tomatoes: 98%

On the Waterfront was based on a long-running press exposé—twenty-
four articles by Malcolm Johnson in the *New York Sun* entitled "Crime
on the Waterfront"—that detailed corruption in the docks and won its
author a Pulitzer Prize in 1949. But it's hard not to see it as something
of a riposte to critics of its director, Elia Kazan, who was notoriously one
of the people to name Hollywood communists to the House Un-
American Activities Committee in 1952 (although Kazan claimed it
wasn't).

In his mid-twenties, Kazan had been a member of the American
Communist Party in New York for a year and a half. When summoned
by the committee, he initially refused to name names but eventually
identified eight. He'd been left embittered when he was tried by the
party for refusal to follow instructions and said that he wasn't willing to
give up his film career for something he didn't believe in. All eight he
named were already known to the HUAC, but it still cost him many
friends—one of whom was noted playwright Arthur Miller.

It was Arthur Miller who had worked on an early draft of the screenplay of this movie when it was called *The Knock*. Kazan agreed to direct
it, and he and the writer went to Columbia Pictures to meet Harry
Cohn. Cohn was onboard in principle but disliked the portrayal of cor-

rupt union officials, finding it anti-American, and asked for them to be changed to communists. Miller—still unhappy about Kazan's decision to name names—refused and was replaced. It's been suggested that Miller's version ended up as his stage play A *View from the Bridge*. The new writer was Budd Schulberg, who jettisoned much of the existing material in favor of writing his own original story.

But this version didn't float either. They took the script to 20th Century Fox, but Darryl F. Zanuck declared that he didn't like a thing about it. Eventually, the project was taken on by an independent producer, Sam Spiegel, who also wanted a mass of rewrites. Under Spiegel's guidance, the key role of Terry Malloy shifted from an investigative reporter to an older divorced man before settling as the ex-boxer/dockworker of the final product. This final incarnation of the leading character was partially based on real-life whistleblowing longshoreman Anthony DeVincenzo. Despite Terry Malloy being portrayed on-screen by Marlon Brando as brave, honest, and tough, DeVincenzo still felt that his privacy had been violated, and when the film came out, he sued the studio for $1 million. The case wasn't settled until 1956, when DeVincenzo was awarded $22,800.

The film won Marlon Brando his first Oscar. Born in 1924, the young Brando had been a poor student, more interested in sport and theater than academia. He was sent to a military academy, where he also developed his love of acting, but he was expelled in his senior year due to his inability to submit to authority. With no qualifications, he ended up digging ditches before his father agreed to pay for him to move to New York and study with Stella Adler. He was a sensation on Broadway in *I Remember Mama* in 1944 and *A Streetcar Named Desire* in 1947.

It was this part that brought him into contact with Elia Kazan, who founded the Actors Studio in 1947 before leaving for Hollywood. Even at this stage of his career, Brando was making life difficult for those around him. The only reason he had been free to accept the job with Kazan was that his costar Tallulah Bankhead had had him fired from *The Eagle Has Two Heads*. But his restless energy and distrust of authority made him an electric screen presence, and his casual and naturalistic style reimagined how screen acting could work.

By the time Kazan came to consider him for *On the Waterfront*, Brando had completed five films and earned three Academy Award nominations. He initially turned down the role of Terry Malloy, and Frank Sinatra had a "handshake deal" to do it, but Kazan still wanted Brando, at least partially because of the bigger budget this would grant. He got actor Karl Malden to direct Paul Newman and Joanne Woodward in a screen test to try to persuade Spiegel that someone like Brando was a better fit for the role than Sinatra. It worked, and when Brando's agent persuaded him to reconsider, the film was on. Sinatra was furious and demanded to be cast in the role of Father Barry instead—but Spiegel had to inform him that Malden had been cast in that part.

When Grace Kelly turned down the role of Edie, Kazan got his casting possibilities down to two—Elizabeth Montgomery (ten years before her starring role on television in *Bewitched*) and another Hitchcock blond—the eventually cast Eva Marie Saint. She had been raised in the area and was offered the part after a successful improvisation with Brando. Terry's brother Charley ended up being played by Rod Steiger after the first choice, Lawrence Tierney, asked for too much money. Steiger had to read with Brando—which was terrifying for him as he'd seen Brando act in the movie version of *A Streetcar Named Desire* and greatly admired him.

The movie was filmed over thirty-six days around the very cold Hoboken, New Jersey, utilizing the docks, workers' slums, bars, churches, and roofs—with the help, it's said, of many of the mobsters the movie was about. Brando would improvise heavily, turning a spoiled take into movie magic when he opted to play with Saint's accidentally dropped glove and riffing with the similarly Actors Studio–trained Steiger—although as the tired Brando had to leave the set every day at 5:00 p.m. to see his therapist, the two men weren't always performing together. Steiger had to read against the continuity guy for much of the famous taxi scene (the window was covered with a blind to avoid the need for back projection).

Upon release, the film was a huge commercial success, but Kazan could never quite escape his notoriety. He was presented with an honorary Academy Award in 1999, which split the audience down the middle. Several of those present gave him a standing ovation—but many more pointedly refused to clap.

BEST OF THE BEST: *ALL ABOUT EVE*

Writer: Joseph L. Mankiewicz; based on *The Wisdom of Eve* by
   Mary Orr
Director: Joseph L. Mankiewicz
Producer: Darryl F. Zanuck for 20th Century Fox
Cast: Bette Davis, Anne Baxter, George Sanders, Celeste Holm,
   Gary Merrill, Hugh Marlowe, Thelma Ritter, Gregory Ratoff,
   Marilyn Monroe
Won: Best Picture, Best Director, Best Supporting Actor (Sanders),
   Best Screenplay, Best Sound Recording (Thomas T. Moulton),
   Best Costume Design (Edith Head, Charles LeMaire)
Nominated: Best Actress (Baxter, Davis), Best Supporting Actress
   (Holm, Ritter), Best Score (Franz Waxman), Best Art Direction
   (Lyle R. Wheeler, George Davis, Thomas Little, Walter M.
   Scott), Best Cinematography (Milton Krasner), Best Film Edit-
   ing (Barbara McLean)
Length: 138 minutes
Budget: $1.4 million
Box office: $8.4 million
Rotten Tomatoes: 100%

Jessica Regan: The kids might be familiar with Bette Davis from the
half-dozen GIFs that do the rounds on Twitter, but to me growing up,
she was a femme fatale in *The Letter*, a broken-down doll monster in
Whatever Happened to Baby Jane? and most potently of all—perhaps
casting the die for my future career choice—the ultimate actress in *All
about Eve*, all turbans and dressing gowns, martinis and dressing downs.
She is not the Eve of the title nor the person who tells us of the
intertwined fates and failings of a group of show-business people who
fall in and out of favor and each other's beds, but she is the center of
this starry galaxy and influences all who orbit her.

Often misremembered as a movie about women being insecure,
cutthroat gorgons to each other, in fact it has two female friendships at
its core that are deeply loving in different ways. Celeste Holm's warmly
beguiling Karen Richards knows she is a member of Broadway star
Margo Channing's court but is supportive and protective of her
friend—every now and then kindly holding her to account when she
goes over the line. Thelma Ritter's superb Birdie may seem like staff

initially, but she is more sibling than employee, as she and Margo snipe at and rib each other in the way only true family can. Birdie clocks Eve's disingenuousness before all the others, and they would have done well to pay attention. Backstage sees more than front of house.

This is a film about people talking in rooms, but as director, Joseph Mankiewicz keeps it light and lively, deploying a freeze-frame and voice-over moment in the first few minutes that feels delightfully fresh. The camera captures every flicker and foible of this brilliant ensemble; not a moment goes to waste. Marilyn Monroe shows up in a golden cameo that manages in a minute to embody everything that is wrong with the power structures of the entertainment industry and the men who make it a meat market.

Which brings us to our true villain. It is not the titular Eve Harrington (Anne Baxter) who will wreak all the vengeance coming to her by leading this lonely life of no true friends but the fabulously monikered Addison DeWitt (George Sanders). Louche and reptilian, his full-blown sociopath plays chess to Eve's checkers. There is nothing more dangerous than a man with no motivation other than always to have the upper hand.

Zingers are delivered with such force they should be registered as lethal weapons. This is a story about people pretending, to audiences, to each other and to themselves. Margo is clinging onto playing the ingénue, Karen is silent about her husband's absences and late-night phone calls, and Eve . . . Eve deceives herself most of all. She is convinced that her machinations will bring about fulfillment, that success will fill the gnawing hole of her damage. "Wherever you go, there you are," Mankiewicz seems to be saying, and no shiny award or plum role will make you whole if you are not straight with yourself and the people around you.

Margo eventually triumphs—perhaps without even realizing—by following her bliss and not the false promise of further prestige. Karen's husband finds his way back, and we are never sure if he was ever lost to her or if it was the fantasies of Eve being spoken aloud, as if she could manifest a relationship with him through sheer want and will.

This is not just a camp classic to be misquoted and misremembered. There are life lessons embedded in this film, but Mankiewicz knows not to preach—people remember more when they laugh. Hurt people hurt people. Keep your friends close and your enemies nowhere to be seen.

You destroy yourself when you go about the business of destroying others. Let go of what no longer serves you. And if you find yourself at a boozy show-biz shindig, always be two drinks behind everyone else, fasten your seatbelt, and I hope, for your sake and your friends' at brunch the next day, that it's a gloriously "bumpy night."

WORST OF THE BEST: *AROUND THE WORLD IN 80 DAYS*

Writers: James Poe, John Farrow, S. J. Perelman; based on the novel by Jules Verne
Director: Michael Anderson
Producer: Michael Todd for United Artists
Cast: David Niven, Cantinflas, Shirley MacLaine, Robert Newton
Won: Best Picture, Best Adapted Screenplay, Best Cinematography (Lionel Lindon), Best Film Editing (Gene Ruggiero, Paul Weatherwax), Best Music (Victor Young)
Nominated: Best Director, Best Art Direction (Ken Adam, Ross Dowd, James W. Sullivan), Best Costume Design (Miles White)
Length: 182 minutes
Budget: $6 million
Box office: $42 million
Rotten Tomatoes: 71%

John Dorney: *Around the World in 80 Days* sometimes feels like it was shot in real time. Jules Verne's classic novel following Phileas Fogg's around-the-world trip is translated into an epic cinematic travelogue, riddled with audience-pleasing star cameos. But somehow the one thing the moviemakers have forgotten to pack is fun. Long swathes of the movie present beautiful photography of far-flung corners of the globe, with the production team only irregularly remembering they're supposed to be hanging it off a plot. At the time, on a big screen, this must have seemed thrilling. It was a world before international travel became commonplace, where the sight of even an elephant was a striking novelty. But now, with foreign vistas and spectacle the click of a cursor away, this approach loses a lot of its appeal.

It doesn't help that a number of these sequences are overextended. There are endless shots of railway tracks, minutes-long flamenco dances, and scenes of Fogg's right-hand man Passepartout proving to be a remarkably adept bullfighter that seem to last longer than most other movies—and this material is infuriatingly reprised just when you think it's safe to relax again. There is practically no sequence in the film that couldn't have been shorter. It's a testament to excess that nonetheless still bafflingly chooses to omit key plot points, such as rescuing Passepartout from some problematically portrayed Native Americans (which happens entirely off-screen) and, perhaps most egregiously, leaving out the actual start of the journey, with the audience left to decipher that the story is now suddenly in Paris without any travel footage or establishing shots to help them out at all.

In addition to the multiple foreign vistas, the film's other big draw is its star-studded guest cast. But here again, director Michael Anderson, producer Mike Todd, or both can't figure out how to sustain the appeal. Initially well integrated into the narrative, the cameos increasingly become an end unto themselves, most clearly with the rote appearance of a silent Frank Sinatra as a random piano player for no obvious reason. Eventually, we reach the nadir of Peter Lorre playing an Asian passenger on a boat, because no one really cares at this point. The film never uses its amazing roster of stars properly. The production team was seemingly unable to figure out what to do with any of them other than just let them be recognizable—leaving the whole thing the cinematic equivalent of Madame Tussaud's, with most of the guest cast literally standing around doing nothing.

As for the main cast, David Niven as Fogg does his best with the material, but he's not been given much to work with and largely just has to be himself and anchor the world around him with a bit of star quality (amazingly, he later said it was his favorite role). He at least emerges largely unscathed, which is more than can be said for Shirley MacLaine, where it would be unkind to dwell on her largely inconsequential brownfaced Indian princess.

The true MVP of the movie is undeniably Cantinflas as Passepartout. Hailing originally from Mexico, where he was a huge box-office star, this dancer, clown, actor, and impresario had been delighting Spanish-speaking audiences since the 1930s. He was born Mario Fortino Alfonso Moreno Reyes, and the origins of his stage name are still mysterious—Cantinflas himself claimed it didn't mean anything—but his admirers included Charlie Chaplin, who once called him the "greatest comedian alive." Here he gives a beautifully physical and likeable clown performance and walks away with the picture (even if they make him a little uncomfortably lascivious in the early stages). But he only completed one other American film—*Pepe* for director George Sidney in 1960. This is also littered with dozens of pointless celebrity cameos, and unlike *80 Days*, it bombed at the box office.

Sadly, watching Mike Todd's movie today, the appeal of Cantinflas isn't enough to hold my attention, given the huge number of missteps and errors of judgment elsewhere. The original novel's story line is a strong and enduring one, so it's a bit strange that the filmmakers opt to start with what appears to be another story entirely—a documentary-style prologue about filmmaker Georges Méliès and how he was influenced by Jules Verne, incorporating footage from *From the Earth to the Moon* and the launch of an unmanned rocket. This decision is made even odder when the movie closes with a jaunty animated sequence that would seem a perfect introduction to the concepts and style of the film yet has been dropped in at the end instead for no readily apparent reason (although if you want to see a better, shorter version of the film and if you're willing to get the cameos only in cartoon form, you can probably just watch these seven minutes).

That end is one of the bigger disappointments in the film and not just in its underwhelming final beat. As the film approaches its last half hour, it runs out of globe and cameos to rely on and so has to find other ways to fill the time. And it's at this point that you glimpse what it could have been. Because now, finally, it opts to fill the screen with fun, and we start to have genuinely entertaining sequences, such as a boat being slowly taken apart, even as its passengers are crossing the sea in it. All this just undermines the first two-and-a-half hours, emphasizing how uninspired they are.

To be fair, a lot of the problems likely come down to producer Mike Todd's cinematic inexperience, with it being—for tragic reasons—his only film. But we have to be honest: it's hard to say if it actually is a film at all. There really isn't enough story or detail here to really count as a movie. It's perhaps best watched in the background while doing something else. Possibly reading a book. Maybe even a globetrotting one by Jules Verne. That'd probably be a better experience.

DID THE ACADEMY GET IT RIGHT?

1950: *All about Eve*

John Dorney: Look, *All about Eve* is brilliant. Obviously, it's brilliant, holding its own against such cinematic classics as *Sunset Boulevard* and *Born Yesterday*, and any one of them would be a worthy winner in any other year. But I've always adored the bafflingly unnominated **The Third Man**, and it's probably the one I choose to watch again most often. Ultimately, though, this is one of those years where it feels like picking any movie over another is a mug's game.

    Jessica Regan: The Academy could hardly get it wrong this year with such an embarrassment of riches on offer. Had they decided to reward the astounding *Sunset Boulevard* or the slick and pacey *The Third Man*, I could hardly remonstrate with either choice. But to give Best Picture to **All about Eve** is just fine and dandy with me. It is so densely packed with nuance and insight. Joseph Mankiewicz holds a mirror up to show business in all its folly and frailty, while consistently entertaining the hell out of us. My enjoyment of it has only increased upon revisiting.

    Tom Salinsky: Even given the wealth of amazing films on display here—*Born Yesterday*, *Harvey*, *Adam's Rib*, *The Third Man*, *Kind Hearts and Coronets*—it's still a photo finish between *Sunset Boulevard* and *All about Eve*. I bow to no one in my admiration of Billy Wilder, and I relish the dark, satirical heart that ominously beats at the center of his film. And yet, I found myself won over by **All about Eve**'s unexpected delicacy and sweetness that give it a tiny extra shade to paint in at the very last minute. Get me to watch them both on the same day next week and then ask me again, and you might get a different answer, but today I'll give it to Mankiewicz over Wilder by the slimmest of margins.

1951: *An American in Paris*

John Dorney: You've got to feel sorry for *An American in Paris*. It's forever going to suffer from not being *Singin' in the Rain*. But that isn't out this year, so my choice for the big prize is Billy Wilder's short, bitter **Ace in the Hole**, a nasty little fable that feels terrifyingly true even now.

Jessica Regan: Technicolor; tap-dancing; and the GOAT himself, Gene Kelly—what's not to love? Well, as amiable a canter through the boulevards of Paris via the backlots of MGM as this is, I didn't fall hard for this one. The film is crammed with culture, treating us to concerts and ballets, as well as Kelly and Caron's mesmeric pairing, all against a backdrop of lavish, unrestrained design. But the wall-to-wall spectacle kept me at a distance emotionally. No such distance is possible in the sweaty confines of **A Streetcar Named Desire**. It is set in a small world among few people, but Tennessee Williams's coruscating writing, Kazan's pitch-perfect direction, and powerhouse performances all around amount to searing, unforgettable, epoch-making cinema.

Tom Salinsky: Gene Kelly is as athletic and charismatic as ever, but the story is as thin as one of Jerry Mulligan's paintings, and it's not clear what he's done to deserve lasting happiness with Leslie Caron (nor what Oscar Levant and Nina Foch have done to deserve a lifetime of loneliness). As MGM musicals go, it's fine and fun, but on balance, I'd rather watch *On the Town* or *The Bandwagon* or *Easter Parade* or even *Summer Stock*. Meanwhile—and especially as I deprived Billy Wilder the previous year—for Best Picture I have to give it to the pitch-black but utterly engrossing **Ace in the Hole**. A commercial flop on its first release, it becomes more prescient with every passing year.

1952: *The Greatest Show on Earth*

John Dorney: Remember how I said *An American in Paris* was always going to suffer from not being *Singin' in the Rain*? Well, *The Greatest Show on Earth* is struck down by the same problem, but this time that film is actually (theoretically) in contention—if bafflingly unnominated in this category. Even if the Gene Kelly classic wasn't there, *Greatest Show* (with its restless inability to decide on what sort of film it even is) would still be a lesser piece than other films from this year, such as *The Lavender Hill Mob* and *High Noon*. But it is there. So, **Singin' in the Rain** should have won.

Jessica Regan: This film suffers from a complaint of the time: plot and character are sidelined in favor of spectacle, as movies were trying everything and anything to get people away from their TV screens and into cinemas. The treatment of people with disabilities is very hard to countenance, and all the animal cruelty on display is stomach-turning, but this is a Cecil B. DeMille joint after all. When the focus shifts, it does become quite absorbing in places, as Betty Hutton and Gloria Grahame bring much-needed sparkle and salty talk. But the Academy of *course* should have given it to **Singin' in the Rain**; wondrous and almost euphoric to behold, it soars and delights like its protagonists' dancing.

Tom Salinsky: Possibly not quite deserving of its reputation as a turkey, this is certainly an odd duck, with many stretches of tedium, but the resolution of the subplot with James Stewart and Henry Wilcoxon's FBI agent is genuinely touching, if arising out of an incredibly contrived situation. But who really cares about any of this? It should have been **Singin' in the Rain**, of course.

1953: *From Here to Eternity*

John Dorney: *From Here to Eternity* is a piece of precision engineering, a finely tuned miracle of a movie that makes you feel every emotion imaginable at one time or another. I have a lot of time for *Shane*, but I think the Academy definitely got it right on this occasion.

Jessica Regan: Everyone remembers the big-screen stylings of Kerr and Lancaster collapsing into an embrace as overwhelming as the ocean that laps around them. But Ernest Borgnine also does wonderful work as a stone-cold sociopath who never falls into mere goon territory. Montgomery Clift is so modern, it's gasp-inducing at times. Sinatra is less Rat Pack, more ragged clown, showcasing his range and not being pretty about it. I find it fascinating in this postwar period to see a film that shows the soldier and the army as being in an abusive, codependent relationship. With every department getting it so right, **From Here to Eternity** is a winner for the ages.

Tom Salinsky: Necessarily bowdlerized to make it acceptable for cinemagoers of the day and equally necessarily streamlined from James Jones's doorstep of a novel, it's the intricate character work and the details of the relationships that makes this sing, almost seventy years after it was made. *Gentlemen Prefer Blondes* is delightful fluff and iconic in its own way, the sight of Brando in *Julius Caesar* is as incongruous as it sounds (although he makes it work!), and William Wyler shows his range and introduces the world to Audrey Hepburn with *Roman Holi-*

day, but I can totally understand the Academy voting for ***From Here to Eternity***, and I think I would have voted the same way.

1954: *On the Waterfront*

John Dorney: *On the Waterfront* loses me in its final stretch, so I have to look elsewhere. I could have been tempted by *Seven Brides for Seven Brothers*, which is fun—but dodgy. In the end, I think I have to go with ***Rear Window***, which manages to take a film set in a single room—the least cinematic setup imaginable—and turns it into a thrilling, visual feast.

    Jessica Regan: There is some exquisite work between Eva Marie Saint and Marlon Brando. Their scenes feel dangerous, not because of anything out of control, but because here are two actors totally alive to each other, and anything could happen. The world around them, though, is inconsistent and even clunky at times. There's no clear timeline that I can discern, and Bernstein's score swamps the subtler moments, as if he didn't trust the material to have enough heft. Where Kazan's effort feels heavy handed, Hitchcock's ***Rear Window*** feels like filigree. Finely wrought but strong enough to withstand its extraordinary constraint, it is a terrifically compelling triumph and so complete in and of itself it deserves the win.

    Tom Salinsky: Sadly, a once-powerful piece of cinema with some epic performances and iconic scenes has dated rather badly, and the moral leaves a nasty taste in the mouth, particularly when director Kazan's personal history is factored in—but also when it isn't. While I'm very fond of *Rear Window*, I was delighted to discover ***The Caine Mutiny***. It might not have the bonkers energy of the film it so obviously inspired—*A Few Good Men*—and it does take a while to get going, but I'm enormously impressed with the nuance of the ending and with Bogart's fascinating portrayal, combining potent male authority with fragile uncertainty.

1955: *Marty*

John Dorney: *Marty* is a small but charming film, with a beautifully sweet, against-type performance from Ernest Borgnine anchoring it at the center. But it's up against some absolute belters—*Lady and the*

Tramp, *Bad Day at Black Rock*, and the truly magnificent *The Wages of Fear*. But I'm giving the prize to Charles Laughton's (at the time shamefully overlooked) classic **The Night of the Hunter**, simply because it's quite unlike any other film, with a disturbing atmosphere all its own.

Jessica Regan: *Marty* feels like an early study of masculinity and very progressive for that reason. The central performance from Borgnine is the heart and guts of the film. He maintains a thread of vulnerability throughout that is highly engaging. It could be seen as the progenitor for small films about ordinary people where not a lot happens— all mumblecore basically. But there is another film that interrogates masculinity and what it means to be a father, a brother, and a son in a much more bombastic fashion and has a performance that is so special, so uncomfortably raw with all its truth and tenderness. While I salute *Marty* and I believe we are indebted to it in many ways for showing the industry that small stories have a place on the big screen, I give my vote to that tranche of Americana, **East of Eden**, starring James Dean in the fullest expression of his talent.

Tom Salinsky: What an extraordinary film *Marty* is—a Richard Linklater film made five years before he was even born. And this year, some of my favorite filmmakers aren't really stretching themselves overmuch: neither *To Catch a Thief* from Alfred Hitchcock nor *The Seven Year Itch* from Billy Wilder are breaking new ground, while the Gene Kelly–Stanley Donen operation reaches for something darker and finds it doesn't quite fit with the rest of their style. Alas, the most successfully innovative film of the year was too much for most critics. The critical and commercial failure of **The Night of the Hunter** meant that Charles Laughton never directed another film, but at least he gave us this strange, compelling masterpiece of fairy-tale horror, with a terrifying Robert Mitchum as the Preacher and a heartbreaking Shelley Winters as the Widow.

1956: *Around the World in 80 Days*

John Dorney: My choice is definitely not Mike Todd's eccentric folly, so what is it? I will admit that I've never liked *The Searchers* as much as I'm supposed to, but that would be a lot of people's top choice. Mine, though, is the ever-influential *The Seven Samurai*, a corking, rainy-day movie par excellence.

Jessica Regan: Good Lord, no. Considering the whimsical premise of the film—a fantastical wager made by an eccentric protagonist—it is a curiously joyless slog that feels more of a schlep than a wondrous journey. I barely consider it a film, diverting as it is at times. I give it instead to that pinnacle of Ealing comedies, *The Ladykillers*—which is just about the funniest, cleverest film of the year. It couldn't be further away from the bloated morass that is the winner and should have won the Best Picture Oscar and everything else.

Tom Salinsky: The winning film is almost unwatchable, for all the reasons we so lovingly detailed earlier. Luckily, I don't have to look too far for a better candidate. One of the last of the great Ealing comedies is eligible this year, and it's probably their best. Brilliantly plotted, wonderfully played, directed with grace and precision, *The Ladykillers* is a masterpiece of black comedy and an object lesson in the craft of moviemaking.

1957: *The Bridge on the River Kwai*

John Dorney: Much as I admire *Paths of Glory*, the cynical early Kubrick masterpiece, its terse fable can't compete with the scale of *The Bridge on the River Kwai*. This ultimate Sunday afternoon movie is a feast for the eyes, with David Lean nailing the epic style at the first attempt. But it doesn't just look amazing. It's got a compelling plot and two fantastic central characters, brilliantly acted by Guinness and Holden, who share one of the greatest arcs in cinema history. It is simply magnificent.

Jessica Regan: In such safe hands, I was expecting lush cinematography, epic storytelling, and a damn good time. What I was not prepared for is how Lean's lens uncovers a kind of insanity at the core of the pageantry and performance of soldiering. Nationalism takes on cult-like qualities when you live, die, and kill for your country, embodied brilliantly by Alec Guinness's Colonel Nicholson, who is institutionalized to the point of mania. Sly humor stops it from ever becoming a slog, and for your forbearance with the running time, you are rewarded with a white-knuckle climax that is as startling as it is satisfying. How could the Academy give it to anything but *The Bridge on the River Kwai*?

Tom Salinsky: This was always going to be a two-horse race. David Lean's epic is far more than a simplistic *Boys' Own* adventure story, and yet, the gung-ho imperialism is celebrated as much as it is interrogated. Painted on a far smaller canvas and without quite as much depth but devastatingly dismantling the lie of the nobility of warfare is Stanley Kubrick's early triumph *Paths of Glory*. In what's virtually a coin flip, I end up giving Kubrick the win. *The Bridge on the River Kwai* is fascinating and brilliantly made, but the closing seconds are slightly clumsy, whereas the unhurried poetry of the final scene of *Paths of Glory* is endlessly sublime.

1958: *Gigi*

John Dorney: *Gigi* is far more boring than any musical about a Bond villain dating a courtesan has a right to be. It shouldn't have won Best Picture, and it certainly shouldn't have won in a year when Alfred Hitchcock's *Vertigo* wasn't even nominated. A movie that is basically ninety minutes of setup for thirty minutes of the most fucked-up relationship you're ever going to see, this breathtakingly complex movie is considered his personal best and one of the greatest films of all time for a reason.

Jessica Regan: What an oddity this is. A musical where everyone stays sitting, a thoroughly unlikeable protagonist, and a cheerily exploitative "romance" at the hollow heart of it all. *Cat on a Hot Tin Roof* is stuffed to the brim with barnstorming performances, Tennessee Williams's verbal savagery, and an iconic Elizabeth Taylor as Maggie the Cat—all fire to Paul Newman's subdued cool. So why the Academy did not see fit to reward such phenomenal work but rather a piece of showy contrivance, I'll never know.

Tom Salinsky: I did everything I could to like this movie, and I almost succeeded, but in the end, it wore me down. Maurice Chevalier, Hermione Gingold, and Leslie Caron are all charming enough, and the songs are brisk and lively, if a bit same-y. But it's still suffocatingly twee and rather pointless, with precious little in the way of character development or worldviews in conflict. Even the songs are disappointingly perfunctory. Far, far better is Orson Welles's late triumph *Touch of*

Evil, which thrillingly melds its pulpy story line to a richer theme and then elevates it with breathtaking camerawork and superb performances. Even the studio-cut version that Academy voters saw in 1958 is amazing. The restored version is close to a masterpiece.

1959: Ben-Hur

John Dorney: *Ben-Hur* is undeniably a bravura piece of filmmaking, a rousing epic of the kind that epitomizes the phrase "they don't make them like that anymore." But that's ultimately its drawback, as it's only a few years in advance of *Lawrence of Arabia*, and as a direct comparison, it's hard not to find the biblical epic not quite technically antediluvian. And this is the year of **Some Like It Hot**, which is a cordon bleu meal in contrast to *Hur*'s multicourse feast. It's great to have them both, but the (in every sense) Wilder film has to take the prize.

Jessica Regan: Director William Wyler fills this bombastic film with all kinds of flourish and restraint, micro-storytelling moments, and macro-action. Our titular protagonist goes through harrowing trials and experiences bone-crunching brutality but chooses love and peace and a world of women. Charlton Heston has terrific chemistry with every actor he comes up against, be it fraternal (Stephen Boyd) or romantic (Haya Harareet) or even Christ, whom we never see. The famous chariot race delivers and leaves more than a few contemporary action sequences in the dust. It is a dead heat with the precisely perfect *Some Like It Hot*, but I find it just so undeniable in terms of scale, ambition, and achievement—it's **Ben-Hur**.

Tom Salinsky: *Ben-Hur* is the very the best possible example of itself imaginable, and it's the role Charlton Heston was born to play. It's hard to argue with most of these awards, but in the other corner is a film so wholly different in its aims, approach, and methodology that to try to judge them by the same yardstick seems absurd. And yet, that's the name of the game, so as impressed as I was with Wyler's epic, I have to cast my vote for Wilder's peerless comedy **Some Like It Hot**. Marilyn Monroe singing "Something Wild," Jack Lemmon at his most frenzied and funniest, Tony Curtis's amazing Cary Grant impersonation, and one of the best curtain lines ever written.

5

THE 1960s

THE OSCARS IN THE 1960s

The first awards of the decade were dominated by John Wayne's passion project *The Alamo*. Wayne himself produced, directed, and starred as Davey Crockett, and the film had a lavish running time of three hours and eighteen minutes. It also cost $12 million to make. Wayne's previous film, *Rio Bravo*, directed by Howard Hawks, cost just $1.2 million. Of the film's budget, $3 million came directly out of Wayne's own pocket, but when it was released, the press hated it. Wayne's only hope now was Oscar glory, and he campaigned like a man possessed, spending a further $1 million on a gigantic campaign that included a press release running to an insane 183 pages. He took out forty-three

	Best Picture	Biggest Earner
1960	The Apartment	Spartacus
1961	West Side Story	West Side Story
1962	Lawrence of Arabia	The Longest Day
1963	Tom Jones	Cleopatra
1964	My Fair Lady	Mary Poppins
1965	The Sound of Music	The Sound of Music
1966	A Man for All Seasons	Hawaii
1967	In the Heat of the Night	The Graduate
1968	Oliver!	Funny Girl
1969	Midnight Cowboy	Butch Cassidy and the Sundance Kid

ads in trade papers. He secured a testimonial from John Ford that read, "*The Alamo* is the most important motion picture ever made. It is timeless. It will run forever."

At first it seemed to be working. *The Alamo* received seven Oscar nominations, including Best Picture, although nothing for Wayne as director or star. Veteran character actor Chill Wills was nominated in the Supporting Actor category—his first nomination in a twenty-five-year career. Seizing his chance, Wills hired his own publicist and mounted his own campaign, which threatened to eclipse John Wayne's in its zeal and vulgarity. As the Oscars approached, Hollywood was turning against the film, and the slogan on everyone's lips was "Forget the Alamo." It had only taken $8 million at the box office by the time it had finished its run. Not bad in 1960 but a disaster for a film that cost $12 million. Wayne never recovered financially, and *The Alamo* won only a single Oscar for its sound.

As it so often is, Best Actress was where most of the drama was found. Just as the papers were full of lurid stories about her stealing Debbie Reynolds's husband, Elizabeth Taylor received her fourth consecutive nomination for her role as a good-time girl in the not particularly well-received *Butterfield 8*. The unfortunate combination of her bad press and its echoes in the kind of character she was playing should have been enough to write off Elizabeth Taylor's chances, but during the voting period, she contracted pneumonia while on the set of *Cleopatra* and had to undergo an emergency tracheotomy. Some newspapers printed the headline that she had died.

By Oscar night, she had recovered enough to attend the ceremony, and almost none of her fellow nominees saw any point in turning up. Only Greer Garson was present to watch a very shaky Elizabeth Taylor helped to the podium to receive her award from Yul Brynner. She gratefully accepted the statuette, walked off the stage, and promptly collapsed in a dead faint. Unable to witness this, a rueful Shirley MacLaine commented, "I lost to a tracheotomy."

The thirty-fifth Academy Awards was the scene of the climax of the feud between Bette Davis and Joan Crawford. Rumors abounded of a fierce rivalry between the two, with Jack Warner said to be using their animosity to manipulate them. By 1961, they were both in their mid-fifties, and neither was getting the quantity or quality of roles she wanted. Crawford suggested that Davis play opposite her as the title character in *Whatever Happened to Baby Jane?* a Grand Guignol horror piece that would have looked violently out of fashion had it not been for Hitchcock's *Psycho* a year earlier. The film was a huge success, but much of the press surrounding the film focused on the way that the feud between the two stars mirrored the antagonism of the characters. Now, all attention was focused on the Oscars.

When the nominations were announced, Davis was included, and Crawford was not. Crawford was furious. This was her project. But she realized that there was a way she could make Davis watch her walk off the stage holding the Best Actress Oscar. She volunteered to collect the award for any absent winner, so when Maximillian Schell read out Anne Bancroft's name (Bancroft was onstage in New York), Crawford swept out in her Edith Head gown to accept the statuette, leaving Davis fuming. Crawford even got herself photographed with the other winners, holding Anne Bancroft's Oscar.

The most-nominated film of 1963 was a British period romp called *Tom Jones*, based on the Henry Fielding novel. A faction of Academy voters was determined to find a homegrown film to stop its momentum, and they settled on *Lilies of the Field*. This story of an African American laborer who builds a chapel for a group of East German nuns had attracted some criticism on its first release. *Newsweek* wrote, "The screen overflows with enough brotherhood, piety and honest labor to make even the kindest spectator retch." But everyone could agree that Sidney Poitier's performance was remarkable, and a big push was made to at least secure him an award instead of Albert Finney.

It worked, and five years after his first nomination for *The Defiant Ones*, Poitier gladly accepted the statuette from Anne Bancroft. However, he later commented, "I'd like to think it will help someone, but I don't believe my Oscar will be a sort of magic wand that will wipe away the restrictions on job opportunities for Negro actors." He was the first person of color to win a competitive acting Oscar since Hattie McDaniel in 1939 and the first to win Best Actor.

One of the more famous stories about *My Fair Lady* is that Julie Andrews, who originated the role of Eliza on Broadway, was passed over in favor of established movie star Audrey Hepburn, despite the fact that Hepburn was not an experienced singer. That didn't stop Jack Warner's production from earning twelve nominations, tied with Peter

Glenville's historical drama *Becket*. But ahead of both was Julie Andrews's own movie debut, *Mary Poppins*, with thirteen nominations.

To Jack Warner's chagrin, Audrey Hepburn had not been nominated for *My Fair Lady*, but Julie Andrews had been nominated for *Mary Poppins*, and it was of course Julie Andrews who duly won. Collecting her Golden Globe a few weeks earlier, she'd cheekily thanked Jack Warner, "without whom this would not have been possible." Now she told the delighted audience "I know you Americans are famous for your hospitality, but this is really ridiculous." Audrey Hepburn stood up to applaud her.

In 1965, the Academy gave Best Actress to another British Julie—Julie Christie, who won for her role in John Schlesinger's *Darling*. This film has the dubious privilege of being the first Oscar-winning performance to include a nude scene. In fact, in 1965, directors became more and more daring with nudity. As well as Christie's bare bottom, you could see naked breasts for the first time in an American film made during the Production Code years in Sidney Lumet's Holocaust drama *The Pawnbroker*. The Hays Office made it clear that this was an exception, which was not intended to set a precedent. But it absolutely set a precedent, and pretty soon the Production Code was routinely ignored.

As the decade came to a close, this trend toward harder-hitting and more complex fare was easy to see. The 1967 Best Picture nominees consisted of two films dealing with race relations; *Bonnie and Clyde* pushing the envelope with violence as well as borrowing techniques from the French New Wave; and *The Graduate*, maybe the most influential film of the crop of nominees, which deals with sex and relationships in a very frank and provocative way for the time.

And then there's the frankly preposterous, ill-conceived, and generally poorly executed *Doctor Doolittle*, a half-assed attempt to cash in on the success of *My Fair Lady* four years earlier. It was a flop, critically panned, and yet managed nine nominations, second only to *Bonnie and Clyde* and *Guess Who's Coming to Dinner*, with ten each. Doubling down on their enormous investment in the film, 20th Century Fox mounted an incredibly lavish Oscars campaign, wining and dining Academy members for weeks. It eventually won Best Original Song (beating "The Look of Love" and "The Bear Necessities") and Best Visual Effects.

A few years later, Universal tried the same trick. *Anne of a Thousand Days* had got rotten reviews when it was released in the United Kingdom, but unwilling to lose their shirts on what had been an expensive film to make, the studio figured its best chance of making its money back was awards. They hastily booked the film for a run at a Los Angeles cinema, just before the Academy Awards deadline. They then organized special Academy screenings, at which they served filet mignon and champagne. It worked—to a point. The film began the evening as the most nominated, with ten mentions, including Best Picture, Best Actor for Richard Burton, and Best Screenplay, but it won only for its Costume Design. Had it won Best Picture, the award would have been collected by Hal Wallis. He was the credited producer for nineteen films nominated for Best Picture—which is a record. If his name sounds familiar, it's because he won Best Picture for producing *Casablanca*.

Now, let us pause for just a moment to discuss something else. How does one become a member of the Academy? There are two routes to membership. One is to have at least two prominent credits on successful movies, then to be proposed by two existing members, and finally to be approved by the Board of Governors. The second route is to win an Academy Award. All winners are automatically members of the Academy. We'll come back to this in a moment.

Hollywood's big new sensation in 1968 was Barbra Streisand. Throughout the 1960s, she'd been releasing records, staging concerts, and making television appearances. She'd already won two Tonys, and she was now starring in her first movie, reprising her stage performance in the Jule Styne musical *Funny Girl*. Clearly, Streisand was going to have a big career in movies, and Academy president Gregory Peck thought her youth and energy was just what the stuffy Academy needed. Why should she have to wait for her second movie or her first Oscar before she became a member? So, he fast-tracked her membership, and at the age of only twenty-six, she was already filling in her first ballot. She also was nominated as Best Actress against Katharine Hepburn, although the favorite was Vanessa Redgrave in *Isadora*.

The presenter for this award was Ingrid Bergman. As she waited in the wings, one of the Price Waterhouse partners handed her the envelope with the following instruction, "Read *everything* inside here." Bergman read out the nominees and then opened the envelope, revealing that the winners were *both* Katharine Hepburn *and* Barbra Streisand. It was a tie. And Streisand, who picked up her statuette with the words "Hello, gorgeous," might have done well to thank Gregory Peck for her win—although she didn't mention him by name. Because he broke the rules for her, she was a member of the Academy at least a couple years early. And because of that she was able to vote in these awards. Presumably she voted for herself, and that one vote was all she needed to tie Katharine Hepburn.

Another happy winner in 1968 was John Chambers, who won an honorary award for his makeup on *Planet of the Apes*. There was no regular makeup award at this stage, and if there had been, presumably Chambers would have had to fend off Stuart Freeborn, who had also turned human actors into what many people thought were even more realistic apes in Stanley Kubrick's *2001: A Space Odyssey*. This landmark film still divides critics and audiences. It wasn't nominated for Best Picture, but Kubrick was nominated as Best Director and for the screenplay he wrote with Arthur C. Clarke, and the film was also nominated for its art direction and its visual effects.

With at least five major effects sequences to create, there were various teams working on solving different visual effects problems, led by—among others—Douglas Trumbull, Wally Veevers, Con Pederson, Tom Howard, and Brian Johnson. But the Academy would only allow up to three names to be submitted. Kubrick's solution was simple. He put his own name down as Special Photographic Effects Director and submitted that to the Academy. This was *2001*'s sole win of the night, and years later, Douglas Trumbull was still grumbling about Kubrick taking all the glory, even though this proved to be the only Oscar that Stanley Kubrick ever won. Trumbull went on to be nominated three times, and he won a Scientific and Technical Award in 1992 and the Gordon E. Sawyer Award in 2011.

Last, we should mention the film *Young Americans*, which won Best Documentary Feature in 1968. Producer and director Alex Grasshoff was thrilled with his win, saying that he and his wife slept with the statuette for several nights. But Grasshoff's enjoyment was short lived because several weeks after the ceremony, it came to light that the film had first been shown in theaters in October 1967 and thus wasn't eligible for this year's Oscars. Grasshoff was asked to surrender the trophy, and the award was given to the runner-up film *Journey into Self*.

While there have been nominations that were scrapped in other years, this is the only time that an Oscar win has been revoked.

THE MOVIES IN THE 1960s

1960 kick-started one of cinema's greatest and most gloriously bonkers decades. All the vibrancy of style, technical innovation, cultural revolution, and social change occurring around the world was reflected in the films of the time, as bold new voices, changing tastes, and increasingly experimental methods got us from biblical epic *Ben-Hur* to sordid New York story *Midnight Cowboy* in ten tumultuous years.

British Social Realist Wave or British New Wave originated in the previous decade, but it was in 1960s that it truly arrived—enjoying commercial, critical, and international success. Hallmarks include gritty, true-to-life characters and locations; natural, unsoftened lighting; and exploration of such themes as class, racism, injustice, and economic disparity, as well as the trope of the angry young man—usually a strident pressure cooker of rebellion, rejection, and frustration.

Saturday Night and Sunday Morning, released in 1960, is a prime example of so-called kitchen-sink drama. *Victim*, starring Dirk Bogarde as a London barrister, was released the subsequent year. It was revelatory for showing how discriminatory laws against homosexuality ruined lives, leaving people vulnerable to blackmail and extortion. Three major figures of this new guard were Tony Richardson (*A Taste of Honey*, *Tom Jones*), Richard Lester (*A Hard Day's Night*, *Help*) and John Schlesinger (*Darling*, *Midnight Cowboy*), who unleashed psychedelia-seasoned anarchy—these were war children after all, now making movies. Out of the BFI's top one hundred British films, twenty-six are from the 1960s, the most-represented decade.

The French New Wave was shaking up the establishment like its British counterpart and challenging the old ways as Italian neorealism was going into decline. Jean-Luc Godard's low-budget, improvised *À Bout de Souffle* (*Breathless*) exemplified this new cinema à la mode. It was Godard's first feature-length film and featured such techniques as jump cuts and handheld cameras, which are still employed to fresh effect today.

In America, it was British director Alfred Hitchcock who would shock audiences and shred their nerves with the release of *Psycho*. Famously killing off its seemingly main protagonist in the first forty-five minutes, it had a modest budget (well under $1 million) and was shot on a spare set using crew members from his television show *Alfred Hitchcock Presents*. Featuring an iconic all-strings score by Bernard Herrmann and a cracking cast—Anthony Perkins and Janet Leigh at the height of their allure—*Psycho* was Hitchcock's biggest commercial hit and would go on to be referenced in pop culture more than any other of his films.

James Bond 007 debuted in *Dr. No* in 1962 against the backdrop of the space race with Russia, and the Cuban missile crisis which had the potential to wipe out a third of humanity. Marilyn Monroe died the same year, plunging Hollywood and the world into mourning—a dress rehearsal for the grief felt the following year upon the assassination of President John F. Kennedy. The woman who defied the HUAC to date Arthur Miller was suspended for refusing to do a film she felt was yet more typecasting. In response, she founded a production company— she hired Laurence Olivier for *The Prince and the Showgirl*, not the other way round, remember. But now she was no more, as the last vestiges of Hollywood's golden age died with her.

1964 saw the release of two significant films that dealt with race but used different cinematic methods. Director Larry Peerce's debut film, *One Potato, Two Potato*, was one of the first truthful explorations of interracial marriage on-screen. Initially banned by the Hays Code, the film was released on 29 July, just a few weeks after the passage of the Civil Rights Act—but a few years before the Supreme Court's 1967 ruling in *Loving v. Virginia*, which decreed state bans on interracial marriage violated the Fourteenth Amendment of the U.S. Constitution. Director/screenwriter Shirley Clarke's feature film *The Cool World* is a semidocumentary look at the rise of the Black Power movement and was the first commercial film venture to be shot on location in Harlem.

Speaking of faux documentaries, the first Beatles movie, *A Hard Day's Night*, directed by Richard Lester, premiered. As Beatlemania erupted worldwide, this innovative film depicted a heightened version of the behind-the-scenes lives of the Fab Four. The Beatles had made their first live TV appearance in the United States on *The Ed Sullivan Show* on 9 February 1964, and America—along with the rest of the world—was under their spell. The swinging sixties was going full throttle.

In 1966, Otto Preminger took out an injunction against Columbia Pictures to prevent them from allowing his film *Anatomy of a Murder* to be shown on television, as he believed ad breaks and edits would compromise his artistic vision. But he was unsuccessful in court, and it was determined that "final cut" only applied to theatrical release and not to television airing. The landmark ruling enabled the dissemination of films across the globe via television long before VHS or streaming existed. There were some drawbacks, of course—the dreaded pan and scan, which cropped off the sides of the picture; or the unmatted frame, which "uncovered" stray boom mics; or hilariously sanitized dubbing of R-rated films shown before the watershed. You may not have been able to choose what films were showing on your terrestrial channels, but it did mean significant access to the canon and the classics.

By the second half of the 1960s, censorship had broken down. America was reckoning with the uprising of marginalized groups as people were organizing and taking to the streets to be heard. The civil rights movement, women's lib, and Stonewall were calling for change, equality, and progress. Against this milieu of social movements and artistic expression, fissures were reaching critical mass in the Code that once ruled content. British films that violated the Hays Code but were venerated artistically—*The Leather Boys*, *A Taste of Honey*, *Alfie*—managed to get released in the United States. *Who's Afraid of Virginia Woolf?* was the first film to get the MPAA production code seal of approval despite containing profanity and frank sexual content. For Antonioni's *Blow-Up*, its American distributor, MGM, circumvented the Code by releasing it through a subsidiary company solely created for this purpose.

Eventually a voluntary ratings system was announced by the Motion Picture Association of America in November 1968. This new system of classification had four categories: G for general audiences; M for mature audiences; R so that no one under sixteen was admitted without an adult guardian (later raised to seventeen); and X so that no one under seventeen was admitted. Classification was largely determined by the themes of the film and the amount of violence and nudity. Confusion ensued, as some people assumed films rated M were more adult than those that were rated R. The X certificate meanwhile was co-opted by the porn industry, who gleefully advertised their movies as X-rated or the meaningless triple-X-rated.

In the first year of this new system, the Best Picture winner was *Oliver!*—the only G-rated film ever to win the award. The very next year, the winner was *Midnight Cowboy*, which was rated X for its first release and is still the only X-rated film to win Best Picture. (It has since been rerated R.)

After various updates in 1969, 1970, and 1984, the MPAA settled on three "unrestricted" ratings: G, PG, and PG-13, plus R and NC-17, which was the new, less tarnished version of X. Having three ratings that were merely advisory undoubtedly contributed to the proliferation of teen movies in the 1980s, as that hinterland between ages thirteen and seventeen was finally recognized and catered to by the ratings system.

With this climate of permissiveness and unrestraint came a creative flourishing. The parameters of American New Wave or New Hollywood are loosely defined—was it a period or a movement?—but broadly speaking, it covers a chapter of filmmaking from the late 1960s to the early 1980s, where the director had authority rather than a studio, and the narrative deviates from classical norms. Such films as *Bonnie and Clyde*, *Easy Rider*, *Cool Hand Luke*, and *The Swimmer* showcase exceptional work from studio-supported auteurs. In 1969, Gordon Parks directed *The Learning Tree*. It was the first feature film by a Black director for a major US studio. This laid track for his follow-up, the hugely successful and highly influential *Shaft*, which was released two years later.

As well as forging new genres, the 1960s elevated existing ones in terrific style. Audiences had never seen anything like Stanley Kubrick's *2001: A Space Odyssey*. It gobsmacked cinemagoers with mind-melting trip-tastic visuals pioneered by Douglas Trumbull, as some semblance of plot wrangled with . . . oh, I don't know, *all of human evolution?* Rather more lo-fi but similarly genre-rattling was George Romero's debut *Night of the Living Dead*, released the same year. Romero's debut film was shot documentary style in 35mm black-and-white for very little money and managed to be all the more terrifying for its bare-bones approach. It transcended its schlocky origins to become hugely influential—giving cinema the template for the modern zombie.

These violent delights have violent ends. In August 1969—in the final year of the decade that preached peace and love on the streets and in so much of its art—Jay Sebring, Abigail Folger, Wojtek Frykowski, Steven Parent, and actress Sharon Tate and her unborn child were found mercilessly murdered in and around the grounds of 10050 Cielo Drive in Beverly Hills. The very next night, Leno and Rosemary LaBianca were murdered in a similarly horrific and senseless way.

It was savagery beyond the pale, and in its aftermath, Hollywood went through a kind of dark mirror. Long-haired hippies seemed suddenly sinister, unfortunately resembling the depraved perpetrators. Free love and unfettered drug taking wasn't the party it had first appeared as people scrambled to explain the inexplicable and understand the unknowable. Patt Morrison of the *LA Times* opined, "Live freaky, die freaky." There was a sense that just by living bohemian, artistic, creative, unconventional lives, these "Hollywood types" had invited this dreadful undoing. This was, of course, not the truth, but it was a feeling that pervaded as night fell over Hollywood (in all kinds of ways) on those awful August evenings. Our corruptibility and capacity for destruction would never be more interrogated or scrutinized through American cinema than in the decade that followed.

THE MAKING OF *THE SOUND OF MUSIC*

Writer: Ernest Lehman, based on the musical; book by Howard Lindsay and Russel Crouse, songs by Richard Rodgers and Oscar Hammerstein II
Director: Robert Wise
Producer: Ernest Lehman for Argyle Enterprises/20th Century Fox
Cast: Julie Andrews, Christopher Plummer, Eleanor Parker, Richard Haydn, Peggy Wood
Won: Best Picture, Best Director, Best Adapted Music Score (Irwin Kostal), Best Sound Recording (James Corcoran, Fred Hynes), Best Film Editing (William H. Reynolds)
Nominated: Best Actress (Andrews), Best Supporting Actress (Wood), Best Color Cinematography (Ted D. McCord), Best Color Art Direction (Boris Leven, Walter M. Scott, Ruby R. Levitt), Best Color Costume Design (Dorothy Jeakins)

Length: 174 minutes
Budget: $8.2 million
Box office: $286 million
Rotten Tomatoes: 84%

The Sound of Music is based on a true story, first revealed in Maria von Trapp's 1949 memoir, *The Story of the Trapp Family Singers*, published to help promote the group following the death of her husband Georg two years earlier. The rights to the story were initially purchased by a German producer in the 1950s, although they were eventually sold to Paramount in 1956. Paramount intended to make a film starring Audrey Hepburn as Maria, but nothing ever came of this. However, one of its directors, Vincent J. Donehue, instead proposed a stage musical for Mary Martin.

Producers Richard Halliday and Leland Heyward bought the rights and brought in the Pulitzer Prize–winning playwrights Howard Lindsay and Russel Crouse to write the book, intending to augment it with traditional Austrian songs. Almost as an afterthought, they also approached Broadway legends Richard Rodgers and Oscar Hammerstein II to compose one song for them, but the composers didn't feel their style would sit well with the planned folk music. They offered to write a complete score instead, and the producers swiftly agreed.

Many details were changed to make the story work—timings were altered, family friends invented, and a marriage born of practicality became much more of a romance. The names and ages of the children were changed, at least partially to avoid confusion as one of them also happened to be named Maria. This narrative thus streamlined, the stage production opened on 16 November 1959 in New York City and was a huge success, running for 1,443 performances and winning six Tony Awards. A film version was now almost inevitable. In June 1960, 20th Century Fox purchased the film adaptation rights for $1.25 million (equivalent to more than $10 million today) against 10 percent of the gross.

In 1962, Fox hired Ernest Lehman to adapt the stage script into a screenplay. He removed or rearranged the order of some of the songs and made significant changes to many sequences to open them up for filming and fully utilize the expensive location work—most noticeably taking the fairly static "Do-Re-Mi" number and turning it into a travelogue montage. While he developed the screenplay, the search for a director began. Fox's first choice was Robert Wise, fresh off *West Side Story*, but he was tied up developing *The Sand Pebbles*. Other directors were approached, including Stanley Donen, George Roy Hill, and Gene Kelly, but they all said no.

In January 1963, Lehman invited one of his favorite directors, William Wyler, to New York City to see the Broadway version. Wyler hated it, but Lehman was on the case. After two weeks of persuasion, Wyler reluctantly agreed to direct and produce the film, and the two men soon traveled to Salzburg to scout locations, visiting seventy-five filming sites, all of which enormously helped Lehman to conceptualize some sequences.

Lehman completed the first draft of the script on 10 September 1963 and sent it to Wyler, who had no suggestions or changes. However, this very reaction meant that Lehman started to doubt Wyler's commitment, so he also arranged to secretly slip the screenplay to Robert Wise, who was very impressed with how Lehman had transformed the material. When Wyler approached Fox asking them to delay production and allow him to direct another film, *The Collector*, Fox chief Darryl Zanuck told him to go ahead with this other project and quickly picked up the phone to Robert Wise; production of *The Sand Pebbles* had been delayed, owing to a fortuitous monsoon.

The part of Captain von Trapp was one that Wise struggled to cast. Actors considered include Bing Crosby, Yul Brynner, Sean Connery, and Richard Burton. The director had seen Christopher Plummer on Broadway, and he quickly rose to the top of the list, but Plummer turned the part down on multiple occasions. It was only when Wise flew to meet him in London and assured him that they could work together on developing the character that Plummer agreed to join the production. The distinguished actor later said he'd been quite arrogant at the time and spoiled by too many great theater roles.

There was only ever really one choice for Maria, though—Julie Andrews. She'd been a smash hit on Broadway in *My Fair Lady*, and the trade papers were full of stories about Jack Warner refusing to cast her in the film version. While this row raged on, Walt Disney had swept in and cast her in *Mary Poppins*—her film debut. Somehow, Wise and Lehman managed to get Disney to show them some of the *Poppins* footage, and they realized that she was effortlessly translating her stage appeal to the screen. After ten minutes, Wise turned to Lehman and said, "Let's sign her before anyone else does."

The only person who wasn't completely sold on the idea of Julie Andrews as Maria von Trapp was Julie Andrews. Already nervous about typecasting, she worried that the sweetness of the theatrical version was awfully close to Mary Poppins. Once again, Lehman had to persuade a star that the character would be further developed and that he, too, wanted to mitigate the more saccharine qualities of the story. Reassured that everyone was pulling the same direction, she signed on. Later she admitted that she wanted the part but feared she had ruled herself out by spoofing the stage version with Carol Burnett in a television comedy sketch called "The Pratt Family Singers" in 1962.

The casting of the children began in November 1963 with more than two hundred interviews throughout the United States and England. Some of the child actors who were interviewed but not selected included Mia Farrow, Patty Duke, Lesley Ann Warren, Geraldine Chaplin, Teri Garr, Kurt Russell, and the Osmonds. Most of those picked had acting, singing, or dancing experience, with the exception of Charmian Carr, who was a model working part time in a doctor's office with no ambition to be an actress. She was called in after a friend sent her photo to Wise's office and had such innate poise and charm that they pretty much immediately decided to cast her.

Singing and dancing rehearsals began in February 1964, with the husband-and-wife team of Marc Breaux and Dee Dee Wood doing the choreography—they'd also worked on Mary Poppins. They found the original staging too restrictive, but this was all new material, better suited for film and the locations. Some of the singing ended up being dubbed—most notably that of Christopher Plummer, whose singing voice was provided by Bill Lee, who only a few months earlier had been replacing David Tomlinson's voice on Mary Poppins. One of the nuns was played by Marni Nixon. Rarely seen on-screen, Nixon was one of Hollywood's busiest "ghost singers," and she had been brought in to dub Audrey Hepburn in My Fair Lady—the part that Julie Andrews created on Broadway. Andrews, of course, was as gracious as ever, telling Nixon she was a huge fan.

The production filmed for a month in Salzburg, where Wise faced opposition from the city leaders when he wanted to use swastika banners. They only relented when he threatened to replace the footage with actual newsreel of crowds in the town cheering Hitler's visit. But the good burghers of Salzburg weren't the only ones regretting saying yes to the film. Despite the assurances that he'd extracted from the producers, Christopher Plummer continued to find the story line cloyingly sugary and twee, later referring to the film as "The Sound of Mucus" and saying that working with Andrews was like being hit over the head with a Valentine's card. However, it's clear they were close friends, both during the shoot and for the rest of their lives, laughing so much during their kissing scene that it needed to be done in silhouette.

Both actors needed alcoholic aid at points. Andrews, who'd never played the guitar before and struggled with strumming and singing at the same time, found it was easier to do if she had some schnapps. And that wasn't the only thing she found hard—during the shooting of the famous opening sequence, Andrews consistently got knocked over by the downdraft from the camera helicopter. And Plummer found himself comfort eating and drinking through the weeks of location work, leading to his costumes having to be adjusted. He hated the number "Edelweiss" enough to beg for it to be cut from the movie and only filmed it after downing several drinks. Years later, on the *Oprah Winfrey Show*, first-time actor Charmian Carr was asked what she learned from the experienced theater performer playing her father. "I learned how to drink!" she replied.

Filming in Salzburg concluded in July, and most of the interiors were shot on Fox sound stages over the next three months. In total, production lasted five months, and the film was finally ready for a sneak preview in January 1965. Despite a handful of curmudgeonly reviews (legend has it that both Joan Didion and Pauline Kael lost their jobs as film critics—for *Vogue* and *McCall's*, respectively—because their negative reviews of this film were so out of step with the readership), the movie became not just a success but also a phenomenon. After four weeks, it became the number one movie at the US box office and held that place for thirty of the next forty-five weeks in 1965. The original theatrical run of the film in America lasted four-and-a-half years.

And *The Sound of Music* went on to charm audiences in almost every country in the world. Two holdouts were the places where the story had originated—Austria and Germany. The original nonmusical film versions of the story were much beloved by German-speaking audiences, and there was little appetite for an Americanized imitation. What were these silly costumes the characters were wearing? That's not what really happened! And what's become of those lovely traditional folk songs? History does not record Rodgers's and Hammerstein's reactions.

The film's Nazi themes also created problems in Germany, where one enterprising cinema owner attempted to avoid giving offense by cutting the entire third act of the film and rolling the credits after the wedding sequence. Robert Wise and 20th Century Fox swiftly intervened, the film's climactic scenes were restored, and the hapless manager lost his job.

BEST OF THE BEST: *THE APARTMENT*

Writers: Billy Wilder and I. A. L. Diamond
Director: Billy Wilder
Producer: Billy Wilder for the Mirisch Company/United Artists
Cast: Jack Lemmon, Shirley MacLaine, Fred MacMurray, Ray Walston, Jack Kruschen, David Lewis, Edie Adams, Hope Holiday, Willard Waterman, David White, Johnny Seven
Won: Best Picture, Best Director, Best Original Screenplay, Best Film Editing (Daniel Mandell), Best Art Direction (Alexandre Trauner, Edward G. Boyle)
Nominated: Best Actor (Lemmon), Best Actress (MacLaine), Best Supporting Actor (Kruschen), Best Cinematography (Joseph La-Shelle), Best Sound (Gordon E. Sawyer)
Length: 125 minutes
Budget: $3 million
Box office: $24.6 million
Rotten Tomatoes: 93%

Tom Salinsky: This is one of those movies in which everything works. It looks sensational, the cast is exemplary, the pacing is perfect, the score is tremendous—even the title font is iconic. But I want to talk mainly about the screenplay—and that means that there will be spoilers. So if you haven't seen this wonderful film yet, close this book, and go watch it. Or skip to the next section until you've had time to acquaint yourself with C. C. "Bud" Baxter, Fran Kubelik, and Jeff Sheldrake.

Billy Wilder became a director largely to protect his screenplays, but this doesn't mean that Wilder had no visual flair or filmmaking talent.

His directing is rarely flashy—not for him the cinema pyrotechnics of Welles or Hitchcock—but he does far more than simply point the camera at the person talking and call, "Action." He blocks and stages scenes brilliantly, he uses the widescreen frame to its fullest, and he's always careful to capture the story in the most engaging way possible.

The best example of Wilder as director is his choice of Fran Kubelik's compact makeup mirror as the object that lets Baxter know that the woman of his dreams was in his apartment with another man. The mirror is cracked, which is itself a potent visual symbol (as Fran says, "I like it that way. Makes me look the way I feel."). Its purpose in the narrative is to turn Baxter's world upside down at the moment that he sees it again. Any object would have done, but the compact is particularly brilliant because it allows Wilder to shoot both it and Baxter's reaction simultaneously. Jack Lemmon's face reflected in that broken mirror tells us everything we need to know about what is happening to that character in that moment.

But the real reason that *The Apartment* works so completely begins and very nearly ends with that screenplay. People who roll their eyes at the "formulaic" nature of the traditional three-act Hollywood screenplay have usually never written one. The so-called formula doesn't do any of the actual writing for you. And what Robert McKee calls "anti-plot" movies—avant-garde films with very little story—usually fail to attract a wide audience. The films that burrow into the collective psyche and stay there are usually the ones in which all the "rules" of screenwriting have been observed—and they've been executed brilliantly. Think *Casablanca*, *The Godfather*, *Star Wars*.

The Apartment starts with a wonderfully juicy situation, full of promise. Nebbishy insurance clerk Bud Baxter is stuck doing favors for his bosses, letting them use his home to entertain their bits on the side. When Baxter gets the promotion he's looking for, far from being able to resign from the affair-enabling business, he discovers he's now assisting his new boss in sleeping with the girl of his dreams. Wilder and Diamond gradually build complication upon complication, situation upon situation, simultaneously keeping Baxter sympathetic while also having him and us recognize that the moral choices he has been making are somewhat less than ideal.

It all comes to a head in that glorious climax on New Year's Eve. Just as Baxter has found the strength of character he needs to choose being able to live with himself over being able to use the executive washroom, Fran Kubelik has found the strength of character she needs to tell Sheldrake to stuff his phony offers of domestic bliss. Finally, these two lost souls can be together.

But there's one more hump in this narrative roller coaster. As she rushes up the stairs toward Baxter's apartment, she hears a sudden loud retort. Fran knows, because we know, that one reason Baxter was sympathetic when she took her overdose is that he, too, once attempted suicide because of love. Fran knows, because we know, that he still possesses the gun he bought for the purpose. There is only one thing that retort can possibly be—and the look of anguish that passes over Shirley MacLaine's face is heartbreaking. Suddenly, cruelly, the lifetime of happiness that she thought was finally going to be hers has been snatched away.

Baxter opens the door, overflowing champagne bottle in his hand, and it's all going to be okay. They resume the game of gin rummy they interrupted. "I love you, Miss Kubelik. I absolutely adore you."

"Shut up and deal."

Look at how many elements have to be set up in order to make this work—the past suicide attempt, the existence of the gun, the incomplete gin game, the fact of it being New Year's Eve, the presence of the champagne. There's even a callback to a seasonally gifted fruitcake for good measure. Not only does none of this feel at the time as if it is being painstakingly setup, planted for the sole purpose of being paid off later, but also when it is all finally, gloriously assembled, we don't sit back and admire the cleverness of the construction. It hits us right in the gut. That's screenwriting of the very highest order.

Could such a brilliant screenplay have been screwed up by the wrong director behind the camera or the wrong performers in front of it? Of course it could. Wilder and Diamond wrote with the principal cast in mind, particularly Lemmon. It's hard to think of another contemporary actor who could have remained as appealing while making such weak choices. For me, *The Apartment* is the story of two people who learn to like themselves and so can finally love each other. Plenty of leading-man actors can play winning heroes whom you want to succeed; and plenty of character actors can play weak, selfish people who make bad decisions. Very few actors can combine both aspects into a single integrated performance, and Lemmon does it without breaking a sweat.

Fran Kubelik is a character whose emotions are kept very firmly in check. Much of the movie is played from Lemmon's point of view—this is a story in which the protagonists often experience the same moment with very different understandings of what is going on. The second time you see this film, watch Shirley MacLaine's face when she leaves work to meet Sheldrake—intending to go see *The Music Man* with Baxter afterward. Everything you need to know about her backstory is written in her eyes. Because Wilder is both cowriter and director, he knows he doesn't need to put this in the script, but it takes a wonderful actor to put it on the screen.

Fred MacMurray and the Four Stooges are breezing through the snappy dialogue in a relaxed way. Wilder's brilliance here is in casting and control of tone. Often described as a romantic comedy, *The Apartment* doesn't have all that much in the way of laugh-out-loud one-liners and contains essentially zero comedy set pieces. But Ray Walston, David Lewis, David White, and Willard Waterman keep the bubbles fizzing in the glass, until the exact moment that Wilder wants the humor to drain away.

And while we're saluting the actors, let's doff our hats to Joan Shawlee, Edie Adams, and Naomi Stevens, who all do much to round out their characters, as well as the marvelous Jack Kruschen as Dr. Dreyfuss, who begins as comic relief, turns out to have a major plot function to fulfill, and then has the unenviable task of stating the premise of the movie—which again manages not to feel forced or contrived in any way.

At the time, *The Apartment* was criticized in some quarters for its low moral standards. From a modern perspective, it looks almost quaint. A small child could watch it and never really understand what was happening in Baxter's place, apart from a little drinking and a little dancing. But that never comes off as coy; it never feels as if Wilder is unable to tell the story he wants to tell. Rather, it all feels of a piece—after all, this is the only love story I know of where neither protagonist ever addresses the other by their first name.

Although the Production Code would be in place for another seven or eight years, this does feel like the end of something. It's the last black-and-white film to win Best Picture until *Schindler's List*. It's the last Billy Wilder masterpiece (as fond as I am of *One Two Three* and

The Fortune Cookie, they're not in the same league as this or *Some Like It Hot* or *Sunset Boulevard*). And it's arguably the last "small" film to win Best Picture until *Kramer vs. Kramer*. The rest of the 1960s and 1970s are big-budget musicals, epic adventure stories, and urgent issue films. The simple pleasure of watching two lonely people find each other, shot simply and told well, would eventually come back in the indie cinema of the 1990s, but it reached its pinnacle here.

ALSO BEST OF THE BEST: *LAWRENCE OF ARABIA*

Writers: Robert Bolt, Michael Wilson; based on *Seven Pillars of Wisdom* by T. E. Lawrence.
Director: David Lean
Producer: Sam Spiegel for Horizon Pictures/Columbia
Cast: Peter O'Toole, Alec Guinness, Anthony Quinn, Jack Hawkins, Omar Sharif
Won: Best Picture, Best Director, Best Original Score (Maurice Jarre), Best Sound Recording (John Cox), Best Color Art Direction (John Box, John Stoll, Dario Simoni), Best Color Cinematography (Freddie Young), Best Film Editing
Nominated: Best Actor (O'Toole), Best Supporting Actor (Sharif), Best Adapted Screenplay
Length: 222 minutes
Budget: $15 million
Box office: $70 million
Rotten Tomatoes: 98%

John Dorney: George Roy Hill, director of *Butch Cassidy and the Sundance Kid*, once said, "If you can't tell your story in an hour fifty, you better be David Lean." *Lawrence of Arabia* is getting close to four, so thank goodness its director is. It's a movie that the word *epic* could have been coined to describe, a visual spectacle that nonetheless conveys a complex story about a complex man with detail and intelligence. It won the big prize at the Oscars a mere three years after *Ben-Hur* charioted away with the same award and could easily be expected to be a similar piece about a straightforwardly unimpeachable hero—and yet it most emphatically isn't, with Lean far more interested in telling a deeper story about the moral quandaries Lawrence presents than delivering a hagiography.

And *how* he tells it. The film is riddled with iconic imagery and cinematography, from Omar Sharif's slow approach across the desert to Peter O'Toole's sand-blown face and one of the greatest jump cuts in movie history. But every striking shot or bravura moment is there in service of the story—in many ways the story *is* the imagery. It's easy to get swept away with the beauty of the cinematography, all shot for real, but it's almost a bait and switch, as just when you've been seduced by the land and by Lawrence, the story swings into a darker place. The strength of Lean is evident in how well he's able to handle both these elements, equally adept with the ugliness of our world as he is with its majesty.

It would be easy for these shifts to leave the film feeling episodic, but Lean opts to keep the film's momentum moving with dissolves and covering big time jumps in hard cuts, which is vital because the film—for its first half, at least—is determined to take as long as possible over everything, to put you in the same place as its characters, and yet this never drags. Long shots draw you in, and it all ends up passing more quickly than a superficially faster-paced, more rapidly cut piece.

And that's not the only example of Lean's skill. Lesser hands could have left this as something of a white-savior piece. But while Lawrence might think he is one, he isn't presented as anything of the sort. He's a pawn, buying into his own myth, and his involvement in Arabian affairs eventually comes over as something of a mess, where it's hard to say if he did any good at all. He often displays the stiff upper lip of the honorable English gentleman, but it tends not to work out well, being undercut every time, each decision leading to death and mistakes he emphatically does not learn from. For all the film's visual feast and scale, its action, excitement, and political intrigue, it's ultimately a small story about a man who doesn't belong. It just happens to be told on a vast canvas.

Given this is a movie with an interval, it's literally a film of two halves, and it's possible to say that the film slightly struggles at the top of the second, moving from a single viewpoint character (Lawrence) to a wider collection, as it shuffles pieces around the chess board to get to the spectacle of the end. Certainly, the presentation of the scenes changes; they become shorter, which makes the storytelling faster, if not necessarily as absorbing. But this is all largely in contrast to the incredibly assured first half and could in fact be said to reflect the character's journey as he moves into murkier circles.

That journey would go for nothing without a stellar central performance. In the central role, Peter O'Toole is pretty much a rock star—an otherworldly, beautiful creature you'd happily follow off a cliff—able to deliver every line with wit, charm, great depth, and a fascinatingly curious asexual quality. This does, however, lead to one slightly problematic sequence, when the film isn't able to commit to the character's sexual assault for censorship reasons, which means his later savagery isn't motivated quite as strongly as it could have been. But that's an unfortunate flaw of 1960s moviemaking in general.

It's not a flawless film from a twenty-first century perspective either, with two central roles played by white actors in brownface (much as they're doing subtle and respectful work), and its complete omission of women (the only Best Picture winner without a single woman featured at all). But when the piece as a whole is playing at such a high level, even these issues can only knock it down so far. It is and always will remain a masterpiece.

DID THE ACADEMY GET IT RIGHT?

1960: *The Apartment*

John Dorney: Well, yes, obviously. *Spartacus* and *The Magnificent Seven* are all-time classics, but *Psycho* is really the only other clear contender for the prize—a showy contrast to Wilder's reserve. It's probably actually more cinematic and should definitely have been on the ticket. However, for me, **The Apartment** remains the richer piece, so I've got no hesitation in going for it, victory-wise.

Jessica Regan: Yes. I wondered if *Psycho* would trouble my conscience somewhat, as it is very dear to me, but the emotional hold this film has on my heart only strengthens upon repeated viewings. There is not a shot, a look, a moment, a beat, or a word that I would change. There is nothing to be improved on, only more treasures to unearth as the years go by. Over time, resonances alter with the weather of your life, and that is how you make a film for the ages. Reader, I am tearing up now at the recollection of it. It is unquestionably *The Apartment*.

Tom Salinsky: Other Best Picture winners may have moved the cinematic arts on further or may have had something deeper and more profound to say about the human condition. *The Apartment* is a simple story about two people who don't like themselves very much and who each gradually becomes a mensch. It is sweetly funny, thrillingly dark, deeply moving, and immaculately constructed. *The Apartment* is my favorite movie.

1961: West Side Story

John Dorney: Is it a scrappy mishmash of disconnected styles and footage? Certainly. But it's also working incredibly hard to try to pull as much as it can out of you, getting full to the brim with energy and invention—which, combined with a rock-solid story and score, means that "Tonight" I'm going to give it to *West Side Story*.

Jessica Regan: Much of the singing is dubbed, and the casting of Caucasian actors to play Puerto Rican characters looks terribly dated. Yet who can resist this most earnest of love stories with its cutting-edge choreography and soaring songwriting? Yes, the street gangs come across as a bunch of theater kids having a dance-off as they pas de bourrée down the streets of New York, but the charm and sincerity of the leads is so appealing I could not put up any resistance. Unashamedly passionate and emotional, it swept me right up into its messy heart. I love *West Side Story* for what it gets right and even more for the parts that don't quite work because it is reaching for the same stars that cross our lovers.

Tom Salinsky: One can only imagine what Jerome Robbins's ideal version of *West Side Story* on film would have looked like, but the version we have is full of compromises, from the actors who don't do their own singing to the recreation in the studio of places we have already seen on location to the bowdlerized lyrics. *The Hustler* doesn't have Robbins's demented ambition, but it is precision-tooled moviemaking with four standout performances and a tragic plot that inexorably delivers its heroes to their inevitable unhappy ending. For me, it's both more fun and more moving.

1962: *Lawrence of Arabia*

John Dorney: Did the Academy get it right with ***Lawrence of Arabia***? Yes. Obviously yes. Totally yes. It's amazing. Do you need any more?

Jessica Regan: An epic resounding *yes*. David Lean presents a story as murky as the cinematography is resplendent. This is a political, labyrinthine film with a complex character at its core. We still go all the way with O'Toole even as we come to increasingly question his choices and wonder about his motives. He is hypnotically good, Bowie-esque in his otherworldliness, and the density of the story is punctuated by proper belly laughs, exquisite turns, and brilliant delivery throughout, so it never loses us but lifts us along with it, keeping hold of our sleeves with a punchy edit or bit of prelapping. Its cinematic vocabulary is such a great leap forward it took a while to find its place, but the Academy—contrary to some critical opinion—understood the significance of ***Lawrence of Arabia*** and rightly honored it.

Tom Salinsky: One of those films that completely and utterly lives up to the hype. Needing every minute of its nearly four-hour running time to completely engross the audience in its story, it darts nimbly between the epic and the personal, the whole affair held together by O'Toole's titanic performance. ***Lawrence of Arabia*** is the quintessential Best Picture winner. The Academy got it wrong by not rewarding the lead actor, as well.

1963: *Tom Jones*

John Dorney: It's definitely a more pleasurable (and short) experience than reading the book, and its crazed, borderline sitcom invention makes it a unique Best Picture winner. But at the end of the day, it's nowhere near as bold and striking a picture as ***The Haunting***—the haunted house movie every other one wants to be. The only way you'll get to sleep after seeing it is if you crack open the Henry Fielding novel.

Jessica Regan: A film as delirious as the decade that spawned it, there is no other winner quite like this one, and I feel I must support the Academy's choice. A refreshingly sex-positive period piece that strikes a cacophonous chord, Albert Finney's performance ensures the center holds, and we follow the action even when it is visceral to the point of repulsion. Tony Richardson, director of the superb *Taste of Honey* from 1961, frays convention with his anarchical, rambunctious, postwar sensibility and takes us on a wild ride. After all, who can resist **Tom Jones**?

Tom Salinsky: Unlike many films from decades past whose advocates claim they are "groundbreaking," "innovative," or a "breath of fresh air," this film actually does feel alive and fresh even after nearly sixty years. The director's tics and quirks never overwhelm the film but evoke the feel of the novel and help the storytelling rather than fighting with it. Despite stiff competition from such classic works as *Hud*, *8½*, and *The Great Escape*, **Tom Jones** more than earns its place among the Academy's Best Picture winners.

1964: My Fair Lady

John Dorney: *My Fair Lady* has an ace up its sleeve—an absolute cracker of a story. With George Bernard Shaw's plot backed up by some belting tunes, the movie would struggle to go wrong. But these benefits also cause it some harm because the combination of fidelity to the play and the need to still include songs means that the second half feels a little overextended—and that's before we even get to the ghastly ending put in against Shaw's wishes. Part of me wants to give it to Stanley Kubrick's brilliant *Dr. Strangelove*, but I'm going to plump for **Goldfinger** instead. It's not my favorite Bond film—it's not even my favorite Bond of the two eligible movies this year—but it is the iconic one, the Bond against which all others are judged. For creating a note-perfect spy thriller that launched a franchise, it feels like the gold standard.

Jessica Regan: What incredible source material this musical has to work with. Interluded between the sparkling songs as light as champagne bubbles are all kinds of meditations on class, gender, privilege, and prejudice. Shaw's dialogue is clear and crackling, the production design is largely superb, and the ending is richly ambiguous. Hepburn is transfixingly good, totally transcending the limitations of her controversial dubbing by the end. But after all that, I give it to the peerless and depressingly prescient **Dr. Strangelove**. A coldly astonishing film elevated by dementedly good performances from Peter Sellers and a chilling George C. Scott embodying the insatiability of a superpower. This peak of Kubrick's oeuvre (and there is more than one) bears repeated viewing and is my choice this year.

Tom Salinsky: I think I've been rather down on *My Fair Lady* in the past, even though I've enjoyed the stage version more than once. I think I was guilty of dismissing it as the "musical where nobody can sing." This time, it caught me in its spell, and Audrey Hepburn in particular is astonishing. But alas, for Lerner, Lowe, Warner, and Cukor, all of this is irrelevant because this is the year in which Stanley Kubrick released **Dr. Strangelove**. Most comedy about unpleasant things makes us laugh by making sure we don't take those things too seriously. Black comedy is comedy that makes you feel the pain as you're laughing, which is why most black comedies either aren't funny enough or aren't really as black as they imagine they are. Kubrick's film is pitch black, laugh-out-loud funny, and I find something new to discover in it every time I watch it. It kills me that it was nominated for Best Picture (and three other awards) and won nothing.

1965: *The Sound of Music*

John Dorney: This year's winner isn't really for me. It is a little too much a film of two halves, and as a musical, it seems to run out of actual songs a long time before even thinking about ending. But it's a huge international success beloved by millions when nothing up against it comes close. So who am I to say it isn't a worthy winner? It clearly connects with a great many people, so **The Sound of Music** has to be my choice, too.

Jessica Regan: Julie Andrews bursts joyously through the serenity of beautifully composed shots in a film far better than its twee reputation would have you believe. Yes, it's a long film, with little in the way of plot twists or complex characterization, but the almost-outrageous charisma of Julie Andrews and Christopher Plummer make it an irresistible prospect right up to and including a rather thrilling escape sequence that sees the film out. The Academy rewarded a film that touched the hearts of the many, not the few. Indeed, it is a wholehearted film. Ignore the begrudgers; let it fill you up and take you to where the hills are alive with **The Sound of Music**.

Tom Salinsky: The first half of this is unarguably wonderful. Andrews shines, bringing a wonderful gawky physicality to Maria—so different from prim and upright Mary Poppins—and stern yet compassionate Plummer finds exactly the right tone. But the middle gets bogged down with a character called something like the Dowager Countess, whose only purpose is to artificially extend the storyline, and by the end, it's run out of songs and has become a new film entirely called *The Trapp Family Escapes the Nazis*. And yet, I can't help but be reminded of how many people adore this film utterly and how much it means to them, so because of that, and because the first hour or so is so magical, I'll slightly grumpily concede that **The Sound of Music** is the rightful winner. Far better at any rate than the plodding *Doctor Zhivago* and—let's be clear—the Academy was never going to give it to *Repulsion*, were they?

1966: A Man for All Seasons

John Dorney: When push came to shove on recording our *A Man for All Seasons* episode, I struggled to pick between it and *Blow-Up*, two very different but equally magnificent films. To avoid having to make a choice, I opted for *Batman* to spoil my ballot paper (as it does contain my favorite scene in movie history—Adam West failing to get rid of a bomb). But really **Blow-Up** is the one of the two that stays in my head and is therefore where I'm casting my vote this time around.

Jessica Regan: *Who's Afraid of Virginia Woolf?* gives me pause and with good reason. This year sees the best of US acting and dialogue pitted against a film that completely embodies the United Kingdom's strengths in storytelling. Taylor and Burton subvert their rocky relationship and tempestuous personas in a firework display of acting that makes for a thoroughly gripping experience. And across the water, Robert Bolt's screenplay, comprised of densely historical subject matter, is made lean and clean and wonderfully accessible by the ensemble's command of his text. Paul Scofield's performance is as strong as his protagonist's conviction, always playing for truth rather than emotion. *Who's Afraid* is a knockout, but **A Man for All Seasons** hits the narrower target—a slow burn for the soul, where resonances increase rather than diminish upon repeated viewings.

Tom Salinsky: *A Man for All Seasons* is about as engaging as a film ever can be, given that the premise is that our hero won't talk and won't say why not, and it's stuffed to the gills with ripe supporting performances. But *The Fortune Cookie* is a deliciously blackly comic moral-ity tale that grips with a vice and won't let go. Walter Matthau is one of my favorite actors, and I love this film in particular. But I also adore *The Taking of Pelham 123*, *The Sunshine Boys*, and *Cactus Flower*, to name only three. He's one of those actors who just improves every film he's in. I'm also a huge Billy Wilder fan, but nothing after this is essential, and there are several outright failures, so even though (as noted) this isn't quite in the same league as *The Apartment*, I still can't resist casting my vote for my favorite filmmaker one last time.

1967: *In the Heat of the Night*

John Dorney: *The Graduate* is a strikingly fun concoction, albeit a bit rough and ready in its second half and a little too fond of using "Scarbo-rough Fair." *Bonnie and Clyde* is even better and feels like the future in a way that our actual winner kind of doesn't. But the things that **In the Heat of the Night** is doing and saying at the time it did and said them are so brave and so important that for me it's easily the worthy winner for its year.

Jessica Regan: Norman Jewison serves up a deeply satisfying and thought-provoking exploration of race relations within the sturdy struc-ture of a whodunnit procedural. The story takes increasingly unex-pected turns and is both affecting and surprising, but Jewison's major triumph is his casting: The fabulous screen pairing of Rod Steiger and Sidney Poitier makes for stunning, sweat-beaded scenes. Skillful, too, is the way in which the film roils with layered dynamics as opposed to expounding in broad strokes. Timelessness is usually a virtue in a film, but in the case of **In the Heat of the Night**, it's a damning indictment of how little attitudes and practices have changed.

Tom Salinsky: So often, films tackling big important social issues made in a previous era seem clumsy and dated, and it's hard to try to imagine the impact that they must have had on first release. Maybe because the performances are so lucid or because the race-relations story line is wrapped up in a murder-mystery plot or just because every-one's committing to making this feel totally authentic, this hasn't dated at all. Against some stiff competition, **In the Heat of the Night** walks away with the title.

1968: Oliver!

John Dorney: I just can't give the Oscar to the most plinky-plonky of musicals about child poverty, entertaining as it undeniably is. There are too many other great films up against it—with an obvious major contender in the form of *2001: A Space Odyssey*, a film that is pretty much pure cinema. Yes, it's infuriating and obtuse and self-indulgent, but I wouldn't cut or change a minute of it. However, **The Good, the Bad and the Ugly** is one of my all-time favorite films—a thrilling, visual spectacular packed with plot and character. It's a close call, but for me the western just sneaks over the line.

   Jessica Regan: Oliver Twist is an unusually passive protagonist but highly relatable as he yearns for those most pressing needs after basic sustenance—love and safety. Ron Moody is elegantly bewitching as Fagin, with a rapidity of delivery that smacks of *Hamilton*. I appreciate, too, the non-Disneyfying of Bill Sykes and Nancy's relationship—Sykes is no cockney rogue; he is a violent, abusive psychopath. When I had a classroom of children raised on Pixar and Disney in my care some years ago, *Oliver!* kept them utterly spellbound. But it has to be **2001: A Space Odyssey**. It is a kind of miracle of a film, so unbelievably lofty in its aims, so inconceivable in its execution—and it's wonderful.

   Tom Salinsky: *Oliver!* is extremely sure-footed, balancing the innocent sweetness of the golden age of movie musicals with the Dickens rogues' gallery of caricatures and the grinding poverty of Victorian London, and Ron Moody is superb as Fagin. But while I'd happily endorse the Academy's pick given the list of nominees, Stanley Kubrick's **2001: A Space Odyssey** is utterly unique in the history of movies, despite various clumsy efforts to reproduce its majesty over the years.

1969: Midnight Cowboy

John Dorney: While I struggle slightly with Dustin Hoffman's very much "acted" performance and the overuse of the otherwise generally lovely "Everybody's Talkin'," **Midnight Cowboy** still manages to triumph for me over the rather more conventional westerns *Butch Cassidy and the Sundance Kid* and *Once Upon a Time in the West* because it's a deeply sad and touching film that is filled with inventive storytelling flourishes and visual flair. It's a small tale that ends up so much more than it needed to be.

Jessica Regan: The direction and editing is startlingly good—it only feels unruly if that's how John Schlesinger wants you to feel. We have just enough fragments to join the dots even if Jon Voight's Joe hasn't, as snatches of his unprocessed trauma appear in his mind unbidden as he goes about the treacherous business of becoming a gigolo. Hoffman is working hard—sometimes too hard—but he and Voight succeed at crafting a begrudging, then poignant, and ultimately tender connection out of mutual need. A host of America's finest character actors deliver one-scene wonders, and New York really does feel like a character in and of itself in this disorienting quest tale. I wouldn't change a beat . . . it's *Midnight Cowboy*.

Tom Salinsky: It's a deeply affecting and confidently made film, with an incredibly winning performance from Voight and a very committed one from Hoffman. It's also far more eccentric and nonliteral than I'd been expecting, which is vastly to its credit. I do feel it runs out of steam about three-quarters of the way through, and I'm not convinced that the mere fact that Ratso dies really gives it any tragic power. *They Shoot Horses, Don't They?* is a (slightly) more restrained piece of filmmaking, but the performances are incredible, and I'm still reeling from that hammer-blow ending.

6

THE 1970s

THE OSCARS IN THE 1970s

During the 1970s, the Academy struggled to find an identity for the Oscars which would make sense in these troubled times. While America was embroiled in Vietnam and trust in institutions faded, the movies themselves became simultaneously more challenging and more commercial, leaving the carefree glamour and glitz of the Oscars looking increasingly old-fashioned and irrelevant.

The 1970 and 1971 awards did without a host, and the next six shows featured multiple emcees, including Carol Burnett, Burt Reynolds, Robert Shaw, and Diana Ross. Bob Hope featured only once in these lineups, at the 1974 show, which was one of the most eventful to date—

	Best Picture	Biggest Earner
1970	Patton	Love Story
1971	The French Connection	Fiddler on the Roof
1972	The Godfather	The Godfather
1973	The Sting	The Exorcist
1974	The Godfather Part II	The Towering Inferno
1975	One Flew over the Cuckoo's Nest	Jaws
1976	Rocky	Rocky
1977	Annie Hall	Star Wars
1978	The Deer Hunter	Superman
1979	Kramer vs. Kramer	Kramer vs. Kramer

although viewers at home only got glimpses of the intense backstage drama. Hope, fellow host Frank Sinatra, and presenter John Wayne were incensed at the winners of Best Documentary Feature daring to read out a telegram from the Viet Cong delegation who were attending the Paris Peace Talks. The backstage row got to the point where Hope had producer Howard Koch pinned up against a wall and insisted on reading out a statement that distanced the Academy from the announcement, while Shirley MacLaine screamed, "Don't you dare!" and Francis Ford Coppola attempted to find a diplomatic solution.

Two years later, the Academy put tyro director William Friedkin in charge, and he assembled a quartet of New Hollywood stars to keep things moving. He even asked screenwriter Lillian Hellman to present an award. As a playwright, Hellman had written *The Children's Hour* and *The Little Foxes*; the latter she also adapted into a movie for Bette Davis in 1941. In 1952, she testified before the House Un-American Activities Committee and refused to name names. She was blacklisted and returned to Broadway. Onstage at the Dorothy Chandler Pavilion, at the age of seventy-one, she described Hollywood's elite as standing up to the communist witch hunt with the "force and courage of a bowl of mashed potatoes." But the humor at this show felt desperate and flat, and when Warren Beatty closed the telecast by saying, "Thank you for watching us congratulate each other," it didn't seem charmingly self-deprecating but rather smug and slightly sour.

Trying to reinvent the Oscars and make them relevant clearly wasn't working. The best Oscars shows from this decade took a different approach instead—luxuriating in nostalgia, sometimes looking as far back as the silent days. After being eliminated from the running at the first Academy Awards, Charlie Chaplin had received a few nominations, notably for *The Great Dictator* in 1940, but he had yet to receive a competitive Oscar or attend a ceremony. In 1952, he recreated the London of his childhood in his Los Angeles studio for the film *Limelight*, in which he plays a washed-up vaudeville comedian. Given its British setting, Chaplin opted to premiere the film back in the country of his birth. The moment he set sail across the Atlantic, the American government revoked his visa, preventing him from returning. Chaplin never made another film in the United States.

But in 1972, he was permitted to re-enter the country to collect an award at the Lincoln Center in New York City. Quickly, the Academy decided to give him a second honorary award, and Chaplin agreed to make the trip to California to receive it in person. At the end of the show, he received a record-breaking twelve-minute standing ovation, following which Jack Lemmon handed Chaplin his signature hat and cane and led the audience in a rendition of his song "Smile." Not a dry eye in the house.

Later that year, *Limelight* got its first release in Los Angeles. And, per Academy rules, that meant that—twenty years after it was made—it was eligible for all the main awards. It was nominated for its score and won, meaning that a mere twelve months after his honorary award, Chaplin won his first and only competitive Oscar. Sadly, he wasn't able to collect this one in person.

Another hallmark of 1970s Oscars is lack of cooperation from nominees or even sometimes winners. For his performance in *Patton*, George C. Scott became the first actor to decline an Oscar, having informed the Academy by telegram that he did not even want to be nominated. When Goldie Hawn read out his name with a delighted squeal, the film's producer, Frank McCarthy, calmly collected the trophy on his behalf. It was never engraved with Scott's name and was returned to the general stock of Academy statuettes.

Although Scott was at pains—before and after the ceremony—to point out that he objected to the process as a whole rather than this particular crop of nominees or his name being included, it is perhaps notable that his antipathy toward the Academy Awards didn't surface until after he lost in 1959, when Hugh Griffith beat him as Best Supporting Actor as part of *Ben-Hur*'s near-complete Oscar sweep. His friends and family said that he desperately wanted that award and that it was only when he didn't win that he realized he had become obsessed to a degree that was unhealthy. That's why and when he vowed never to have anything further to do with the Academy Awards.

In 1961, when he was nominated for *The Hustler*, he attempted to withdraw his name from the race—but no mechanism existed by which this could be accomplished. He said then, "I take the position that actors shouldn't be forced to out-advertise and out-stab each other." Reigning Best Actor Burt Lancaster retorted, "He's under no pressure to take any ads. All he has to do is *not take any ads*."

Now, declining Oscars became the thing for politically minded male movie stars to do. Marlon Brando, suddenly back at the forefront of

American cinema, was nominated as Best Actor for *The Godfather*, despite the story being far more oriented around Al Pacino's character than Brando's. Brando won, but he sent one Sacheen Littlefeather in his place. Brando had written her a long speech, but she was buttonholed in the audience moments before the Best Actor Award was due and warned by Academy officials not to speak for too long. This is what she ended up saying:

> Hello. My name is Sacheen Littlefeather. I'm Apache, and I am president of the National Native American Affirmative Image Committee. I'm representing Marlon Brando this evening, and he has asked me to tell you in a very long speech, which I cannot share with you presently because of time, but I will be glad to share with the press afterwards, that he very regretfully cannot accept this very generous award. And the reasons for this being are the treatment of American Indians today by the film industry—excuse me—and on television in movie reruns and also with recent happenings at Wounded Knee. I beg at this time that I have not intruded upon this evening and that we will in the future, our hearts, and our understandings will meet with love and generosity. Thank you on behalf of Marlon Brando.

You may read on some parts of the internet that this woman's real name was Marie Louise and that she was born in California, as if Brando had hired a pretend Native American from Central Casting. In fact, her mother was from Phoenix, and her father was from the White Mountain Apache and Yaqui tribes. She was already an activist before her contact with Brando, and she continues working to further the interests of Native Americans, particularly in Hollywood, to this day. She wasn't playing the part of a Native American to further her acting career, as some have insinuated.

The Godfather and its sequel (also a Best Picture winner) are now seen as landmark films, but despite winning Best Picture, the first installment's only other wins were for its screenplay and Best Actor. Although both Coppola's film and Bob Fosse's *Cabaret* started the night with ten nominations, *Godfather* only won three, and *Cabaret* won eight—making *Cabaret* the film that holds the curious record for the most Academy Awards without winning Best Picture.

The 1972 awards got off to a very shaky start. Charlton Heston, booked to open the show, had gotten a flat tire on the way to the venue and was late, so Clint Eastwood was pushed out in his place. Eastwood explained what had happened and grumbled, "So who do they give the job to? A guy who hasn't said three lines in twelve movies." He started reading out Heston's cue cards, full of jokes about Moses and the Ten Commandments, until eventually Heston was able to take over—Eastwood mock-keeling over with relief that the ordeal was at an end.

1973 saw the first female producer, Julia Philips, collect an award for Best Picture (for *The Sting*), and Lina Wertmüller became the first woman to be nominated as Best Director (for *Seven Beauties*, which received three other nominations but which left empty-handed). Other moments to treasure include the streaker at the same awards. American photographer Robert Opel darted across the stage completely naked just before the end of the show, prompting a nimble-minded David Niven, taking his turn as emcee, to muse, "Isn't it fascinating to think that probably the only laugh that man will ever get in his life is by stripping off and showing his shortcomings?"

Then at the 1978 awards, the Oscars finally found its perfect emcee in television chat-show host Johnny Carson. Famously welcoming the audience to enjoy "two hours of sparkling entertainment spread out over a four-hour show," he made the broadcast his own, and he went on to host four out of the next five ceremonies.

The following year, Best Actor went to bookies' favorite Dustin Hoffman for *Kramer vs. Kramer*. Following Brando's and Scott's refusals, there was some speculation that Hoffman would do the same. In 1974, he had called the awards "obscene, dirty and no better than a beauty contest." Although he admitted to mixed feelings, he devoted about a third of his speech to thanking the crews on films who don't win Oscars and actors who are out of work, and he said that he refused to believe that he beat any of the other nominees or that any of them "lost"—he did eventually accept the award with grace and eloquent gratitude. Possibly, just possibly, normal service was about to be resumed.

THE MOVIES IN THE 1970s

Widely hailed as the ultimate decade in cinema, the 1970s has become something of a sacred cow in film discourse. Unquestionably some of the finest American screen acting can be found in this decade, the exuberance of the 1960s refined into more nuanced and truthful choices. Progressive actors like Jane Fonda; Ellen Burstyn; Meryl Streep; Jack Nicholson; and the triumvirate of Robert De Niro, Al Pacino, and John Cazale (and so many of their peers) truly moved the art of acting forward in ways we hadn't seen since the days of Method in the late 1940s and early 1950s. But it is not an unimpeachable period in film. Despite its many achievements, the preponderance of troubled male narratives created a pervasive homogeneity in terms of perspective.

Hollywood was facing a financial slump in the first half of this decade, but the resuscitation of the disaster movie improved its fortunes considerably. *Airport* sparked a hugely successful franchise, putting Universal back in the black and quite a few veteran movie stars and national treasures in various states of peril. Other studios took note, putting out films that followed a similar formula of real-time danger and starry ensembles. *The Poseidon Adventure* from 20th Century Fox; *Earthquake* also from Universal; and *The Towering Inferno*, for which Warner Bros. and Fox joined forces, all turned in big profits and thrilled audiences across the United States and beyond.

MASH, *Patton*, and *Tora! Tora! Tora!* kicked off what would be an intense preoccupation of 1970s filmmakers: war. Specifically, the Vietnam War, which spawned a subgenre all its own. The war was entering its third decade; it loomed so large that even non-Vietnam films, such as the Korea-set *MASH* and the survival mini-epic *Deliverance*, felt like allegories of this interminable conflict. Echoes were everywhere. Vietnam veterans were now a section of society, and culture reflected this. The legacy of trauma was examined with as much intensity as the war itself. Personal, revelatory films, such as *Coming Home*, occupied the same space as the orgiastic imaginings of *The Deer Hunter* and *Apocalypse Now*, where the war in turn becomes an allegory for the darkness that seemingly lurks in the hearts of men and will inevitably run amok given the right circumstances.

If explorations of masculinity in the cinema of the 1970s could be Venn-diagrammed into sections of "Retribution," "Outsider," and "War," the circles would all intersect with the two *Godfather* films and *Taxi Driver* at its heart. These dominant themes are exemplified with lush period detail and familial blood bonds by Francis Ford Coppola and with grit, New York grime, and vigilante-wrought viscera by Martin Scorsese. In both cases, at the center is a protagonist who had fought for his country in one war or another.

All the President's Men tells the story of journalists Woodward and Bernstein and their exposé of the Watergate scandal involving President Nixon. The film came out a mere two years after Nixon's resignation. *Network* is a searing critique of capitalism and predicted which way the wind was blowing regarding the media not just covering the news but also creating it. *The China Syndrome*, although fictional, shows the risks involved when nuclear power is subject to the whims of human frailty.

The 1970s was the third-most violent decade in US history, with homicides in New York peaking in 1976. Corruption from the top and violence thriving on the streets of cities that had run out of money meant that revenge franchises flourished. The *Dirty Harry* and *Death Wish* series proved very popular, as did antiheroes like Popeye Doyle (*The French Connection*), Randall P. McMurphy (*One Flew over the Cuckoo's Nest*), and Travis Bickle (*Taxi Driver*). Their narratives provided the audience with a kind of catharsis. Rough justice meted out, institutions confronted by "mavericks," or a "rigged" system challenged—these all became sights that were satisfying, even reassuring.

Jaws lived up to its moniker by being an absolute beast at the box office. It was the first film to push past the $100 million mark, largely due to a huge TV ad campaign and the fact that it opened in an unprecedented 460 cinemas—one of the first films to really open nationwide. The blockbuster was well and truly established, and summer would never be the same. Its director Steven Spielberg was twenty-seven years old.

If Spielberg birthed the blockbuster, then George Lucas was surely midwife to the mega-franchise. He founded Industrial Light and Magic (ILM) in 1975 to create visual effects for his forthcoming film *Star Wars*. Lucas had wanted to hire Douglas Trumbull, who was responsible for much of the visual wizardry in *2001: A Space Odyssey*, but

Trumbull was already committed to Spielberg's *Close Encounters of the Third Kind*, so he suggested his assistant John Dykstra.

Dykstra assembled a team of college students and upcoming artists and went to work in a warehouse in Van Nuys, California. The never-before-seen visuals in *Star Wars* did exactly what Lucas intended—they set a precedent and a bar as high as the cosmos they depicted. ILM went on to become world leaders in their field, and even if you are not a *Star Wars* fan, you have most certainly enjoyed their work in one or all of the following small sample of their credits: the *Indiana Jones* series, the *Harry Potter* series, the *Jurassic Park* series, the *Back to the Future* trilogy, many *Star Trek* and *Mission Impossible* films, *Who Framed Roger Rabbit*, the *Terminator* sequels, and the Marvel Cinematic Universe films.

Steadicam was invented in the mid-1970s by Garrett Brown. It was a new system that allowed the camera's motion to be fluid and smooth, even if the operator was traveling over uneven terrain. This was an enormously freeing invention, creating immediacy in motion without the costly and time-consuming laying of dolly tracks or the juddery effects of traditional handheld camerawork. It was deployed to great effect in Best Picture winner *Rocky*, allowing us to get in the ring and clearly follow the action of the fight, as well as to follow Sylvester Stallone on his run up those famous Philadelphia steps during his training montage.

Horror was no slouch in the 1970s either. 1973 was a standout in particular, with unforgettable films *The Exorcist* and *Don't Look Now* both released, as well as more schlocky but nevertheless cherished fare *The Omen*, *The Wicker Man*, and *Theatre of Blood*. *Halloween* came out in 1978—if not inventing then certainly solidifying the slasher-film subgenre—and it was embraced by audiences.

Special mention must be given to the creepily compelling *Rosemary's Baby*, directed by Roman Polanski, and Stanley Kubrick's *The Shining*, which—in a decade of era-defining performances from Jack Nicholson (*One Flew over the Cuckoo's Nest, Five Easy Pieces, Chinatown*)—gave us his arguably most iconic moment, hacking through a door, maniacal, axe-wielding, and gleefully uttering the monstrously repurposed catchphrase "Heeeeere's Johnny!"

Post–Hays Code audiences were becoming increasingly acclimatized to graphic images after a decade of free love and America letting its hippy hair down to turn on, tune in, and drop out. This metastasized in the 1970s, as porn came out of the dark shadows of "dirty movie theaters" and into the flickering light of mainstream cinemas with such enormously popular films as *Deep Throat* and *Emmanuelle* enjoying long, hugely profitable runs and, in the case of *The Devil and Miss Jones*, a four-star review from critical luminary Roger Ebert. The "golden age of porn," as it became known, spanned 1969 to 1984 before home video killed it off, as depicted in the later film *Boogie Nights*.

Sex in 1970s films was rarely straightforward and was often a nihilistic activity in such disturbing and complex films as *Klute* and *Looking for Mr. Goodbar*. Both have tremendous central female roles, but punishment, peril, or death often followed sexually liberated single women enacting their desires. *Network* is a noteworthy exception, as Faye Dunaway's Diana Christensen enjoys an almost comically efficient orgasm and then carries on with her evening. But *Mean Streets* and *Saturday Night Fever* shame women for sexual availability. The latter's scene depicting this is particularly disturbing, as it occurs after a gang rape witnessed by our leading man—who not only does nothing to intervene but also is not the least bit critiqued for his inaction or for shaming the victim, which results in a suicide attempt. But everyone just remembers the dancing. . . .

Sex was weaponized not just by characters but also in some cases by filmmakers. Bernardo Bertolucci, a venerated 1970s "master," traumatized a nineteen-year-old Maria Schneider by insisting she film a scenario that wasn't in the shooting script of his 1972 film *Last Tango in Paris* but that he had devised himself with Marlon Brando. *Coming Home* has the decade's most tender and revelatory sexual encounter as Jon Voight's paraplegic veteran Luke gives Jane Fonda's military wife Sally her first orgasm. We could have used more scenes like that—and we certainly could have used intimacy coordinators to protect actors from exploitation, but it will be more than four decades before that becomes a standard industry term and requirement.

Before we could rent films on video, watch dedicated movie channels, or stream content over the internet, there was an LA-based premium cable outlet called the Z Channel, which started in 1974 and continued until the late 1980s. It was significant in that it helped all kinds of movies reach all kinds of audiences. It programmed festivals hits, foreign films, rare classics, and hidden gems and sometimes provided redemption for critically acclaimed films that hadn't fared so well on initial release. Producer Charles Joffe told filmmaker Xan Cassavetes in a documentary about the channel that the primary reason Woody Allen's *Annie Hall* won the Academy Award for Best Picture in 1977 was because it had played so often on Z Channel in the weeks running up to the voting. Cinephiles owe the channel quite the debt of gratitude for shaping some auteurs, such as Quentin Tarantino and Jim Jarmusch, and promoting the work of others, from Robert Altman early on and later Oliver Stone.

The 1970s is perhaps the most influential decade of the cinema for good reason. Treasures abound, and many of its films and filmmakers endure. But its impact has meant a propagation of certain narratives and practices, keeping the scope of mainstream and much of art-house cinema narrower than it could have been for decades to come. Put simply and a little crudely, these films made by men about men inspired the next generation of men to make more films about men. The Academy rewards these films, so more get made in their template.

If this seems like an extreme assertion, consider that Lina Wertmüller was the first woman to be nominated as Best Director in the Academy's history, and from then until the ninety-second awards held in 2020, only four—yes four—more women directors have gone on to be nominated. To be so far from parity is shameful. That anything outside of the Caucasian experience was considered fringe by the industry was racist—*is* racist.

The uncritical venerating of this decade makes me uncomfortable in light of these facts. Many bright and brilliant white male minds did fantastic, astonishing work. This would not be a problem if they hadn't been the *only* minds invited by Hollywood to create worlds, influence future filmmakers, be rewarded by the Academy, and therefore be put in a position to reward similarly conceived work, thus shaping film discourse for generations to come. It puts me in mind of a quote from *Act Accordingly* by Colin Wright that came to me via Michaela Coel: "There are as many perspectives as there are people." The 1970s, for all its bold claims to be the greatest decade in cinema, cannot claim to reflect this.

THE MAKING OF *THE FRENCH CONNECTION*

Writer: Ernest Tidyman; based on the book by Robin Moore
Director: William Friedkin
Producer: Philip D'Antoni for Philip D'Antoni Productions/20th
   Century Fox
Cast: Gene Hackman, Fernando Rey, Roy Scheider, Tony Lo Bian-
   co, Marcel Bozzuffi, Frédéric de Pasquale
Won: Best Picture, Best Director, Best Actor (Hackman), Best
   Adapted Screenplay, Best Film Editing (Gerald B. Greenberg)
Nominated: Best Supporting Actor (Scheider), Best Cinematogra-
   phy (Owen Roizman), Best Sound (Theodore Soderberg, Chris-
   topher Newman)
Length: 104 minutes
Budget: $2.2 million
Box office: $75 million
Rotten Tomatoes: 98%

It's the early 1970s. Director William Friedkin has completed four
films, and none has been particularly successful. He was something of
an idealist, convinced that movies could change the world, and this was
reflected in his last film—*The Boys in the Band*—a relatively dark picture about gay characters in a New York apartment celebrating a birth-
day. As you might expect, it wasn't terribly popular. Friedkin was living
with Howard Hawks's daughter at the time and, frustrated, he took the
opportunity to ask Hawks what the veteran director thought of his movies. Hawks said that he thought they were lousy and suggested people
didn't want stories about personal problems or any of that "psychological shit." Friedkin, Hawks opined, should make an action film with a
good chase in it.

Enter *The French Connection*. The film is based on Robin Moore's
book of the same name, an account of a real international conspiracy. It
documents the criminal exploits of Corsicans Paul Carbone and Jean
Jehan (among others), who were smuggling heroin from Turkey to
France and then on to the United States, and the attempts to catch
them. In 1961, NYPD detectives Buddy Egan and Sonny Grosso uncovered one of their schemes involving a French television celebrity called
Jacques Angelvin and a Buick car. The detectives seized 112 pounds of
heroin, which not only set a record but also was about as much heroin

as the NYPD estimated was coming into the country every year. Carbone and Jehan had been importing about that much every two weeks.

While it was a huge bust, almost nobody involved in the incident
served any jail time. Jean Jehan, for example, continued to arrange
drug-smuggling operations across Europe—partly because French law
enforcement saw him as a hero of the resistance. He eventually died
peacefully of old age in Corsica. Nonetheless, the novel was ripe for
cinematic exploration, and it came to Friedkin.

He's said that the film is an impression of the case rather than
specifically the one described by Robin Moore, but Popeye Doyle and
Buddy Russo are fairly explicitly based on Eddie Egan and Sonny Grosso. Egan was known as Popeye because he always had his eyes open,
and Grosso was nicknamed Cloudy because of his morose nature. In
addition, the tactics used by Gene Hackman in the film very much
resemble those used by the cops in real life. They genuinely would go
into bars and cause panic until suspects revealed themselves, and then
Egan would ask violent non sequiturs while his partner asked really
specific questions as a ploy to trip up suspects into confessing. Egan and
Grosso were on set for every day of shooting to ensure it came off as
genuine, and both make cameos. Egan appears as Doyle and Reese's
lieutenant, and Grosso plays one of the FBI narcotics agents assigned to
the case.

Gene Hackman wasn't the first choice for Popeye Doyle. The role
was initially offered to Steve McQueen, but he declined because he
thought the script was too much like *Bullitt*. Paul Newman wanted too
much money. Lee Marvin hated New York City cops. James Caan
thought the character was too unlikable. Jackie Gleason thought that
the story was depraved—but he was considered box-office poison anyway. Robert Mitchum thought the screenplay was garbage. Peter Boyle
turned down the role because he wanted more romantic parts. Yes, you
read that right: Peter Boyle. Rod Taylor actively pursued it, but it was
actually offered to Jimmy Breslin. Breslin wasn't even an actor; he was a
journalist. And the only reason he was eventually fired was because they
realized he couldn't drive.

When they eventually got around to Hackman, they didn't even
audition him. It seems like they just asked if he could drive and then
sent him straight to wardrobe. Hackman was a little bit uncomfortable
about the racist dialogue he was going to have to utter but then spent a

week on the New York streets with Eddie Egan and realized that the script reflected reality.

One of the interesting other pieces of casting in film is Fernando Rey as the main French heroin smuggler. Friedkin was very keen on Luis Buñuel's 1964 film *Belle du Jour* and had been impressed by the performance of Francisco Rabal, who had quite a small part in the film. Friedkin didn't know the name of the actor but could remember that he was Spanish, and so he asked his casting director to find the Spanish actor from the Buñuel film. The casting director thought he must have been talking about Buñuel's 1970 film *Tristana* starring Fernando Rey and offered him the part. When the production team finally figured out what had gone wrong, it transpired that Rabal was unavailable and in any case spoke neither French nor English, so they stuck with Rey— although they ended up redubbing his French dialogue (according to some sources).

Friedkin wanted to give the film a documentary feel, shooting on real locations instead of building sets, and the production used a lot of guerrilla tactics. The traffic-jam scene on the Brooklyn Bridge was achieved by setting up an actual traffic jam on the real Brooklyn Bridge, without any permits. Of course, at least one thing that would probably help you, if you're determined to grab shots illegally, is to have two cops on the payroll and on set every day to smooth over any problems with the city. There was no budget for a proper dolly, so tracking shots were achieved by putting the camera operator into a wheelchair and pushing them along.

Despite Hawks's (possibly apocryphal) advice, the original script did not include the very famous car chase in the middle of the film. Friedkin, who preferred not to use storyboards, claims that he and producer Philip D'Antoni sketched out the sequence walking around New York. Their original idea was to have Popeye driving down subway tunnels, but this was beyond their limited budget.

When filming started, traffic was cleared for five blocks in each direction. They shot between 10:00 a.m. and 3:00 p.m., and off-duty New York police officers teamed with assistant directors to direct traffic. The production had permission to control traffic signals on streets where they ran the chase car, but then the chase illegally spilled onto areas where there was no traffic control, forcing stunt drivers to evade real cars and pedestrians. The crash that occurs midway through the chase involved a local man who was driving to work when his car was struck by the picture car. He wasn't hurt, but the producers did (of course) pay for his repairs. Hackman did a lot of his own driving, and when his car hit a concrete pillar, filming on the chase was declared over—even though Friedkin complained he didn't have all the coverage he needed.

Almost everyone playing the gangsters and the dealers in the shoot-out at the end are actual off-duty police officers who worked on the original case. One of the crew said, "If you're not Gene Hackman, Roy Scheider, or someone who worked with Luis Buñuel, chances are you're an off-duty cop in this film."

The film was released in October 1971 and became a huge hit, collecting around $75 million worldwide, from a budget of less than $2 million. It won five Oscars from its eight nominations, including Best Director for Friedkin and Best Actor for Hackman. A sequel followed in 1975, with John Frankenheimer taking over as director. Although well reviewed, it cost more and made less than the original, and no further awards or nominations (or sequels) were forthcoming.

BEST OF THE BEST: *THE GODFATHER*

Writers: Mario Puzo, Francis Ford Coppola
Director: Francis Ford Coppola
Producer: Albert S. Ruddy for Alfran Productions/Paramount
Cast: Marlon Brando, Al Pacino, James Caan, Richard Castellano, Robert Duvall, Sterling Hayden, John Marley, Richard Conte, Diane Keaton
Won: Best Picture, Best Adapted Screenplay, Best Actor (Brando)
Nominated: Best Supporting Actor (Caan, Duvall, Pacino), Best Costume Design (Anna Hill Johnstone), Best Film Editing (William Reynolds, Peter Zinner), Best Sound (Bud Grenzbach, Richard Portman, Christopher Newman)
Length: 177 minutes
Budget: $6 million
Box office: $250 million
Rotten Tomatoes: 98%

Tom Salinsky: Watching *The Godfather* again, what strikes me immediately is how confident it all is, how sure it is of itself and the effects it is creating. Coppola was nobody's first choice as director (Be honest: Would you have given this project to the director of *Finian's Rainbow*?), and he fought with Paramount and their head of production, Robert Evans, over almost every creative decision—including the casting of Pacino and Brando. Yet, looking at the finished film, it's hard to imagine that he didn't have the whole creation completely clear in his head from the first day of location scouting to the last day of mixing and dubbing.

That isn't to take anything at all away from the amazing team of collaborators he assembled. Indeed, what hits home as the film opens is the iconic Nino Rota score and the incredible photography by Gordon Willis. Salvatore Corsitto's eyes emerge from the inky blackness, and he states the theme of the piece very boldly—almost too boldly—but we're too bowled over by the power of the imagery and the score to notice.

Brando dominates the first half of the film—teetering on the brink of caricature—but having made some highly outré initial choices, he underplays for much of the running time. And in the opening scenes, Pacino's Michael is almost as much of an outsider as Diane Keaton's Kay. But gradually, almost without us noticing, this becomes Michael's story. Two sequels and countless memes later, it's easy to forget that—as Sonny, Tom Hagen, and even Clemenza all jockey for power—it isn't initially obvious that it's softly spoken young war veteran Michael who can, will, and must assume his father's toxic throne.

It isn't the killing of police captain McClusky that seals his fate—although that sequence is justly famous. It's the shot of him standing guard outside the hospital. Poor Enzo is trembling with fear—unable to light his own cigarette. Michael is alert but calm. He can do this. It's a quiet moment in a movie that doesn't hold back from making a lot of noise, but it's a key one.

Pacino's careful delineation of the character's rise in influence and collapse into moral compromise is an acting master class. But despite that (and despite a number of later, rather more hysterical performances), there's nothing showy about what he's doing here. He lets Brando stuff cotton wool in his cheeks, stroke cats, and peel oranges. Then he quietly steals the film from under the nose of the man who revolutionized screen acting.

He gets tremendous support across the board, of course, from James Caan, Robert Duvall, Talia Shire, Diane Keaton, John Cazale, and all the minor players who seem utterly authentic and truthful, like they walked off the pages of Mario Puzo's novel. But the novel is far messier, pulpier, more obvious (and more weirdly obsessed with the sizes of male anatomy) than the screenplay, which Puzo and Coppola crafted together.

Michael's sojourn in Sicily threatens to kill the momentum, but *The Godfather* benefits from these moments of reflection. Not only do they deepen our understanding of the characters, but they also make the explosions of violence shocking, unpredictable, and real. Don Vito is an old man, thinking about succession as soon as we meet him. His death hardly comes as a surprise. But James Caan's athletic and virile Sonny is a devastating loss—until you pause to reflect on how much blood is already on his hands.

And this is maybe the thing that guarantees that *The Godfather* will endure. It isn't fair to say that Coppola has no interest in glamourizing the Mafia. As revolting as the horse-head scene is, we can't help but admire the ruthlessly efficient problem solving it reveals. But part of the point of *The Godfather* is how seductive this lifestyle is. And that's why Kay is such an important character. In this very male film, she isn't given very much to do, alas, but her perspective is crucial. She's seduced by the allure of this exciting world of money, freedom, and power. By the time Michael flatly denies that he ordered the killings at the end of the story, she's no longer capable of hearing the truth. She's become completely enmeshed in the appeal of the Corleone's brutal world. And before we judge her too harshly, we realize—so have we.

WORST OF THE BEST: *PATTON*

> **Writers:** Francis Ford Coppola, Edmund H. North
> **Director:** Franklin J. Schaffner
> **Producer:** Frank McCarthy for 20th Century Fox
> **Cast:** George C. Scott, Karl Malden, Michael Bates, Edward Binns, Lawrence Dobkin
> **Won:** Best Picture, Best Director, Best Original Screenplay, Best Actor (Scott), Best Sound (Douglas Williams, Don Bassman),

Best Art Direction (Urie McCleary, Gil Parrondo, Antonio Mateos, Pierre-Louis Thévenet), Best Film Editing (Hugh S. Fowler)
Nominated: Best Original Score (Jerry Goldsmith), Best Cinematography (Fred J. Koenekamp), Best Special Visual Effects (Alex Weldon)
Length: 170 minutes
Budget: $12.6 million
Box office: $61.8 million
Rotten Tomatoes: 96%

John Dorney: If you're interested in the life of General Patton, it's worth watching the opening five minutes of this movie. This sequence, featuring George C. Scott parading in front of a vast US flag, speaking dialogue written by Francis Ford Coppola, is excellent and justifiably famous. But you might as well just switch off straight away afterward, as you're never going to learn more about this complex man than you will from that opening scene. Which is probably for the best because as the cliché goes, *Patton* is three hours of your life that you're not going to get back. And that's because it's three hours of the life of a rather unsympathetic, war-mongering sociopath and narcissist that never quite goes beneath his skin.

That's not to say that a film can't feature an unlikeable protagonist—of course it can. But this one doesn't have that much to add, even the sense that Patton was particularly good at his job (he tends toward infighting with the people on his own side rather than the enemy). It's never entirely clear what we're supposed to think about him, whether we root for him or against him, with the film failing to commit to a side so completely that it's easy to have both a left- and right-wing reading of it. Is he a war criminal or a brilliant maverick? To a certain degree, it works as a mirror, with the film reflecting your own position back at you—but that doesn't really tell us anything about the man himself and ultimately makes for a weaker story.

So, if the story's lacking, there has to be something else to fill the gap. And there really isn't much. The movie feels desperately keen to be *Lawrence of Arabia* but has none of the epic sweep or visual style, feeling at times almost TV level in its direction. It's filled with jarring hard edits and scenes that simply stop, covering awkward exposition with newsreel in the laziest way imaginable. For a war movie, it's surprisingly weak on the battle scenes, with most of them underwhelming, sterile, or off camera, and it's simply far too long. Endless scenes of tanks and walking and a whole scene of Patton literally directing traffic would lend the movie a constipated pace, even if it had much more story to be going on with, but it really doesn't.

Stories in general (pun not intended) are largely about change and evolution—someone emerging at the end in a different place from where they started. And Patton doesn't change, which might be acceptable and interesting in a shorter movie but feels like a waste of time at three hours. We don't learn who he was before the war—or even just away from it—with only a cursory mention of a wife to clue us in. If we get any impression of Patton at all, it's largely down to a barnstorming, scenery-chewing central performance from George C. Scott. It doesn't really have much depth, complexity, or interiority, but it is at least entertaining.

And there are other positive notes—quite literally. The score by Jerry Goldsmith is subtle and haunting, with an elegant motif that sticks in your head. But ultimately, it's the Wish.com version of a David Lean epic, partway between a pound-shop *Kwai* and a half-decent episode of *Columbo*, and it just goes on and on without feeling the urge to be heading anywhere in particular or to be saying anything all that interesting. Upon viewing it, I was compelled immediately to text a friend, "Never feel the need to watch *Patton*." It's a position I would happily maintain to anyone today.

DID THE ACADEMY GET IT RIGHT?

1970: *Patton*

John Dorney: *Patton* is a deeply dull film, and while its chief rival, **MASH**, is flawed, it's nonetheless very entertaining and significantly shorter. Plus, it led to the genesis of a classic sitcom, and other than *Everyone Loves Braveheart*, how many Best Picture winners can claim that?

Jessica Regan: It's a poorly made film about an unpleasant, unhinged warmonger with flat visuals, bad editing, and—most unforgivably—no point of view on Patton the man at all. My choice this year is the somewhat-undervalued ***Ryan's Daughter***. Gross miscasting of

Robert Mitchum as a reserved Irish schoolmaster aside, it is a small story concerning a handful of people in a tiny village, writ large by master of the epic David Lean. It is also quietly progressive in its attitude toward sexuality, judging the judgers and sympathizing with the casualties of repression.

Tom Salinsky: One of a handful of really duff films to have won Best Picture, *Patton* is unfocused and very dull and looks like a made-for-TV movie. Maybe because there are so many better films to choose from, I'm going to pick a real obscurity. *The Rise and Rise of Michael Rimmer*, written by Peter Cook and John Cleese (among others) and starring Cook, is as savagely satirical now as it was when it first released. Overlooked even at the time, it's richly deserving of a wider airing.

1971: *The French Connection*

John Dorney: It's a very strong year and a pretty good list of Best Picture nominees, with the exception of the rather tedious *Nicholas and Alexandra* and possibly *Fiddler on the Roof* (which you really have to be in the right mood for). I'd probably have put the insanely watchable *Dirty Harry* on the list instead of the Russian melodrama—and I would have also tried to find room for *Klute.* From the ones that were actually nominated, I've got a lot of time for *A Clockwork Orange* and *The Last Picture Show*, too. On any other day, any of them would have felt like a worthy winner. But ultimately, I'm going to say the Academy did get it right because **The French Connection** just doesn't feel like anything else.

Jessica Regan: It's not my favorite film of 1971 by any means. *A Clockwork Orange* means a lot to me and did much for my appreciation of Kubrick, but I'm not sure I would want to live in a world where it won. *The French Connection* succeeds in its intentions, and I understand what it's trying to do, but **Klute** does a lot of the same things and does them better—or at least in a way that I connect with—and the chemistry between Jane Fonda and Donald Sutherland isn't talked about nearly enough.

Tom Salinsky: Amid all the year's tough-cop dramas, a couple of breezy comedies escaped the Best Picture list—Elaine May's *A New Leaf* and Ken Russell's loopy *The Boyfriend*. I was also very taken by the immensely progressive *Sunday Bloody Sunday*, with a fantastic performance from Peter Finch. But although I have a lot of time for *The French Connection*, another determinedly eccentric film feels to me like it has more texture and more heart. Who but Robert Altman could have set his tale of entrepreneurial prostitution in the Old West to the songs of Leonard Cohen? My pick would be ***McCabe and Mrs. Miller***.

1972: The Godfather

John Dorney: Of course, it's ***The Godfather***. While there are aspects I don't entirely like—Brando always seems to be doing an act to me—it's hard to deny this film's heady majesty. *Deliverance* and *Cabaret* are memorable classics, but the Mafia saga casts such a shadow that its victory is something else that can't be refused.

Jessica Regan: Like a fine wine, it is full bodied and everything you want from a Best Picture winner. It requires a deep level of engagement to follow the shifting alliances and changing fortunes of these ruthless but always compelling protagonists. It is sumptuous, transportive, and a film that you don't watch passively. You experience it wholly. My goodness, it's ***The Godfather***.

Tom Salinsky: Believe the hype. ***The Godfather*** is one of the great pieces of American cinema. Beautifully shot by Gordon Willis (unnominated!) with pitch-perfect performances from all concerned, it's a chilling meditation on the meaning of family, power, status, and honor. It's a testament to how deeply invested we are in the characters that for many people, me included, the worst thing Michael does is lie to Kay's face. *Cabaret* is a remarkable film, as well, of course, but it's Bob Fosse's bad luck that he was up against this juggernaut.

1973: The Sting

John Dorney: *The Sting* is a fun piece of fluff, but that's ultimately all it is. A film that wants to trick you and nothing more. I've nothing against entertaining films, but for the title of Best Picture, a movie needs to do something more than entertain. Oddly enough, this is pulled off with aplomb by *The Sting*'s predecessor: *Butch Cassidy and the Sundance Kid*. But that wasn't out this year, and among the films that were, ***The Exorcist*** carries the most weight.

Jessica Regan: I applaud *The Sting* for its light touch, a trait often underrated by the Academy, but alas, it's not for me. I appreciate we have the benefit of hindsight, and few could have foretold its cultural impact in the years to come, but it is truly impressive for a genre film such as ***The Exorcist*** to be nominated, and I wish it had gone all the way. It shook up the world. It is a tent pole in the evolution of horror and a damn good story well told and unnervingly well acted.

Tom Salinsky: On rewatching, *The Sting* is not without charm, but it's a rather empty, soulless confidence trick of a movie. Incredibly shocking on first watching but repaying return visits rather better is the iconic ***The Exorcist***—which was nominated in as many categories as *The Sting*, but Academy voters didn't follow through.

1974: *The Godfather Part II*

John Dorney: My favorite film of this year is the other Francis Ford Coppola film nominated for Best Picture, *The Conversation*—a quiet character study with a devastating ending that's haunted me for decades. But we're not here for favorites; we're here for the best, and objectively speaking, ***The Godfather Part II*** is probably the best film of the year, even with incredibly strong competition from *Chinatown*.

Jessica Regan: It may be called ***The Godfather Part II***, but it is the mother of all sequels. This film would be a worthy winner if it had done half as much. As it stands, we get not one but two narratives, each perspective enhancing the other with context and comparison. We are so immersed in the fates of the Corleone brothers that we become almost complicit in their spiritual and fleshly transgressions. We get a new unforgettable character—Hyman Roth, played to perfection by that pioneer of New Method, Lee Strasberg. We get Robert De Niro comfortably filling Brando's shoes as only he could. We get New York of old and older again, Sicily, Cuba—we get a perfect film that rightly gets the Oscar. *Bellissima!*

Tom Salinsky: In a ludicrous year that includes two Mel Brooks classics, the first original Monty Python film, and the sublime *The Taking of Pelham 123* and where every Best Picture nominee is beautifully crafted and thoroughly entertaining, I still have little hesitation in saying that the Academy got it right. ***The Godfather Part II*** is arguably less iconic than its amazing progenitor, but it is more subtle, more complex, richer, and bolder. Together, they are an unparalleled achievement in American cinema.

1975: One Flew over the Cuckoo's Nest

John Dorney: Did the Academy get it right? Definitely. This year might be the best set of nominations ever, with every picture vying for the title an absolute corker. But for sheer tragic power and the ability to move you from laughter to tears in a heartbeat, it's pretty much impossible to beat *One Flew over the Cuckoo's Nest*.

Jessica Regan: *One Flew over the Cuckoo's Nest* is masterfully directed, superbly acted, and brilliantly adapted. It can stand and indeed demands repeated viewings, and it is worth selecting a different protagonist to focus on each time. Jack Nicholson is outstanding, as is every single actor in every single frame. It has the most humanity of all the winners of this decade, showing how any of us can come undone, whichever side of the nurses station you find yourself on.

Tom Salinsky: Miloš Forman's film has been assembled with an enormous amount of skill and care. The cast spent weeks rehearsing together, and the time spent there has really paid off. It's a photo finish between this film and *Dog Day Afternoon*, and I also have a lot of time for *Barry Lyndon*, despite its weak central performance. But *Jaws* almost seems to be running a different race, such is its enormous cultural impact. This impact wasn't altogether positive, but Spielberg's film is far deeper, more thoughtful, more humane, and more literate than pretty much any summer blockbuster that came after it—and yet it will still scare the living shit out of you at the same time.

1976: Rocky

John Dorney: *Rocky* is a charming film, an easy and enjoyable watch that defies most of the clichés of sports movies—mainly by virtue of not really being about sport at all. But much like its hero, while it deserves to be in the race and even to last the distance, it doesn't really deserve to win. *Taxi Driver* is just such a bold piece of cinema, in every sense, with its use of sound and photography feeling so much more advanced than its rival. It's a hugely intense experience and is the obvious winner.

Jessica Regan: As much as I would like to give the Oscar to a film that's full of heart and striving, that possesses an underdog innocence and kind, loving relations between consenting, enthusiastic adults, as well as a thrilling climactic fight, I am giving it to grubby, grimy *Taxi Driver* in all its ugly beauty. Deceptively paced, it has something more to unpack on every viewing. There is simply nothing like it, and there hasn't been since—as much as 2019's *Joker* pays lip service. Do yourself a favor, and go straight to the source. Enjoy Scorsese and De Niro, Foster and Keitel announcing their talent as loudly as the sirens on the streets they're trawling.

Tom Salinsky: *Rocky* creates an appealing hero and has him win a personal victory against impossible odds. *Taxi Driver* creates a hateful hero and has him fail at almost everything, even his hoped-for self-actualization via heavy artillery. But whereas *Rocky* passes the time, Scorsese's masterpiece holds me in a vice and won't let me go.

1977: Annie Hall

John Dorney: *Annie Hall* is a film I've never liked as much as I feel I'm supposed to. It tends not to linger too long in my memory. It changed Woody Allen's career—but *Star Wars* changed the whole of cinema. And it's easy to forget that that's in part because it's really good: a genuinely thrilling tale of good versus evil, with a great cast of characters, wit, energy, and an ambitious epic scale. Popcorn cinema at its best, it's really hard to top.

Jessica Regan: Although it has an utterly beguiling central performance from Diane Keaton and features some truly hilarious sequences and killer lines, it suffers from jarring moments of callousness from Allen's script and a general thinness that make it an altogether diverting film but not exactly a towering achievement. Those words are reserved for *Star Wars*, an art-evolving masterpiece. Although not to my taste, it remains undeniable, as all Best Pictures should be—whatever your personal preferences.

Tom Salinsky: *Annie Hall* is dazzlingly inventive, of course, always ready with another gimmick, device, style, or joke—and those jokes are top drawer. But how can you argue with an era-defining film like *Star Wars*? Now awash in endless prequels, sequels, and spin-offs, the original still feels unbelievably fresh and alive—particularly if you're able to get your hands on the "despecialized" version. I also want to give a shout out to *Sorcerer*, William Friedkin's brilliant remake of the terrifying *The Wages of Fear*, overlooked by audiences at the time, who assumed it was some kind of sequel to *The Exorcist*. It isn't.

1978: *The Deer Hunter*

John Dorney: *The Deer Hunter* teeters back and forth on the dividing line between art and pretention for the majority of its length and probably falls mainly into the latter, indulging itself in its own worthiness. That's something that can't really be said of **Superman the Movie**, a joyous piece of positivity that remains a gold standard for its genre decades later, anchored by one of the most remarkable and underrated central performances in movie history. The tendency of the Academy to overlook genre films in favor of weaker, more "important" pieces begins here, and the Oscars are all the poorer for it.

    Jessica Regan: *The Deer Hunter* starts well but, for all its worthiness, disintegrates into a histrionic, masochistic fantasy. Michael Cimino seems to be telling us every step of the way, "This is a *serious and important* film," with its indulgent length and protracted sequences of suffering, breaking men literally and figuratively. **Invasion of the Body Snatchers** is far more honest. It sets out to be an entertaining genre movie but is so well executed that it becomes more than the sum of its parts. It is prescient, a warning, and more relevant now than ever in this age of irrationalism.

    Tom Salinsky: In what's a very thin year, I can understand how a film as unusual and as potentially powerful as Cimino's could win, and while I wouldn't go quite as far as to say that Cimino swindled the voters, I will say that this film doesn't nourish me in any meaningful way, and some elements of the plot are far more ridiculous than anyone involved seems to be aware of. As tempted as I am by the central performance in *An Unmarried Woman* or the expert marrying of social commentary and sci-fi thrills in *Invasion of the Body Snatchers*, the film that I think best stands up today from 1978 is Paul Schrader's **Blue Collar**, about a trio of assembly-line workers (Richard Pryor, Harvey Keitel, and Yaphet Kotto) who pull off a heist. I'm not sure I would have voted for it in any other year, but it has a sureness about it that is keenly missing from many other 1978 offerings.

1979: *Kramer vs. Kramer*

John Dorney: *Kramer vs. Kramer* is okay, I suppose, but it's a resolutely ordinary film that I find rather forgettable, a problem not helped by the fact that its central premise seems utterly unremarkable in the twenty-first century. You'll have a far better time watching *The Muppet Movie*, which was also out this year and has it beaten in almost every department—*Kramer* wishes it had anything in it as good as "The Rainbow Connection." But on a purely cinematic level, the obvious winner is the insane ***Apocalypse Now***, which is about as rich a filmic concoction as you're likely to get.

Jessica Regan: I'm aware that I cannot begin to appreciate the effect the telling of this story had on audiences and the subsequent impact it had on society at the time. My issues of its smallness and televisual feel were not shared by contemporary critics, and it was praised by many as destigmatizing something that so many people found themselves going through. *Manhattan* is a film that lit a fire within me to move to a big city when I grew up (I did) and find that tribe who would appreciate "Rhapsody in Blue" and Jean Renoir (I did; they're the cowriters). But it is desperately tainted by Mariel Hemingway's underage story line and Allen's real-life pursuit of her. I will never watch it again, but I saw it when I was young and knew less and loved it so. My pick is ***Alien***—thrilling, original, and shocking and featuring an unforgettable protagonist and an iconic nemesis.

Tom Salinsky: Although Dustin Hoffman does fine work, Meryl Streep is even better, and it hurts the movie that she gets so much less screen time than he does. And although this isn't the film's fault, its depiction of a lone male left to survive a life of domesticity, which seemed fresh and urgent in 1979, seems dated and trite to me now. Because the Academy obviously wasn't going to pick *Life of Brian* (and I marginally prefer the joyous nonsense of *Holy Grail* anyway), I think a film that showed far more ambition in both themes and execution—even if actually it isn't a personal favorite—is ***Apocalypse Now***.

7

THE 1980s

THE OSCARS IN THE 1980s

This is the decade in which the Academy's taste and that of the mass audience start to drastically diverge. In the 1940s and 1950s, you could almost always find the Best Picture winner somewhere in the American box office annual top ten, sometimes at number one. There are only three Best Picture winners outside the top ten for their year from 1951 to 1979, and they're all in the top twenty.

But in the 1980s, there was only one Best Picture winner that was number one at the domestic box office—*Rain Man*. And *The Last Emperor* ended up as twenty-fifth for the year, a new low for a Best Picture winner (and most of its money was earned *after* its Oscar success). So,

	Best Picture	Biggest Earner
1980	Ordinary People	The Empire Strikes Back
1981	Chariots of Fire	Raiders of the Lost Ark
1982	Gandhi	E.T. the Extra-Terrestrial
1983	Terms of Endearment	Return of the Jedi
1984	Amadeus	Beverly Hills Cop
1985	Out of Africa	Back to the Future
1986	Platoon	Top Gun
1987	The Last Emperor	Three Men and a Baby
1988	Rain Man	Rain Man
1989	Driving Miss Daisy	Batman

what we're seeing is a division opening up between popular films and award-winning films—which is a distinction that wasn't present for the first half of the Academy's existence. Now, the combination of the rise of the auteur director in the early 1970s and the rise of the summer blockbuster in the late 1970s gives us these two Hollywoods existing side by side.

As early as 1980, smaller films were winning big awards. *Ordinary People*, directed by Robert Redford, was made for barely $6 million, and it won Best Picture. But although Donald Sutherland was expected to get a Best Actor nomination for *Ordinary People*, none was forthcoming. In fact, Donald Sutherland has never been nominated for an Academy Award, although he did get an honorary award in 2017. It's hard to know what's worse—being nominated eight times without a win, like Peter O'Toole, or the Academy never even acknowledging your existence, like Donald Sutherland.

And that same year, the Best Director category also brought a new tradition—that of the Academy giving the prize to someone better known for their acting. Redford was the winner, and he was also the third director to win for his debut film, following Delbert Mann for *Marty* and Jerome Robbins for *West Side Story* (and followed by James L. Brooks, Kevin Costner, and Sam Mendes).

As well as Redford and Costner, the list of actors with Academy Awards for directing includes Richard Attenborough, Clint Eastwood, Ron Howard, Mel Gibson, and Warren Beatty—none of whom has an Academy Award for acting. But Barbra Streisand, once fast-tracked to Academy success, was now shockingly overlooked, with no nominations at all, despite writing, directing, and starring in her 1983 smash hit *Yentl*. Amy Irving was nominated for Best Supporting Actress, and the film won Best Musical Score—but lost Best Original Song to *Flashdance*, despite having two nominated songs and *having Barbra Streisand sing them*.

In 1981, *On Golden Pond* earned ten nominations and brought Hollywood legends Henry Fonda and Katharine Hepburn together for the first time. Both were nominated, in Fonda's case for only the second time since *The Grapes of Wrath* in 1940. That year, he lost. This year, he won, setting a record for the biggest gap between first nomination and successful win. Katharine Hepburn was on her twelfth nomination, and this gave her her fourth win—still a record for any actor in any category. The record holder for nominations is Meryl Streep, who this year gained her third for *The French Lieutenant's Woman* (only her sixth film and her first leading role).

Accepting his award for writing *Chariots of Fire* the same year, Colin Welland had echoed Paul Revere, telling Hollywood, "The British are coming." That film had been backed by Goldcrest, founded by Canadian Jake Eberts and British producer David Puttnam in 1977. It had been more than a decade since a British film had dominated at the Oscars, and it briefly seemed as if Welland's words were coming true because Goldcrest's big film of 1982 had been a huge commercial hit and had secured eleven Oscar nominations. However, *Gandhi* was the last British film to win Best Picture until *The King's Speech* in 2010, and that was distributed by the Weinstein Company.

In one of the Academy's less-noble moments, Best Animated Short for 1982 went to Zbigniew Rybczyński, director of the elliptical film *Tango*, who was not exactly given VIP treatment. His name was deemed unpronounceable by presenter Kristy McNichol. His speech was mangled by his interpreter, and Matt Dillon tried to usher him off the stage as the orchestra started to play "That's All Folks." Finally, when he stepped outside for a much-needed cigarette, the security guard clocked his sneakers and refused to let him back in, despite his plaintive cries of "I have Oscar"—pretty much all the English he knew. He spent the rest of the evening in a police cell.

1986 should have been Steven Spielberg's year. Between them, films directed by Steven Spielberg had been nominated for thirty-six Oscars (including three Best Picture nominations) and won fifteen awards— but none of those statuettes had his name on them. He had been nominated as Best Director three times but never won, and he'd not been nominated for *Jaws*, even though that film was nominated for Best Picture.

Various explanations were proffered—he's too young, he's too arrogant, he's too successful—or maybe he's not making the kind of films the Academy favored in the 1980s. Directors who made "serious" films like *Gandhi*, *Amadeus*, and *Reds* were catching the Academy's eye. Well, now Spielberg had directed what was his most "serious" film to date. *The Color Purple* is an adaptation of the book written by Alice Walker in 1982, tracing the life of a poverty-stricken African American woman through the first half of the twentieth century. Whoopi Goldberg and Oprah Winfrey both made their film-acting debuts, and both received nominations. And they weren't alone.

In total, *The Color Purple* was nominated for eleven Academy Awards, tying *Out of Africa* at the top of the list. But although his film was nominated for Best Picture, again Spielberg was not nominated as Best Director, unlike the directors of the other four films nominated for Best Picture. In his place, the Academy had voted for Akira Kurosawa, whose film *Ran*, based on *King Lear*, had not been submitted by Japan as Best Foreign Language Film. In response, American director Sidney Lumet had launched a campaign to have Kurosawa nominated as Best Director, which evidently worked.

But Spielberg's failure to secure a Best Director nomination was pretty much unprecedented. In the previous fifty-seven years, the Academy had nominated one film for eleven or more Oscars thirty-two times, and in every case but one, the director had been among those nominated. The only other exception was in 1942, when Sam Wood was not nominated for directing *The Pride of the Yankees*—and that was when there were ten Best Picture nominees and five slots for Best Director.

Stanley Donen, who was producing the Oscars this year, apparently offered Steven Spielberg the chance to present Best Actor, which he declined. But Donen nevertheless thought it necessary to include a new song for Irene Cara to sing during the ceremony, which was called "Here's to the Losers" and which celebrated famous films that had been nominated for Best Picture without winning—including *Jaws*, *Raiders of the Lost Ark*, and *E.T.* And worse was to come. As the evening wore on, *The Color Purple* evaded the voters again and again, until at the end of the night, it had lost every single one of the eleven Oscars it had been nominated for, equaling the dismal record set by *The Turning Point* in 1977. By way of a consolation prize, the Directors Guild gave Spielberg Best Director, and the following year, Spielberg received the Irving Thalberg Memorial Award at the age of forty-one.

In 1988, it was decided that the Academy Awards were getting tired, and so the board engaged the services of flamboyant producer Allan Carr to liven things up. He devoted almost twelve minutes to the opening number, which has been described as the lowest point in the entire history of the Academy Awards and infamously featured Rob Lowe singing "Proud Mary" (with rewritten lyrics) to an actress dressed as Snow White.

It seemed to dawn on Carr only very slowly that his attempt to revitalize the Academy Awards had been a disaster. On camera that evening, after the show was over, he was full of smiles and enthusiasm. But the papers the next day took him to pieces. The ceremony was heavily criticized in general, and that opening number was described as "one of the most grotesque television performances in history" and "deserving of a permanent place in the annals of Oscar embarrassments."

Then, as Carr was licking his wounds, he received a call from Frank Wells at the Walt Disney Company. Perhaps Carr imagined that this was finally going to be one of those messages of congratulations that he had been expecting to flood in. Actually, Wells was complaining that Carr and the Academy had used the Disney version of Snow White without permission and that they were preparing to sue on the basis that their use of her was "unauthorized and unflattering" and that the Academy had "abused and irreparably damaged" the character. The Academy dug in its heels briefly before issuing an apology, but the nightmare wasn't over yet.

Just over a week after the ceremony had taken place, the Academy received a letter signed by seventeen of Hollywood's great and good— namely, Julie Andrews, David Brown, Stanley Donen, Blake Edwards, John Foreman, William Friedkin, Larry Gelbart, Sidney Lumet, Joseph L. Mankiewicz, Paul Newman, Alan J. Pakula, Gregory Peck, Martin Ritt, Mark Rydell, Peter Stone, Billy Wilder, and Fred Zinnemann. It began,

> The 61st Academy Awards show was an embarrassment to both the Academy and the entire motion picture industry. It is neither fitting nor acceptable that the best work in motion pictures be acknowledged in such a demeaning fashion. We urge the president and governors of the Academy to ensure that future award presentations reflect the same standard of excellence as that set by the films and filmmakers they honor.

Shell-shocked, the Academy set up an Awards Presentation Review Committee headed by Gilbert Cates to figure out how this had happened and what could be done to avoid it in the future. One of the recommendations from Gilbert Cates's committee was to end the practice of the producer's role being unpaid. They agreed that an honorarium of $150,000 should be offered to the next producer of the telecast. That turned out to be one Gilbert Cates—who ended up producing more Academy Awards shows than anyone else.

For the last Oscars of the 1980s, Cates chose Billy Crystal as emcee. He'd been a nightclub and TV comedian since the late 1970s and had broken into movies first with a brief appearance in *The Princess Bride* and this year with his first leading role in *When Harry Met Sally*. He came bounding out to the strains of "It Had to Be You" and asked the happily applauding audience, "Is that for me, or are you just glad I'm not Snow White?"

THE MOVIES IN THE 1980s

John Lennon was assassinated at the age of forty outside his building in New York on 8 December 1980. The death knell of the revolutionary spirit of the 1960s definitively rang out. Cinema of the 1980s concerned itself less with high-minded ideals of hope and change and more with earthly desires and fleshly pursuits. Money, greed, venality, narcotics, and erotic transgression were themes and motifs that came up again and again in all genres, from serious drama (*Wall Street*) to comedy (*Trading Places*, *Working Girl*) and that staple of this decade, the erotic thriller (*Rollover*, *9½ Weeks*). The American dream had mutated from picket fences and apple pie to opulent suites, shoulder-padded escorts and cocaine-contaminated hundred-dollar bills.

It wasn't just the grown-ups who were all about the Benjamins. I remember being goggle-eyed at glamorous teens in John Hughes films who seemed to have no concept of their wealth and appeared impossibly sophisticated. To quote ultimate 1980s teen Ferris Bueller, "I asked for a car; I got a computer. How's that for being born under a bad sign?" If the 1970s is the decade of men in brown suits, the 1980s is all about the boys—the teenage boy to be exact. Old-world influences, European masters, themes of masculine dissipation, and urban desolation gave way for the new and the shiny and the very, very horny. David Rosenthal sums up the moviemaking mind-set of the time in his 1983 article for *Rolling Stone*: "Make 'em loud, make 'em mindless, make 'em laugh."

History was made when thirty-five-year-old Sherry Lansing became the first woman to head a major studio when she became president of production at 20th Century Fox. Under her three-year steerage, the studio enjoyed such acclaimed hits as *Taps*, *Chariots of Fire*, and *The Verdict*.

Speaking of presidents, Ronald Reagan was the first and only professional actor to be elected president of the United States, his two terms soaking up the decade. In 1981, Reagan survived an assassination attempt by John Hinkley Jr., who believed this action would impress Jodie Foster, the focus of his obsession since seeing *Taxi Driver*. Strikingly, the gritty New York of Scorsese's controversial masterpiece underwent a yuppie makeover in film; less Skid Row, more Fifth Avenue. Slick-haired suits dictating megadeals into their brick-sized cell phones and bug-eyed floor traders with sleeves rolled up became common sights in American movies.

The young Turks of the 1970s continued to have a strong showing, with Spielberg straddling multiple genres and enjoying enormous blockbuster success with *E.T. the Extra-Terrestrial* and the terrifically entertaining *Indiana Jones* franchise. But, as we've seen, he failed to convert box-office returns into Oscar glory, even when tackling a piece of serious fiction like *The Color Purple*. Having a largely Black cast was considered financially risky in Hollywood in 1985 (despite the recent success of *Beverly Hills Cop* with a young Eddie Murphy). But Spielberg persisted, casting Whoopi Goldberg in the lead role, which led to Roger Ebert declaring her performance the greatest film-acting debut of all time.

But it wasn't only Oscar voters who weren't happy with Spielberg's rendering of Alice Walker's novel. In fact, it was dogged by controversies, with protests often on both sides of issues within and surrounding the film. This is in no small part due to the paucity of representation of non-Caucasian people in American film. In his excellent article for the *Chicago Tribune*, Clarence Page asserts, "The real issues should be Hollywood's lack of balance in its all too infrequent depictions of Black life and its lack of Black participation in the industry's decision-making."

George Lucas and his team made one of the most successful sequels of all time, thrilling audiences around the world by pulling off that rarest of feats—making a second installment of a franchise that is as well received, if not more so, than the first. *The Empire Strikes Back* was a box-office smash, giving the fans everything they wanted and then some. It remains an outlier, though, as a lot of beloved films were followed up with bad sequels or turned into terrible remakes during this decade: *Psycho 2*, *Jaws 3D*, *Staying Alive*, and *To Be or Not to Be*, to name a sorry few.

In fact, sequels became an all-pervasive feature of the movie industry, feeding the gaping maw of demand for video rentals. The great format war had been won by VHS over Betamax. Although the latter boasted a higher-quality picture (some say), it was VHS's easier tape-transport mechanism and crucially its longer recording capability that put a video recorder in every home, priming the market for the home video revolution that had failed to take off with Laser Disc.

The 1980s is arguably cinema's most demented decade in terms of visual vocabulary: No effect was too nascent; no novelty, too cheap; and no plot, too daft, it seems. Envelope pushing in terms of effects led to some terrific triumphs. *Tron* was the first feature film to make extensive use of computer animation. Other technical innovations can be found in such classics as the *Back to the Future* trilogy, *Alien* and its sequel, and *Blade Runner*—as well as some arguably noble failures, like *Popeye*, *Krull*, *Dune*, and a whole heap of hot garbage besides. For every John Carpenter (*The Thing*, *Escape from New York*), there were dozens of shockingly bad imitators, such as Jim Wynorski (*Chopping Mall*) or Donald G. Jackson (*Hell Comes to Frogtown*) making straight-to-video films focused mainly on hyperarousal—not very hard when you're catering to fourteen-year-old boys hanging out at their local Blockbuster. But I'll not deny there's the odd lotus in the mud: films made with passion and blind conviction that might resemble a fever dream but cannot fail to entertain. From *Sleepaway Camp* to *Ladyhawke*, there was something for everyone on the video-shop shelves.

The more deranged aspects of the 1980s did allow for some truly original auteurs to thrive. If you strayed from the mainstream, you could find all kinds of unconventional sustenance in the queer pastiches of John Waters (*Polyester*, *Hairspray*); the body horror of David Cronenberg (*Scanners*, *Videodrome*, and most famously *The Fly*); the unsettling originality of David Lynch (*Blue Velvet, Dune*); and Kathryn Bigelow's eventual cult classic *Near Dark*. Yes, I am aware there are less women in that sentence than men called David, so you could conclude it was a better decade for Davids than female directors and you would be . . . correct.

Comedy wasn't all gross-out and *Saturday Night Live* alumni antics. This decade did platform some truly incredible comedic actresses: Lily Tomlin (*9 to 5, All of Me*); Bette Midler (*Down and Out in Beverly Hills, Ruthless People*, and *Big Business* with Tomlin); and Shelley Long (*The Money Pit* and *Outrageous Fortune* with Midler). I am grateful that I grew up watching women being hilarious and having leading roles in their forties. But what is deeply troubling is the casual attitude toward rape and assault in the proto-incel flick *Revenge of the Nerds* or even John Hughes's *Sixteen Candles*. These films equate intoxication as consent and passed-out or disoriented women as fair game. There is behavior depicted in every decade that is no longer considered acceptable, and I'm not naïve to this. But I find it chilling to consider that these misogynist narratives were targeted at impressionable minds and even more troubling to consider the kinds of attitudes that those minds may have internalized as a result.

It took a while for the 1980s to deal with burgeoning female sexuality as a central theme. But in 1987, a little film called *Dirty Dancing* was released, and its impact reverberated with teenage audiences around the world. Written by Eleanor Bergstein and produced by Linda Gottlieb, it was initially given an R rating, depriving the film of its target audience—but after some wrangling, it managed to procure that all-important PG-13. It went on to become a tremendous hit, and it is still finding new delighted audiences today. The triumph of this film lies in its ability to stitch together issues often treated as shameful—such as abortion and female desire—into a story of joy. It shames the lack of access to safe abortion facilities, not the character who is very nearly a casualty of that. Baby won't be punished for gyrating with Johnny. Hell, she won't even be put in the corner.

The building of multi- and megaplexes proliferated in the 1980s in line with film-production output. In turn, the "family film" evolved, as smart and involving scripts looking to have cross-generational appeal were enhanced by dazzling visuals. *The Dark Crystal* and *Labyrinth* seared themselves onto the imaginations of children of the 1980s, while such stand-alone films as *The Goonies* and *Stand by Me* could be enjoyed by kids, teens, and adults alike.

The decade ended on a fiercely independent note. Greed and grossout gave way to maturation and minimalism, a development epitomized by *sex, lies, and videotape*. Written in eight days and shot in five weeks by Steven Soderbergh, it is a curiously blank film—it could be set anywhere. Interiors and costumes are muted in a way that feels antithetical to the beefcake men and pneumatic women running from space lasers set to synth soundtracks that elsewhere filled cinema screens. The only novelties here are Soderbergh's nifty storytelling, his use of elliptical editing, and nonsynchronous sound. It was made for $1.2 million. When it won the Palme d'Or at Cannes, it was acquired by Miramax and went on to make $100 million.

In 1989, Spike Lee's *Do the Right Thing* gave us a day in the life of Brooklyn residents as they intersect on a steaming New York Street in a heatwave-fueled pressure cooker of racial and generational tensions. The film remains depressingly relevant, as Tambay Obenson writes in *Indie Wire* thirty years on: "Inspired by the racially-motivated killings of a Black man named Michael Griffith and an elderly Black woman named Eleanor Bumpurs (shot by the New York Police Department, no less), *Do the Right Thing* served and still serves as a window into a country that has historically devalued the lives of African Americans."

At the end of the 1980s, we find ourselves at the very beginning of the wealth of independent films to come. The combination of young bloods who had grown up on the films of the 1970s, and Miramax realizing that low-budget indies could be hugely profitable, would change cinema forever. But before we dismiss this outré decade in terms of taste and style, in favor of the indie explosion of the 1990s, let us savor a time that catered to the dreams and desires of all the wonderful people out there in the dark: the adults experiencing the sensationalist filmmaking of De Palma and Verhoeven, the teens enjoying a wickedly subversive group of girls called the *Heathers*, and children of the 1980s being carried off on Indiana Jones adventures, on never-ending stories to galaxies far, far away. Just give *Howard the Duck* a miss.

THE MAKING OF *AMADEUS*

Writer: Peter Shaffer, from his play
Director: Miloš Forman
Producer: Saul Zaentz for Orion Pictures
Cast: F. Murray Abraham, Tom Hulce, Elizabeth Berridge, Simon
    Callow, Roy Dotrice, Jeffrey Jones
Won: Best Picture, Best Director, Best Adapted Screenplay, Best
    Actor (Abraham), Best Art Direction (Patrizia von Brandenstein,
    Karel Černý), Best Costume Design (Theodor Pištěk), Best
    Makeup (Dick Smith, Paul LeBlanc). Best Sound (Mark Berger,
    Tom Scott, Todd Boekelheide, Christopher Newman)
Nominated: Best Actor (Hulce), Best Cinematography (Miroslav
    Ondříček), Best Film Editing (Nena Danevic, Michael Chandler)
Length: 161 minutes
Budget: $18 million
Box office: $90.4 million
Rotten Tomatoes: 93%

There's a saying: "Salieri didn't murder Mozart, but Pushkin for sure murdered Salieri." You can find evidence to support some occasional antipathy between the two men, but the idea that Salieri was the instigator of Mozart's demise is not taken seriously by scholars. Writer Alexander Pushkin, however, realized that this alleged rivalry could be the basis of a good drama—and so a myth was born. With Pushkin's short play as an inspiration, playwright Peter Shaffer wrote a script of his own for the United Kingdom's National Theatre in 1979, describing it as a "fantasia on the theme of Mozart and Salieri." He later said he was faithful to the spirit of the truth, with a basis for everything, although the overall piece is fiction.

Director Miloš Forman was in the audience for the first preview of the production. He'd not been keen on the idea of seeing a biography of a musician, having seen many that were deathly dull, but found the piece so impactful that he apparently spoke to Shaffer during the interval and told him that if the second act was as good as the first, he'd make a film of it.

Forman did enjoy the second half and soon met with Shaffer to develop it into a movie, telling him, "You realize, everything will be different." Shaffer's plays had been adapted for screen before, but Forman wanted to impress on him that theater embraced stylization, whereas film aims for realism. As an example, Shaffer's play includes a Greek chorus of local gossips—the Venticelli, or "little winds." Such overt theatricality didn't mesh with Forman's more grounded vision of the story. This established, the two men spent four months working on the script, Monday to Friday, spending a lot of that time listening to Mozart's music. In fact, Shaffer viewed music as the lead character of the story, so when the script was complete, they approached famed conductor Neville Mariner to be the music director. He agreed to be involved on one condition: that not a single note of Mozart's music would be changed.

Forman felt that casting was the most important part of the process, thinking that if the director casts it right, he doesn't have to be there anymore. He saw hundreds of actors for the lead roles, including actors who'd played the role onstage to great acclaim—such as Ian McKellen who'd won a Tony for his Salieri. But Forman didn't want known faces; he wanted the audience to just see Mozart and Salieri (which ruled out a Broadway Mozart, Mark Hamill). Other possible Mozarts included Tim Curry, Mel Gibson, Peter MacNicol, and a young Kenneth Branagh. Andrew Lloyd Webber claims he was offered the role but turned it down. One studio had offered to fund the film if Mozart enthusiast Walter Matthau played the role, despite being several decades too old. Forman refused and eventually settled on Tom Hulce.

Salieri contenders included Sam Waterston and Burt Reynolds. The eventual casting, F. Murray Abraham, originally came in to audition for the role of Rosenberg, in which he was apparently just "okay." But during one audition session, Miloš Forman asked him to stay and read Salieri against a potential Mozart. His reading was brilliant, and he became Forman's choice for the role. He felt that Abraham was frustrated by his position in the industry and was basically Salieri on-screen and off.

One Broadway original Forman did want in the film was Amy Irving as Constanza—but Forman was planning to film in the Czech capital city of Prague, and she couldn't face six months abroad. So Meg Tilly was cast as Constanza, and the rest of the cast fell into place. All the actors kept their natural accents—the better to help them focus on their performances.

Prague at that time was under communist rule. Forman, who was considered a traitor for becoming an American citizen, had previously had one of his movies banned there. In order to get the permits he needed, he had to agree to various demands from the Czech government, including going to his hotel every night he was there and having his driver be his best friend from the old days—because everyone knew what would happen to that friend if something politically untoward should occur during filming.

The production team was often followed around by the Czech secret police, who caused a lot of trouble. The archbishop refused filming permission after being told by a secret policeman they'd film nonexistent orgy scenes in his palace. And Forman and the cast spoke about their fears that a Fourth of July prank—the unfurling of the American flag in the concert hall and the singing of "The Star-Spangled Banner" by the large cast and crew—would lead to their arrests for inciting rebellion. (They knew the secret police had witnessed this—they were the half of the extras and the crew who didn't join in with the singing.)

Many suspected that their hotel rooms had been bugged. Abraham himself witnessed one cast member frantically searching for a recording device—looking in the chandelier, under the bed, everywhere he could. When he eventually found a plate on the floor, he unscrewed it with a knife—and immediately heard the chandelier in the room below crash to the ground. They left the room very quickly.

The first scenes shot were those with old Salieri, which gave the other actors a chance to work and rehearse on their own (Hulce particularly was working incredibly hard for weeks learning to mime playing the music exactly). This also had the effect of keeping Abraham separate from the rest of the cast and built up a wall between them. His resentful feelings toward, for example, the bond between Hulce and Tilly, basically mirrored those of his character—which he later said was a "director's dream."

But other aspects of that dream became a nightmare. Tilly—who Forman felt had basically nailed the part even before filming started—tore her ligament during a street soccer game with some children, so she had to leave the role. Hulce and the crew flew back to New York and saw sixty possible replacements in a single weekend. They narrowed it down to two choices—but couldn't make a final decision in the time left, so they brought both over to Prague. And Forman still couldn't decide, so the two women hung out together for a week, eating together every night. Eventually Forman decided the other actor was "too pretty," so the role went to Elizabeth Berridge—who reacted rather wryly to his reasoning.

The film was completed and released to great success, but Forman had to trim or remove a number of scenes. Later, he decided to restore around twenty minutes of deleted material in a DVD director's cut, wanting the best life for the film when the length no longer mattered. Curiously, this is the only version of the film that's easy to obtain today, and while Forman's frustration at having to cut cherished material is understandable, few people think the restored scenes add much except length. And while this isn't the time or the place to start getting into a whole Greedo-shot-first debate, it does mean that *Amadeus* belongs on a short list of Best Picture–winning films that are hard or even impossible to see in their original Oscar-winning versions. Other examples include *Wings*, *The Broadway Melody*, *All Quiet on the Western Front*, *Tom Jones*, and *Lawrence of Arabia*.

BEST OF THE BEST: *PLATOON*

Writer: Oliver Stone
Director: Oliver Stone
Producer: Arnold Kopelson for Hemdale/Orion
Cast: Charlie Sheen, Tom Berenger, Willem Dafoe, Keith David, Forest Whitaker, Francesco Quinn, Kevin Dillon, John C. McGinley
Won: Best Picture, Best Director, Best Film Editing (Claire Simpson), Best Sound (John K. Wilkinson, Richard Rogers, Charles "Bud" Grenzbach, Simon Kaye)
Nominated: Best Supporting Actor (Berenger, Dafoe), Best Original Screenplay, Best Cinematography (Robert Richardson)
Length: 120 minutes
Budget: $6 million
Box office: $138.5 million
Rotten Tomatoes: 88%

John Dorney: It's a mark of the impact that *Platoon* has that when the writers of this book watched all the Best Picture winners together, this was the one of only two that nearly caused a member of the team to walk out of the viewing. Not because it was a poor movie—the usual reason one might bail partway through—but because it very much isn't. This movie is an unflinching portrait of a dark time in American history and a tough and grueling watch, but it is nonetheless a piece that should be seen, even if simply to bear witness to the atrocities within.

Many Best Picture winners deal with war, and *Platoon* isn't even the first of them to deal with Vietnam. But in contrast to the languid pace and artistic pretensions of *The Deer Hunter*, it is visceral and raw, blunt and relentless, and most importantly feels true—an insider's eye on the horror and the mess of that awful conflict. There are no moments of levity, no let-up. You are trapped in the jungle, and you can't get out.

The film is so committed to this claustrophobia that it doesn't even allow the faint respite of initially seeing the soldiers at home before being shipped out. It's breaking the rules from the get-go, ignoring the traditional war-movie setup of a training montage and "men on a mission." Instead, we have a team who are just there, in every sense, moving around, doing minor tasks, and simply trying to fill time and survive. They are literal cannon fodder.

And it continues to be structurally unusual, perhaps even structureless. Its chief conflict is between the rival soldiers played by Willem Dafoe and Tom Berenger—yet our viewpoint character is Charlie Sheen's Chris Taylor, who for the first half at least is writing letters home and narrating the story without being able to influence its outcome. But this always feels like it's the point—to be pointless. This isn't a neat story with traditional beats and is probably at its weakest when it veers the closest to having an actual plot. There's just enough story there to keep you going, but really the whole thing is largely an illustration of what life happens to be like when you're in that environment. And what it is, is horrendous.

Sheen moves toward the center of the film as it progresses, and the slow build of character beats start to pay off, with many great choices from its young star, who even manages to make something of his sparsely used voice-over narration—something that can often come across as clunky and ill-judged but works remarkably well here. The film always avoids making the Hollywood choice, with its nominal hero not portrayed as a saint but as a man who could turn to the dark side and who is disgusted by the fact that that's a possibility. Even the killing of his nemesis toward the end of the movie is treated with restraint and a lack of viscera, taking a moment that could easily have become filled with meaningful "acting" and leaving it grubby.

It's not perhaps a film for the ages, not least because it's not one you're going to be keen to watch more than once—but it's undeniably impressive. Director and screenwriter Oliver Stone knows exactly what effect he wants to create, and he creates it. This isn't one of those simplistic morality tales we might have seen in earlier war films. This isn't a jolly "Boy's Own" adventure; it's not glamorous and full of bravery; it's the truth. War is stupid and messy and grim and filled with death and waste. The film ends with a voice-over saying that the people who survived have an obligation to pass on what they've learned. And that's what Stone is doing here: passing it on. *Platoon* makes you think, and it makes you feel. And what else are movies for?

WORST OF THE BEST: (NEARLY) ALL OF THE OTHERS

Tom Salinsky: As tough a choice as Best of the Best was for the 1960s, the choice of Worst of the Best for the 1980s was even tougher. We wimped out of the choice there, and we're doing it again here. Our book, our rules. And this does mean throwing some perfectly good movies under the bus. There's nothing terribly wrong with *Rain Man*. Even people with an autism-spectrum diagnosis were grateful that the condition got some more mainstream attention, and it's not the fault of a single film that *autism* went on to become a lazy shorthand for "people who are incredibly rude but we put up with them because their near-magical problem-solving ability is worth it."

And the 1980s' Second-Best of the Best, were we giving that prize out, would easily go to *Amadeus*—a really good play with a fascinating relationship at its core, that is necessarily streamlined a bit in its move to the big screen but never feels confined and features a very good performance from Tom Hulce and an outstanding one from F. Murray Abraham. The music isn't bad either.

But when you look at the rest, and when you look at the "Did the Academy Get It Right?" section, you'll discover that this decade generally failed to engage us a group. For us to all be unanimous in picking the Best Picture winner as our favorite is a fairly rare occurrence (it happens about 20 percent of the time), but in this decade it only happens once—and that was for *Platoon*. For some of us, the very male-heavy intensity of the 1970s was already a bit of a slog. But the 1980s is the principal reason we didn't record the podcast by going through the movies in chronological order. We'd never have gotten past 1985.

There are various reasons for these movies being a struggle. The schism between box-office success and critical adulation, which starts opening up in the late 1970s, cracks wide open here. Intimate family dramas take the place of the bone-crunching violence of Cimino and Coppola, which in turn took over from the widescreen epics of the preceding twenty or so years. And the movies have stopped competing with TV and started to imitate it. So this is an era of Best Picture winners that often have low stakes and little cinematic ambition and that didn't find a mass audience when they were first released. Academy voters picked out Bertolucci's *The Last Emperor* in the same year that American cinemagoers flocked to see *Three Men and a Baby* directed by Leonard Nimoy. I'm not a huge fan of either, but Mr. Spock's film at least makes me feel something.

The decade starts as it means to go on with *Ordinary People*, which in many ways is the "patient zero" of the plague infesting this run of Best Picture winners. Well, maybe that was *Kramer vs. Kramer* the previous year—and actually *Ordinary People* isn't nearly as bad as some of its successors. Sitcom star Mary Tyler Moore takes the soap opera material and works wonders with it, absolutely refusing to allow even a hint of sentimentality to slip through her implacable armor. The rest though is . . . fine. A perfectly serviceable drama about a family in crisis and the different ways in which they struggle to get through it—but honestly, nothing you couldn't see done equally well in a dozen other movies or TV shows, just with a bit more star power here from the likes of Judd Hirsch and Donald Sutherland.

Far more disappointing is *Chariots of Fire*, which just seems a bit drab today. It's a not uninteresting slice of history, and the locations look yummy, but sports movies need to get the viewer completely invested in the success or failure of the team or individual in question, and it's hard for me to get all that involved in the largely self-inflicted problems of this gang of amateur athletes, especially when neither the script nor the direction is working at all hard to raise the stakes. The central conflict of the whole plot is resolved in a single, cheerful conversation between several decent chaps all keen to do the right thing. Perfectly watchable stuff on a Sunday afternoon, and Ian Holm is terrific—but this surely can't have been the best, most innovative, most striking movie of the entire year.

Gandhi was one I was dreading. It brought back memories of being sat behind a rickety desk, watching a VHS copy on a television wheeled into the classroom by a teacher who barely knew how to operate it. I generally don't like flabby biopics that pedantically record every detail of a famous person's life without being able to give the narrative any real momentum or power. Maybe because my expectations were set fairly low, I actually found Attenborough's history lesson more engrossing as a grown-up, and Ben Kingsley does a superb job in the leading role. But for all that, it doesn't have the epic sweep that Spielberg or Scorsese or David Lean would have given it, and I found myself nodding along, saying, "Gosh, how interesting," rather than ever being caught up in the moment.

Part of the problem is that the project was supported by the Indian government, and so its ability to be critical of Gandhi is severely constrained. There's one fascinating scene, early on, between him and his wife where it's just briefly suggested that his devotion to the cause would bring problems as well as benefits. But the moment swiftly passes, and the rest is all restrained delivery of factual material and no nuance.

Terms of Endearment is a real oddity—a bonkers world populated by eccentric people with names like Aurora Greenway and Flap Horton. We hang out with these folks for a while as they unite, part, squabble, and make up. Eventually, the film is over, and I'm left wondering just what the point was. Larry McMurtry's novel was part of a longer sequence, and maybe that's why this feels like three episodes from the middle of a long television series. But it's still just not terribly interesting—although it's always a pleasure to see Shirley MacLaine again. And she manages to bed Jack Nicholson! You go, girl.

If *Gandhi* was a relief, then *Out of Africa* was a crushing disappointment. Even if you set aside the distasteful colonial overtones, this still feels incredibly thin. Not for the first time, Meryl Streep works wonders with an underwritten part, and a woefully miscast Robert Redford cruises by on sheer star wattage, but it ends up feeling almost like a documentary, in which Karen Blixen and Denys Finch Hatton calmly reminisce about their time in Nairobi without getting too overwrought. How strange that in the 1970s, it was required for stars—especially the men—to wail and moan and chew the scenery to win awards; whereas, in this decade, the Academy only seems to recognize *repression* as the highest form of artistic endeavor. But repressed emotion needs to be handled with great care, lest it becomes absence of emotion and thus absence of engagement.

The Last Emperor is the best example of this. Having secured permission to film inside the Forbidden City, Bertolucci creates some indelible images, and there's a sub–James Bond mini-movie in the middle, which is rather good fun. But given the Shakespearean ingredients out of which the plot is made, it's stunning how underplayed and undercooked everything is.

The decade ended with *Driving Miss Daisy*. Like *Amadeus*, this is a play on film. Unlike *Amadeus*, this feels like one. Director Bruce Beresford and screenwriter/playwright Alfred Uhry ignore the wider social issues and bet everything on the relationship between Jessica Tandy and Morgan Freeman. (To be fair, this was never likely to even remotely resemble a Spike Lee joint.) Tandy is fine, but Freeman plays every scene the same—it might be my least favorite Morgan Freeman performance, and he's an actor I usually find incredibly engaging. And the grudging respect they feel for each other, which slowly becomes affectionate interdependence, never has enough specificity, detail, or nuance for me to truly care. The malaise of the decade is still here—yet another low-key, soapy family drama, shot like a TV show and plotted with tiny, grudging spoonfuls of incident, somehow appealed to more Academy voters than any other movie.

When we look back on the cinema of the 1980s with fondness, the productions we remember are the big, crowd-pleasing family films, like *Back to the Future* and *Big*, or the amazing horror movies, like *A Nightmare on Elm Street* and *The Thing*, or the iconic comedies, like *Beverly Hills Cop* and *Airplane!* and, of course, the action blockbusters, like *Raiders of the Lost Ark* and *Die Hard*. But the 1980s wasn't just about packing teenagers into multiplexes. Even ignoring all the following films, which we would have voted for, you could still have had *Broadcast News*, *Blue Velvet*, *Stand by Me*, *Blade Runner*, *Once Upon a Time in America*, *When Harry Met Sally*, *The Long Good Friday*, *Das Boot*, *The Verdict*, *Cinema Paradiso*—all of them perfectly plausible Best

Picture winners, but none of them were picked, few of them were nominated, and some were ignored completely.

This trend isn't irreversible. While the chasm between the public's taste and the Academy's would never close, there were some far more interesting films added to the list over the course of the next thirty years. And nobody ever said watching every single Best Picture winner was going to be an unalloyed joy. Onward!

DID THE ACADEMY GET IT RIGHT?

1980: *Ordinary People*

John Dorney: It's certainly an awful lot better than its reputation and is well worth your time. But it's up against a number of all-time classics, and really, it has to wait in line behind them. *Raging Bull* is iconic and obviously brilliant but has never really been to my taste, and *The Elephant Man* didn't quite land for me either. *The Empire Strikes Back* and *Airplane!* are much more my kind of thing and really deserved nominations, but I have to give it to another film that didn't get nominated—in fact, it actually got nominated for the inaugural Golden Raspberry Awards (or Razzies), satirical awards which highlight the worst of Hollywood's output each year. That's **The Shining**, which is stunning and unique, rich and heady in atmosphere, and terrifying to this day.

Jessica Regan: *Ordinary People* is a fine film. I greatly admire Redford's direction, and some career-best performances are coaxed out of these already-legendary actors. There is so much truth and so little ego in the storytelling. I wish more films found that balance. *The Empire Strikes Back* left an indelible mark on cinema and raised the bar of sequels forever. But Stanley Kubrick's **The Shining** unnerves, unravels, and terrifies at every turn. These are not cheap thrills or easy jump scares. These are unforgettable images, iconic performances, and electrifying sequences that scorch themselves onto the psyche of the watcher.

Tom Salinsky: *Ordinary People* is a film that seems at first to be about to sprawl, Altman-like, but that actually gathers the threads of its narrative and binds them almost too tightly together by the end. The performances are immaculate—for which debutante director Redford deserves a lot of credit—but while I don't think this was a terrible decision by the Academy, this ends up feeling a little small to me. In general, I found this to be rather a thin year, but *The Elephant Man* has as much humanity and pathos as Redford's film—and it feels richer and is certainly more visually striking, even if the last twenty minutes have nothing new to say.

1981: *Chariots of Fire*

John Dorney: I feel bad saying it, but it's a no. *Chariots* is definitely enjoyable, but it's not quite well put together enough to get Best Picture when it's in a straight race against *Raiders of the Lost Ark*, which is a thrill ride like no other. It does what it wants to do perfectly and will be watched and enjoyed for decades to come. It's the only possible winner.

Jessica Regan: Featuring an astonishing ensemble, this film is layered in its subtle explorations of competing, othering, and the dearth of purpose that victory can leave in its wake. It flows like a race, with its prelapping sound, a surging iconic score, and a script that gets the blood pumping with such lines as "I am dedicated to the pursuit of excellence, and I will carry the future with me!" Elegantly economic, it does not spoon-feed exposition or thematic intent. It is unshowy but not thin, period but not prettified. I give the gold to *Chariots of Fire*.

Tom Salinsky: Although it's well observed and beautifully acted, the surprisingly low stakes and meandering plotting make it a comfortable and reassuring watch rather than a challenging and exciting one. *Raiders of the Lost Ark* by contrast was electrifyingly exciting on its first release, and by and large, it still holds up today. Possibly its ambitions are limited, but it is an ideal version of what it is attempting to be.

1982: *Gandhi*

John Dorney: It's easy to be wary of *Gandhi*, an incredibly long biopic of the sort that the Academy often rewards egregiously. But Richard Attenborough's passion project is by no means as dull as you might expect, even if it never quite becomes an actual piece of cinema. The best film of the year, however, is undeniably Steven Spielberg's evergreen classic ***E.T. the Extra-Terrestrial***, a joyous watch that will sweep you up time and time again.

Jessica Regan: As an Irish person who moved to the United Kingdom some fifteen years ago, I was astonished to discover how little my English contemporaries knew of their country's colonial history. I therefore approached this film a little cautiously, aware that you can take me out of Ireland, but you cannot take the Irish out of me—no matter how much I endeavor to approach the material with a benevolent neutrality. Happily, I was continuously impressed with this clear-eyed and unflinching handling of historical events. Atrocity is atrocity, and there is no glory in an empire built on the backs and with the blood of other peoples. Much like the man, ***Gandhi*** isn't perfect. But it is a great deal more than a history lesson and a deserving winner, in large part thanks to an extraordinary performance by Sir Ben Kingsley, which runs through it like a central nervous system from which all feeling springs.

Tom Salinsky: *Gandhi* is an important film and a necessary film that avoids many (but not all) of the traps of the reverential biopic, and Ben Kingsley is sublime. But watching it, I yearn for a David Lean who could shoot it with a bit more flair and pace it with a bit more energy. Ultimately it feels like journalism rather than drama. For a simpler tale but shot with incredible panache and full of equally compelling performances, there's Spielberg's astonishing ***E.T. the Extra-Terrestrial***, which will also pull your heart right out of your chest. I'm aware that's two Spielberg crowd-pleasers in a row, but there's a real art to creating these family films that endure, and I'd put both of these up against the likes of *Casablanca*, *Gone with the Wind*, or *Grand Hotel* any day and not feel at all embarrassed.

1983: *Terms of Endearment*

John Dorney: If there was an Oscar for "stupidest character names," this movie would be a worthy winner. For Best Picture, not so much. There's a lot to like here. It's enjoyable enough for a weekend afternoon. But this is the year of my favorite Scorsese movie, ***The King of Comedy***, so that has to take the top spot for me.

Jessica Regan: This film fizzes with frank and funny dialogue, particularly from Debra Winger. MacLaine and Nicholson are surely having at least as much fun playing their scenes as we do watching them, and James L. Brooks is always a safe pair of hands. It is not exactly undeniable, but it is effective. But, in a moment of total unity with my cohorts, it is the scandalously overlooked *The King of Comedy* that gets my vote for possessing levels of wit, subversion, and pertinent social commentary of which a contemporary director—such as, ooh, I don't know, let's say Todd Phillips—could only dream.

Tom Salinsky: Did they not see *The King of Comedy*, or did they not get it? Either is possible, and while it tends not to be brought up in the same breath as *Taxi Driver* or *Goodfellas*, this is one of Scorsese's most complex and challenging films, and I vastly prefer it to the brutish and repetitive *Raging Bull*.

1984: *Amadeus*

John Dorney: Filled with stirring performances and stirring music, all in service of a dazzling script, *Amadeus* is an easy winner for me. Who cares that it's not really true? What it's saying is, and that's probably more important.

Jessica Regan: Under the powdered, pushed-up artifice presented in each frame, there is great depth here. Surprising performances and stunning production design—not to mention the actual music of Mozart—make *Amadeus* a truly captivating experience and one that I have revisited more than once. But for me, the greatest achievement in filmmaking in 1984 was *1984*. In one of the most faithful and stunningly rendered cinematic adaptations of a book—a seminal, seemingly unfilmable book at that—John Hurt gives a career-best performance as Winston in George Orwell's cri de coeur against fascism and all its attendant dehumanizing impulses and expressions. I wish it seemed horribly dated and unforgivably miserable now, but it remains an urgent and essential film. If you are a fan of Adam Curtis documentaries in particular, this one's for you.

Tom Salinsky: Peter Shaffer's excellent play survives and thrives under Miloš Forman's direction, and the performances of Hulce and especially Abraham are sublime. In a sea of unambitious if crowd-pleasing Hollywood fare, only Sergio Leone's *Once upon a Time in America* really stands out—but a combination of an even more complex reediting and reissuing history than Forman's film and some very dodgy sexual politics forces me to rule it out, thus handing **Amadeus** the win. It's not a win by default, though. This is a richly complex film with something genuinely new to say about pride, creativity, ego, and celebrity.

1985: *Out of Africa*

John Dorney: Well, let's get it out of the way, first up. It's not *Out of Africa*. Best Picture has to be one of two. In the spirit of being ultra-picky, with a heavy heart, I can't give it to the dazzling, inventive, but ultimately slightly scrappy *Brazil*—a movie that is, nonetheless, an all-time favorite of mine. Instead, I'm going for the peerlessly rewatchable **Back to the Future**, a film that has a reasonable claim to being the most purely enjoyable movie of all time.

Jessica Regan: Redford. Streep. Stunning scenery. High-necked blouses. What could go wrong? Well not a lot, but it just doesn't go very right. Streep might play the "good" kind of colonizer, but she remains hard to root for and invest in, considering the setup. Even her dashing lover can't stomach her impulse for ownership for more than a few twilight picnics at a time. And so, to my favorite film of the year: **The Purple Rose of Cairo**. It is surely Woody Allen's most original and at times surprising work, perhaps because he concerned himself with telling a cracking yarn with magic realism rather than curated projections of his neuroses and dysfunction. This is a proper Hollywood fairy tale with a Grimm-like resolution that unsettles as much as the previous action has delighted.

Tom Salinsky: No, this is overlong and very pedestrian stuff from director Sydney Pollack, who fails to find the drama or the beauty in this true-life adventure, despite strong work from Redford and Streep. 1985 is an embarrassment of riches, from arguably Woody Allen's finest (*The Purple Rose of Cairo*) to the perfect family adventure comedy in *Back to the Future* and the return of Kurosawa with *Ran*. But **Brazil** is an amazing achievement and the kind of film that a bolder Academy could and should have recognized.

1986: *Platoon*

John Dorney: This year has a lot of personal favorites of mine—like *Little Shop of Horrors* and the endlessly rewatchable *Aliens*. But while they're undeniably more fun than **Platoon**, they're ultimately not as true. It may not be a movie to watch for entertainment purposes, but it's the most powerful and affecting and as a result is an easy choice for the win.

Jessica Regan: It sickens the soul to watch **Platoon**, but I think that is the correct reaction to the massacre of Vietnamese people and the monstering of young American men. There is no specific mission for these soldiers—much like there is no meaning to this war. It just goes on and on, a circle of suffering experienced and inflicted and so on and so forth. Barely tolerable but quite brilliant, Oliver Stone tells the truth of war in all its banality, repetition, and ruination.

Tom Salinsky: I'm generally rather allergic to Oliver Stone, finding his bombastic directing style exhausting and rarely finding what he has to say very interesting. *JFK*, for example, is an absurd exercise in demented style over paper-thin substance. I was totally unprepared for the raw power of this film. It feels absolutely authentic, horrifying, and true. Amid some very entertaining but very lightweight fare, **Platoon** is the only choice for Best Picture.

1987: *The Last Emperor*

John Dorney: *The Last Emperor* is a surprisingly plausible winner from the list of nominees, all of which are decent and fine movies but very few of which cross the line into stellar. But to win the award for Best Picture, I feel there needs to be something more. I was tempted by the ever-subversive and brilliant *Robocop*, which is probably genuinely deserving of a Best Picture nomination—and even more tempted by the evergreen miracle that is *The Princess Bride*. But the best has to be Louis Malle's beautiful and delicate **Au Revoir Les Enfants**, a piece of pure heartbreak.

Jessica Regan: An edifying and unique work of cinema that suffers from its essence being bowdlerized by the choice to make it an English-speaking rather than a subtitled film. Sensuous and transportive but hard to connect to emotionally, the film meditates on how regimes tend to be replaced with other regimes, and history's mistakes are repeated, just with different labeling. But in a decade preoccupied with coming of age, I think the peak of it all is the Swedish film **My Life as a Dog**, directed by subsequent Hollywood hire Lasse Hallström. It manages to be epic and delicate, heartfelt and humorous, and it enchanted and held me as preteen when I was experiencing all kinds of physical and social discombobulation. A personal pick but a very worthy one.

Tom Salinsky: On its face, *The Last Emperor* has a lot going for it—big themes, amazing locations, a window into unfamiliar history. What it doesn't have is any guts. It never pulled me in emotionally. Elsewhere, this is very much the year of a boy's-eye view of World War II, with Spielberg's sweeping but unfocused *Empire of the Sun* and John Boorman's *Hope and Glory*. But Louis Malle's **Au Revoir Les Enfants** is absolutely devastating and easily my film of the year. Unaccountably, it managed to lose Best Foreign Language Film to the engaging but far less resonant *Babette's Feast*.

1988: *Rain Man*

John Dorney: *Rain Man* is a very strong film in a very strong year, anchored by a brilliant performance from Tom Cruise. But it isn't **Who Framed Roger Rabbit**. The only flaw this family classic has is that it makes what it's doing look easy—and it does so much. Yes, it's filled with technical wizardry that seems mind-blowing even now, but there's a lot more going on. It's a masterpiece of world-building, backing up a rock-solid noir pastiche plot, layered with a touching story of a man recovering his soul—and that's before you even get to the performances of a charming Bob Hoskins and a terrifying Christopher Lloyd. It's truly remarkable.

Jessica Regan: An engaging film rather than a stone-cold winner. Everyone remembers Dustin Hoffman's tics and tricks, but for me Tom Cruise gives the performance of the film, effortlessly conveying his shock, fear, and confusion when his brother becomes sensory-overwhelmed. But the film that seduced me with sadistic machinations and sensuality was **Dangerous Liaisons**—full of beautiful people being thoroughly ugly in their dealings with each other. It is such a clutch of career bests, with John Malkovich, Glenn Close, and Michelle Pfeiffer never better; Christopher Hampton's outrageously good script; and Stephen Frears conducting proceedings masterfully, gleefully dancing us around the room in a whirl of powdered wigs and corsetry and then bringing us sharply to a shattering denouement.

Tom Salinsky: A richer and subtler film than its pedigree (and the year of its release) might suggest. *Rain Man* isn't the most complex or ambitious film ever to win Best Picture, but next to the rather stagey *Dangerous Liaisons*, the trivial *Working Girl*, the slender *The Accidental Tourist*, or even the very entertaining but ultimately hollow *Big*, it looks like a worthy winner.

1989: Driving Miss Daisy

John Dorney: *Driving Miss Daisy* is another one of those films that really isn't its reputation. Yes, it's not brilliant, but it's perfectly fine and was probably a very solid stage play. But as a piece of cinema, it's lacking, particularly when contrasted with **Do the Right Thing**. Spike Lee's classic is flawed, but it's riddled with kinetic energy and a heat that burns up the celluloid, while its key moments feel depressingly relevant more than thirty years later. It's not the perfect choice, but it's the right one.

Jessica Regan: Oh. Oh no. Look, this is a fine movie . . . of the week. Two strong central performances struggle and just about succeed against unambitious cinematography and seemingly underfunded production design, but the workmanlike direction does not make for a film that will age well. While I salute the exploration of internalized biases held by the protagonists as much as the racism shaping their dynamic, this feels like a mealy-mouthed choice by Hollywood, opting for a film that pays lip service rather than tackles race relations head on. If the Academy had made the right choice, they would have picked **Do the Right Thing**.

Tom Salinsky: Not quite a filmed record of a stage play but barely more than a decent TV movie, *Driving Miss Daisy* doesn't trample through the painful history of America's emergence from segregation in the way that, say, *Green Book* does, but nor does it seem especially interested in it, which makes it a pretty lightweight watch. Either *Do the Right Thing* or *Glory* would have been better choices if the Academy wanted to reward a film tackling this subject, but both have some weak spots. Michael Lehmann and Daniel Waters's **Heathers**, while never a likely candidate for Oscar glory, is pitched precisely at the right level all the way through, and even the studio-mandated happy ending works.

8

THE 1990s

THE OSCARS IN THE 1990s

The 1990s is the Gil Cates/Billy Crystal era. Cates oversaw nine out of ten of these shows, and Crystal hosted seven out of ten. When you picture the Oscars, if you picture Billy Crystal singing parody songs about each of the Best Picture nominees, then you are a child of the 1990s and grew up watching these shows. Or the highlights package shown the following day.

This is also the era of war in the Middle East, and at the 1990 ceremony, an airport-style metal detector was installed to scan everyone entering the building—guests, presenters, staff, and nominees. Among

	Best Picture	Biggest Earner (worldwide)
1990	Dances with Wolves	Ghost
1991	The Silence of the Lambs	Terminator 2: Judgment Day
1992	Unforgiven	Aladdin
1993	Schindler's List	Jurassic Park
1994	Forrest Gump	The Lion King
1995	Braveheart	Die Hard with a Vengeance
1996	The English Patient	Independence Day
1997	Titanic	Titanic
1998	Shakespeare in Love	Armageddon
1999	American Beauty	Star Wars: Episode I—The Phantom Menace

the presenters was eighty-eight-year-old Bob Hope, who introduced a montage of stars recalling the first film they saw. Hope's name had become synonymous with the Oscars over the years. He first hosted the show in 1939 when *Gone with the Wind* won Best Picture and he comfortably holds the record with a further eighteen appearances as host and a number of other presenting slots besides. This was his last appearance on the Academy Awards stage, and he was also the only exception to the security rules. As Academy spokesperson Bob Werden put it, "You can't ask Bob Hope to walk through a metal detector. He's like the American flag."

We think of #OscarsSoWhite and people thanking their same-sex spouses as being distinctly twenty-first-century phenomena, but in March 1992, the LGBTQ community was out in force, and their target was Hollywood in general and the Oscars in particular. A week or two before the ceremony, Paul Verhoeven's *Basic Instinct* had been released. This film had been widely criticized for its depiction of LGBTQ characters as soon as the script leaked. Four of the film's main female characters, including Sharon Stone's, are lesbian or bisexual; all are portrayed as unstable, man-hating stalkers and killers. Pressure groups attempted to get changes made, but Paul Verhoeven stubbornly filmed Joe Eszterhas's screenplay as written.

So, Queer Nation and other protest groups turned their attention to the Oscars. Both *The Silence of the Lambs*—with its cross-dressing, possibly transgender serial killer—and *JFK*—with its stereotypically gay character and liberal use of homophobic slurs—were coming under fire, and protesters did their best to disrupt the red carpet, but by and large, the police prevented them from causing too much chaos. However, the protest made itself felt in other ways. Several presenters and recipients, either onstage or during press Q and As, mentioned the AIDS crisis, the protests, or related issues. Many presenters and winners wore red AIDS ribbons. Lyricist Howard Ashman won the award for Best Song, which was collected on his behalf by his partner, Bill Lauch, who told the audience, "Howard and I shared a life together, and I am very happy and very proud to accept this for him. But it is bittersweet. This is the first Academy Award given to someone we have lost to AIDS." Director Debra Chasnoff won the award for Best Documentary Short and thanked her partner, making her the first person to come out at the Oscars.

Protestors hoped that Jodie Foster would come out at the ceremony, but she did not. She did say afterward, "Protest is American. It's not against the law. Criticism is also good. Anything other than that falls into the category of undignified. But criticism is very important." A final attempt to disrupt the ceremony itself failed. A man in a tuxedo who had bought tickets to the ceremony began yelling out statistics related to the AIDS crisis as John Candy was introducing a Best Song performance, but he wasn't picked up by cameras or microphones, and he was swiftly removed, so TV audiences were none the wiser.

It's hard to say if it had an impact or not. True, the rest of the 1990s included many more sympathetic LGBTQ characters in Hollywood movies, including from Jonathan Demme, who returned two years later with *Philadelphia*, but it seems likely that the tide was turning anyway. However, Hollywood is a town that prides itself on its liberal ideals, and at the very least, the protests may have brought some self-proclaimed liberals up short and got them to question some of their values and actions. A couple years later, Tom Hanks seemingly "outed" his high school teacher. In fact, he had full permission from Rawley Farnsworth, who was only mildly bemused at how Hanks had known he was gay in the first place. The incident is the basis for the not-very-interesting Kevin Kline film *In & Out* released in 1997.

In 1993, the Academy finally handed a statuette to Steven Spielberg. *Schindler's List* had the most nominations, twelve, and won the most awards, seven, including—at last!—Best Director for Spielberg himself. And Spielberg's career coincides with that slow switch in the Academy's priorities, which began in the 1980s. At first, blockbuster action films that made a lot of money did get some Oscar love—*Star Wars* and *Raiders* were both nominated for Best Picture, for example. But from the 1980s onward, the list is dominated by films like *Out of Africa*, *Born on the Fourth of July*, and *My Left Foot*.

That's why the inclusion of *The Fugitive* on the list of Best Picture nominees alongside *Schindler's List* is so surprising. It's a very well-made action thriller, but it isn't based on a book to give it some literary cred, it doesn't have true-life tragedy to give it gravitas, it isn't a period piece, nor is it shot in a particularly novel way. I'd bet good money that almost nobody reading this can name the director without looking it up. And yet it got seven nominations, and Tommy Lee Jones won Best Supporting Actor. This is the last such film to be nominated—there are a few comedies-with-heart that sneak through (*Four Weddings and a Funeral, Little Miss Sunshine, Juno*), but at this point, the door was closed to action thrillers, unless they had some other artistic component, at least until 2009, when the number of Best Picture nominees doubled.

Meanwhile, the Academy found new ways to frustrate filmmakers. Two films in particular had specific campaigns around them. One was the documentary *Hoop Dreams* about wannabe NBA players in inner-city Chicago. No documentary had ever been nominated for Best Picture, but the movie had opened so strongly that New Line thought it was worth a shot. The Academy seemed to be taking the idea seriously, and it did earn a nomination for Best Editing. But not only was it overlooked for Best Picture (to no one's great surprise), but it also didn't even get nominated as Best Documentary—a prize everyone had assumed it was going to win!

This omission is partly due to the fact that the nominating process for documentaries is a bit eccentric (and it was overhauled after this). And the process for awarding the Best Foreign Language Film is even more bizarre. Rather than survey all the non-English-language films released in the calendar year and vote for a top five, as you might expect, the Academy asks official bodies in each country to select exactly one film for consideration, following which an Academy committee makes the determination about which films get nominated. This is why the trophy has generally been seen as being awarded to a country rather than an individual (although these days, the director's name is inscribed on the base of the statuette).

But—which country? To illustrate the problem, let's look at Krzysztof Kieślowski and the *Three Colors* trilogy. *Three Colors Blue*, released in 1993, was rejected as Poland's entry because it was made in France and the actors spoke French. *Red* had won all sorts of American awards for Best Foreign Language Film in the run-up to the nominations, and Kieślowski assumed all he had to do was follow the precedent set by *Blue*, and all would be well. *Red* takes place entirely in Geneva, and everybody in it speaks Swiss French. But the Academy wouldn't accept it as a Swiss film because the director, writer, and cinematographer were Polish—despite the fact that a year earlier they had ruled that a film made by a Polish director, writer, and cinematographer was not a Polish film. Thankfully, *Red* was eligible for the other awards, and

Kieślowski did end up with a nomination as Best Director and for his screenplay, and the film was nominated for its cinematography, but no Oscars were forthcoming.

And speaking of non-English-language films, one unexpected entry on the 1995 list of Best Picture nominees was the Italian film *Il Postino*. Massimo Troisi was a huge star in Italy but almost unknown in the United States. He'd put the project together himself with British director Michael Radford—but he collapsed on set a week into filming. Troisi hadn't told anyone that he desperately needed a heart transplant. He refused to abandon the film, even though he was only able to work for two hours a day, so a lot of the time you're looking at his stand-in. The day after filming finished, Troisi died in his sleep. Michael Radford recalled that at Troisi's funeral, some mourners gasped in shock when they saw his stand-in paying his respects.

The film was distributed in the United States by Miramax, who hoped it would get a nomination for Best Foreign Language Film, but when Italy elected to submit *The Star Maker* instead, Miramax's hopes seemingly vanished. And despite the excellent reviews it had gotten back in June, *Il Postino* wasn't featured on many critics' end-of-year top-ten lists either. So, in characteristic style, Miramax decided to campaign hard for Oscars, sending out five thousand screeners and soundtrack CDs, organizing poetry recitals, and publishing trade ads throwing Italy's film commission under the bus for refusing to submit a film directed by an Englishman. However, the real reason they didn't submit the film was that it had already been released in Italy the previous year, and so it was no longer eligible. *The Star Maker* did end up with a nomination, but the winner of Best Foreign Language Film was the Dutch movie *Antonia's Line*—the first time this award went to a film directed by a woman.

In the event, *Il Postino* got five nominations—including two posthumous ones for Troisi, who contributed to the screenplay as well as starred in the film—and one for Best Picture, which also included a posthumous nomination as one of its producers, Mario Cecchi Gori, had died before the film was released. Alongside Troisi, with nominations for both her performance and her scriptwriting was Emma Thompson. Although she didn't pick up Best Actress for *Sense and Sensibility*, she did win as its screenwriter, making her the first person—and so far the only person—to win Oscars for both acting and writing (she'd already won Best Actress for *Howard's End*).

Other nominees for Best Actress in 1995 included Elisabeth Shue, who played a hooker falling in love with an alcoholic in *Leaving Las Vegas*, and Sharon Stone as a high-priced call girl who gets involved with a mobster in *Casino*. And over in the Best Supporting Actress category, we find a win for Mira Sorvino as a prostitute in Woody Allen's *Mighty Aphrodite*. This trend was picked up in a *New York Times* article entitled "Play a Hooker and Win an Oscar," in which they note that this preoccupation was as old as the Academy Awards themselves; the first winner of Best Actress was Janet Gaynor in *Street Angel*, in which she plays a prostitute. But the actual winner of Best Actress for 1995 was Susan Sarandon in *Dead Man Walking*, in which she plays a nun. Make of that what you will.

During the 1990s, films from independent studios began to dominate the awards. Look at the list of Best Picture nominees in 1996: *Fargo* from the Coen brothers was made by Polygram with money from Working Title. *Secrets & Lies* was produced by Thin Man, Ciby 2000, and Channel 4. *Shine*, the story of pianist David Helfgott, was distributed by Fine Line Features with around a dozen small production companies on its credits. And *The English Patient* was distributed by Miramax. Only *Jerry Maguire*, the fifth nominee, had anything like a major studio backing it. It was distributed by Tri-Star, owned by Sony, who also owned Columbia.

Normal service was resumed the following year, when James Cameron's *Titanic* earned fourteen nominations and won eleven Oscars. It tied the record for the most nominations with *All about Eve* (and later *La La Land*), and it tied the record for the most wins with *Ben-Hur*. It was the most expensive movie ever made, beating the previous record holder *Waterworld*, but unlike *Waterworld*, it was an enormous hit, beating previous box-office record holder *Jurassic Park* and making $2.2 billion at the worldwide box office. Even today, more than twenty years later, it's still only beaten by *Avatar* and *Avengers: Endgame*, and it was number one at the American box office for a staggering fifteen consecutive weeks, including over the Oscars weekend. After this, only *The Lord of the Rings: The Return of the King* managed to win Best Picture and be the number one box-office film of the year.

The seventieth Academy Awards also received the highest recorded ratings of any Oscars broadcast—57 million Americans tuned in to watch Billy Crystal hosting for the sixth time. He told the audience, "The Oscars is just like the *Titanic*. We're huge. We're expensive. And everyone wants us to go a lot faster." But as the 1990s wore on, Academy Awards shows bloated. It took four hours and two minutes for *Saving Private Ryan* to battle *Shakespeare in Love* (which resulted in Spielberg winning Best Director but *Shakespeare* winning Best Picture). New producers were hired to try to trim it down the following year. In fact, it ran seven minutes longer.

And—incredibly—the Academy managed to lose dozens of statuettes this year. Two weeks before the ceremony, fifty-five Oscars, packaged up and bound for Beverley Hills, disappeared from the courier company's tracking system. The Academy scrambled to get new statuettes made in time and meanwhile offered a reward—first $25,000 and then $50,000—for news leading to their recovery. Finally, somebody spoke up. A dockworker had found the boxes and, upon realizing what the contents were, panicked and dumped them in an alley. By the time they were recovered, three had gone missing. One turned up three years later in Florida during a drug bust. The other two have never been found. Maybe due to the Academy fearing that winners wouldn't accept statuettes with such a grimy history, it was the hastily-constructed replacements that were handed out at the ceremony.

THE MOVIES IN THE 1990s

There never was nor will there ever be a decade more personal to me than this one. My transition from child to adult coincided with the rise of American independent film, the new auteurs, as well as huge evolutionary strides in effects and digital filmmaking. I remember clandestinely watching the films of Tarantino, Scorsese, and Coppola at sleepovers in my friend Fiona's house in Clonmel. No pillow fights and hair braiding for us, just total immersion in whatever latest art-house offering we could prize from her brother's vast collection of gems and curiosities. At fourteen, I staked out a pub near where a film was being shot in County Clare just to meet Richard E. Grant (no dice) and Ewan McGregor (thrilling success—and his parents too!). I read every issue of

Empire magazine forensically from the age of twelve, and I credit it mightily with my ability to write these words. Sensing my obsession, my parents schooled me in the ways of the classics, curating my viewing with the films they grew up on and were inspired by. How fortunate was I to fall in love with cinema right when it was reinventing itself. Right—back to the facts as much as possible but unlike the tagline of one of my favorite films of the decade: this time it's personal.

Terminator 2: Judgment Day was released in 1991. The first film to have a budget reaching $100 million, it was feverishly anticipated and ecstatically received. It combined cutting-edge CGI with Stan Winston's stunning animatronics (and even some twin actors in the cast) to create seamlessly integrated, jaw-dropping visuals that hold up to this day. The CGI in the film is used very judiciously, and it is interspersed with the solidity of practical effects, making the incredible believable and its dystopic future imminent. The bar would not be raised again so significantly until some eight years later with the release of the Wachowskis' kung-fu effects-fest *The Matrix* in 1999.

Time Warner's New Line Cinema could definitely sense which way the wind was blowing and created Fine Line Features specifically to produce and distribute art-house films. Its notable successes included Robert Altman's *The Player* and the hit documentary *Hoop Dreams*. It was instrumental in supporting what film critic B. Ruby Rich termed New Queer Cinema, exemplified by Gus Van Sant's *My Own Private Idaho*, in which River Phoenix plays a gay hustler. Characters in NQC films often live on the fringes of society, rejecting heteronormativity and convention in general. Crucially these were films being made by and about the LGBTQ community and urgently so. The AIDS crisis was continuing to unfold after an abominably callous and slow response by the Reagan administration. Queer stories in cinema normalized and humanized the community most affected by HIV/AIDS, unlike grimly unrelatable statistics or the scaremongering ad campaigns that abounded at the time.

An important determination was made at the top of the decade. In *Buchwald v. Paramount*, the court found Paramount's method of calculating net profits was invalid. Art Buchwald claimed that the idea for *Coming to America* was stolen from his treatment. He was placated by being told he would receive payment if the film was made and turned a profit. Despite it making $288 million at the box office, Paramount claimed the film had not turned a profit, as defined in Buchwald's contract, and had paperwork to support their view. This phenomenon of films making a ton of money but not turning a profit on paper was known wryly in the industry as "Hollywood accounting." Paramount's net-profit formula was determined by the court to be "unconscionable." Fearing a wave of lawsuits, Paramount paid $900,000 to Buchwald. But part of the terms of the settlement meant the decision was vacated. A win for Buchwald but not for profit participators everywhere, it did halt the practice of studios accepting unsolicited materials, fearful of costly litigation.

Jodie Foster's Clarice in *The Silence of The Lambs* and Linda Hamilton's Sarah Connor in *Terminator 2* showed us a new kind of female protagonist—capable and with determination and strength that comes from, and not in spite of, being a woman or a mother. In *Thelma and Louise*, a young Brad Pitt provides the pretty window dressing to the serious foregrounded female-friendship story. Young male stars of this period—Johnny Depp (*Edward Scissorhands*, *Cry-Baby*); Keanu Reeves (*Point Break*); and, before his tragic untimely death, River Phoenix (*My Own Private Idaho*)—had a more complex masculinity than their 1980s counterparts. Hypermuscular movie stars had an almost unreal or camp quality to them—Arnold Schwarzenegger and Sylvester Stallone made nearly as many comedy films as action dramas. Everyman Tom Hanks, Tom "Can Do Everything" Cruise, and Mel "Can't Ever Look at You the Same Way Again" Gibson were the biggest box-office hitters of the 1990s, but Jim Carrey was Hollywood's first $20 million man—ironically for one of his poorest-performing films, *Cable Guy*. Ah the 1990s . . . To put it in the popular surfer parlance of the time: Lotta cool shit but a lotta white dudes.

Miramax, founded by brothers Harvey and Bob Weinstein, began as a distribution company, acquiring the rights to films that might not otherwise get theatrical or VHS releases in the United States. They cannily identified documentaries and work by European auteurs that did well on the festival circuits and would appeal to American cinephiles. In 1992, they acquired the distribution rights to the film that everyone in Cannes was talking about, a low-budget heist movie called *Reservoir Dogs*, directed by one Quentin Tarantino. It was the debut of the decade, claret drenched and ultraviolent, showcasing an aptitude for cracking dialogue and ingenious technique by a bold new talent.

Tarantino was not alone. A slew of distinctive filmmaking voices emerged in a proliferation of creativity not seen since the 1970s. Taiwanese director Ang Lee released six films in nine years, including *Eat, Drink, Man, Woman* and *Sense and Sensibility* (his first English-language film) to international commercial success, critical exultation, and a plethora of awards. Baz Luhrmann's breakthrough film *Strictly Ballroom* follows the progress of an unlikely pairing at a ruthlessly competitive dance tournament. It delighted international audiences with its kaleidoscope of camp and kitsch, while its more outlandish extremes were balanced by a deep sincerity at its core. Luhrmann followed it up by blowing up the Bard and the box office with his hyperkinetic retelling *Romeo + Juliet*.

Robert Rodriguez remade his own indie gem *El Mariachi* (self-funded by participating in medical trials) as *Desperado*, starring Antonio Banderas and Salma Hayek. Allison Anders's *Gas Food Lodging*, about a truck-stop waitress played by Fairuza Balk, was internationally garlanded and won her the New York Film Critics Circle Award for Best New Director in 1992. Anders continued to make films with female-centered narratives, including *Mi Vida Loca*, about growing up in LA's inner city, and the Scorsese-produced *Grace of My Heart*, about a fictional singer-songwriter played by Illeana Douglas. She went on to be awarded the MacArthur Genius Grant and a Peabody for her distinctive work.

Tarantino followed up *Reservoir Dogs* with *Pulp Fiction*, an unclassifiable, inimitable (although many tried), and cool-as-all-hell nonlinear ensemble film comprising intersecting stories and indelible characters over the course of a few days in LA. Miramax initially fought Tarantino's demands for control over casting and final edit. Tarantino's agent counted down from fifteen on the phone as Harvey spluttered protestations, until his brother Bob intervened, and they secured the script. Relief abounded when Bruce Willis signed on and they were able to presell the international rights, thus recouping the entire $8.5 million budget before Tarantino had exposed a single frame of film. From then on, Tarantino and Miramax (now owned by Disney but operating largely independently) were off to the races, establishing themselves—for better or for worse—as the defining auteur and studio of 1990s cinema.

In Denmark, Lars von Trier (*Breaking the Waves*) and Thomas Vinterberg (*Festen*) founded an almost anti-auteur movement with their

Dogme 95 manifesto. It comprises a set of particular constraints that filmmakers of the movement committed to, such as shooting entirely on location and using only diegetic sound and natural lighting—except when this would result in an underexposed image. The film format had to be Academy 35mm, and the director must not be credited. The aim was to forgo aesthetic preferences and any kind of unreality—down to not having a prop that wasn't already present at the location—in favor of the pursuit of truth, raw and unconfuted. The directors were there to facilitate this process, not impose their own vision.

As Britpop was having a cultural moment, so was UK cinema. Danny Boyle's fantastically taut and well-acted movie debut *Shallow Grave* received a lot of critical attention, and he more than fulfilled the promise he showed there with his follow-up *Trainspotting*, helped by a star-making performance from Ewan McGregor and just about everyone else involved. Everything from the acidly begrimed production design to the impossibly cool soundtrack, as well as screenwriter John Hodge's brilliant adaptation of Irvine Welsh's mold-breaking novel, amounted to a messy masterpiece prompting a raft of breathless "Cool Britannia" and "The British Are Coming!"-style headlines.

They were not wrong. UK cinema had a very strong showing this decade. *Four Weddings and a Funeral* and *The Full Monty* were Oscar-nominated, BAFTA-winning, international box-office smashes. Mike Leigh did some of his finest work with *Naked* and *Secrets & Lies*; Antonia Bird directed no less than five films, including the controversial *Priest*; and Shane Meadows, who began his career in the second half of the decade, won the triptych of top prizes at the British Independent Film Awards in 1999 for what was only his third film, *A Room for Romeo Brass*.

Now, I'm not saying there were no bad nights at the movies in the 1990s because there were plenty of flops and follies—*Hudson Hawk*, *The Postman*, *Cutthroat Island*, and *Godzilla*, to name an ignominious few. But on the whole, mainstream output was less derivative and more varied than in subsequent decades. Franchises, however excellent some of them are, can have the unfortunate effect of inducing economic extremes. Studios can reasonably expect a healthy return no matter how inflated the budget or questionable the quality of the script because a loyal fanbase will almost certainly turn out, regardless of reviews. Franchise, remake, and sequel ubiquity brought about not an erasure but certainly a decline in the medium-risk movie, as did the preponderance of Oscar-bait films that seemed to be created for the sole purpose of winning awards. Harvey Weinstein (more about him in later chapters, as you can reluctantly imagine) went from being a savvy distributor to an Oscar-hunting uberproducer, making costly, starry work that often lacked the bratty, fringe-fueled fire his fortunes were forged in.

Which brings us to 1999, sometimes referred to as the last great year in movies. Whether you agree or not, it's hard to argue that it was anything other than crammed with bangers. *Fight Club*, *The Matrix*, and *Being John Malkovich* marched to their own beat and were critically and financially rewarded for it. But even your average four-star effort was better than some years' top films. The likes of *Toy Story 2*, *The Green Mile*, *The Talented Mr. Ripley*, *The Thomas Crown Affair*, and Doug Liman's *Go* didn't change the world, but they were moving and well made or classy and clever or all the above. Maybe it was the last year in which films were better than they needed to be—rather than not as good as they should have been.

Snuck out to a few LA theaters to qualify for the 1999 Oscars, before a wide release in early 2000, I'm claiming *Magnolia* as a fitting finale to the decade of the indie auteur. A mosaic of a film that still manages to feel cohesive, it is exhilaratingly good, wholly original and hewn from the most universally human parts of us—the broken, the abandoned, the hurt, and the hopeful. Progress would refract and retract many times in the subsequent era of post-9/11 paranoia, porn on demand, the shocking lack of representation, and the continued allowance of serious abuses and appalling behaviors to occur in every part of the industry.

A formative decade in so many wonderful ways but as it closes out to make way for a new century, I think of William H. Macy's barnstorming bar scene in Paul Thomas Anderson's aforementioned millennial masterpiece and his Quiz Kid Donnie Smith's warning: "We may be through with the past, but the past is not through with us."

THE MAKING OF *TITANIC*

Writer: James Cameron
Director: James Cameron

Producers: Jon Landau, Cameron for Lightstorm Entertainment/
Paramount Pictures, 20th Century Fox

Cast: Leonardo DiCaprio, Kate Winslet, Billy Zane, Bill Paxton,
David Warner, Frances Fisher, Gloria Stuart

Won: Best Picture, Best Director, Best Art Direction (Peter Lamont, Michael D. Ford), Best Cinematography (Russell Carpenter), Best Costume Design (Deborah Lynn Scott), Best Film Editing (Conrad Buff, Cameron, Richard Harris), Best Original
Dramatic Score (James Horner), Best Original Song (James
Horner, Will Jennings), Best Sound (Gary Rydstrom, Tom Johnson, Gary Summers, Mark Ulano), Best Sound Effects Editing
(Tom Bellfort, Christopher Boyes), Best Visual Effects (Robert
Legato, Mark A. Lasoff, Thomas L. Fisher, Michael Kanfer)

Nominated: Best Actress (Winslet), Best Supporting Actress (Stuart), Best Makeup (Tina Earnshaw, Greg Cannom, Simon
Thompson)

Length: 195 minutes

Budget: $200 million

Box office: $2.195 billion

Rotten Tomatoes: 89%

Titanic happened because James Cameron was a bit of a shipwreck
junkie. Wanting a legitimate reason to do a dive of what remained of the
world's most famous ship, he decided that making it part of a movie was
the easiest way. He pitched the project to 20th Century Fox, with
whom he'd previously made *Aliens* and *The Abyss*. Fox thought of him
mainly as an action director, and they were a little bemused when he
presented them with a three-hour romantic epic. But they wanted an
ongoing relationship with him as a director, so they decided to set sail
together.

Now with a check from a big studio in his pocket, Cameron began
his exploration of the wreck, participating in several dives over a period
of two years. No one had attempted to capture images this way for a
major movie before, and the footage he shot wasn't as high quality as he
would have liked (so although some of this material is in the film, it's
supplemented with model shots and full-sized sets in a water tank). But
seeing the remains of the ship firsthand did give him a sense of how
RMS Titanic was more than just a story—it was a place where real

people had died. Feeling a responsibility to honor them, he also dived in on his screenplay.

Cameron initially claimed he could make the film for $80 million, but it soon became clear that the actual cost would be *slightly* higher, and Fox started looking for ways to spread the risk. In a highly unusual move, they agreed to partner with another studio—Paramount—who supplied an extra $65 million in exchange for distribution rights in the United States. However, Fox was still responsible for any future budget overruns—and there were many.

A lot of the costs were incurred by Cameron's attention to detail, with sets built to match the blueprints of the original ship. Fox bought forty acres of waterfront in Mexico, where they constructed a water tank that could hold 17 million gallons and a full-scale reconstruction of most of the ship (albeit one that was only partially a working set). To facilitate filming of the sinking, the poop deck was built on a hinge to raise it from zero to ninety degrees. One difficulty was that the ship was only completely built on the starboard side (to match meteorological data), but the ship had docked on the port side in Southampton. This meant the filming had to be done in reverse and the image inverted in postproduction.

Leonardo DiCaprio and Kate Winslet agreed to do the film on the basis of a long outline written by Cameron before the script was complete. DiCaprio was initially hesitant, but Winslet tracked him down at the Cannes Film Festival to persuade him, as she didn't want to do it with anyone else. On first meeting, Winslet felt he was so impossibly attractive that she would feel awkward doing romantic scenes with him. But they quickly discovered a shared sense of humor, and the shoot bonded them so strongly that they're still close friends to this day.

This is likely because filming was an incredibly stressful experience, cementing Cameron's reputation as the scariest man in Hollywood who would sometimes end up screaming at his crew through a megaphone while swooping down into their faces on a camera crane. Winslet in particular suffered, chipping a bone in her elbow, worrying that she'd drown (and on some mornings hoping she'd die just to get it over with), and getting hypothermia when barred from wearing a wetsuit. Unsurprisingly, she had to be persuaded not to quit. Other people couldn't be persuaded, and many left the production. Those who stuck it out include three stunt players with broken bones, and people who caught colds, flu, kidney infections, and more besides. The lengthy shoot left everyone completely exhausted.

The wildest story about the filming of *Titanic* happened during the first two months' shooting in Canada. Eighty people fell ill, and fifty were taken to hospital when their shellfish chowder was spiked with the hallucinogenic drug PCP. Cameron realized what was happening when the director of photography was leading a conga line and the assistant director was talking to him over a walkie-talkie while looking straight at him and stabbing him in the cheek with a pen. Cameron forced himself to vomit but was left with bloodshot eyes that made him look like the Terminator. The person responsible was never found but may have been a disgruntled crewmember who took this revenge before walking off the production.

The filming had been intended to last 138 days, but it ended up being 160. Costs also spiraled, eventually reaching $200 million—more than $1 million for every minute of screen time. Fox executives got understandably anxious and suggested an hour of cuts even as the film was still shooting. Cameron responded with his typically robust form of diplomacy, yelling at them, "You want to cut my movie? You're going to have to fire me! You want to fire me? You're going to have to kill me!" Ultimately, executives were unwilling to start over and lose their entire investment, so they backed down—though it helped that Cameron offered to forfeit his share of the profits as a sweetener (something they initially rejected as an empty gesture because they didn't expect there to be any profits).

Cameron was able to complete the shoot and edit the picture his way, but he did admit to some anxiety about how the project would turn out. During the editing process, he taped a razor blade to the inside of a wooden box with a sign on it reading, "Break glass if movie sucks." He had written the script listening to the work of musician Enya, and now he offered her the chance to work on the soundtrack. But when she turned him down, he went to his old colleague James Horner—another person he'd had a tumultuous relationship with—and this proved to be very successful choice. Horner's widely acclaimed score became one of the best-selling music albums of all time—and this was in no small part due to the incredible popularity of the film's hit song "My Heart Will Go On," which spent ten weeks at number one in the United States.

However, this element at least of *Titanic*'s enormous triumph was not part of James Cameron's master plan. The director hadn't wanted any songs with lyrics in the film, but James Horner wrote the piece in secret, with words by Will Jennings, and he asked Celine Dion to record it before even mentioning the song's existence to Cameron. Dion recorded it in a single take, despite having had a lukewarm reaction when she heard the demo. Horner carefully waited for Cameron to be in an amenable mood before presenting it to him, and Cameron reluctantly agreed to use it in the film—at least in part to pacify the anxious studios. Maybe the song would be a hit, even if the movie flopped.

The movie didn't flop.

In advance of its opening, many critics and studio bosses had predicted that it would be a colossal failure—this was an albatross of a film, deservedly slated for its vast hubris and prodigious cost. Even the director feared the worst, later saying he spent the last six months on it certain that Fox and Paramount would lose $100 million. But it struck a chord instantly, selling out theaters on its opening weekend and earning almost $30 million in two days. Once the enormous commercial success of the project was assured, James Cameron's profit participation agreement was honored in full. This *Titanic* was very far from a disaster.

BEST OF THE BEST: *THE SILENCE OF THE LAMBS*

Writer: Ted Tally, based on the novel by Thomas Harris
Director: Jonathan Demme
Producers: Kenneth Utt, Edward Saxon, Ron Bozman for Orion Pictures
Cast: Jodie Foster, Anthony Hopkins, Scott Glenn, Ted Levine, Anthony Heald
Won: Best Picture, Best Director, Best Adapted Screenplay, Best Actor (Hopkins), Best Actress (Foster)
Nominated: Best Film Editing (Craig McKay), Best Sound (Tom Fleischman, Christopher Newman)
Length: 118 minutes
Budget: $19 million
Box office: $272 million
Rotten Tomatoes: 96%

Jessica Regan: Released in the United States on Valentine's Day as something of a sick joke, this film changed procedurals forever. Graphic crime-scene photos, face-offs with a plexiglass divide, meticulously sadistic killers, and captions at the bottom of the screen have become such standard tropes it's easy to forget that mainstream audiences had never before seen anything like *The Silence of the Lambs*. It is far more unrestrained than Michael Mann's classily compelling *Manhunter*, an earlier adaptation of the Thomas Harris novel *Red Dragon*. Here, Jonathan Demme explodes the source material by centering a performance so twisted and terrifying that it almost tips this psychological thriller into full-blown horror.

For a film whose action is often set in confined spaces, the cinematography is starkly stunning. It all takes place in basements, offices, morgues, and prison cells—all potentially uncinematic, but elegant edits and sleight of storytelling hand (as well as a dread-inducing score) sell us a bigger experience. I find the shots we get from Clarice's point of view as she negotiates myriad microaggressions and clumsy or unsettling advances particularly laudable. The film elegantly tracks the attendant exhaustion of such interactions. We experience acutely the male gaze so fixed on her as she moves through spaces, from randomers at the airport to the night-vision goggles that cut through the dark to see her flailing, wide-eyed, and terrified. We observe the men observing her throughout the film, and now we are given Buffalo Bill's vantage for the neck-clawing climax.

Demme uses the language of cinema not to just direct or misdirect but also to heighten engagement. For example, in one sequence, the camera zooms in on the pen of the prison guard, and we know, "Uh oh, Hannibal is about to wreak some terrible havoc," so we're expecting it when it comes. We think we know where we stand in terms of story because we have been led to believe we are in on it with the storytellers. But this works against us to confound our expectations for the final act. However, this doesn't devalue our earlier investment—it increases it.

All these elements make the movie work, but the acting from all involved makes it sing. Is there a more audacious performance in a Best Picture winner than Anthony Hopkins's otherworldly Lecter? Hopkins attributes his distinctive vocal twangs and sneers to a mash-up of Katharine Hepburn and Truman Capote, and it all pings perfectly off the prison walls, piercing Clarice's composure with every snarled syllable.

And so to Clarice. Jodie Foster famously lobbied hard for the role, and she brings that same conviction of being the right woman for the job to every scene she's in. Her stoicism anchors Lecter's bombast; her integrity balances his shapeshifting. Her implacable pursuit of bad men who hurt and kill women is utterly convincing as she bats away doubters and keeps her empathy a part of her professionalism. There is a gaucheness and purity to Foster's performance. So much flickers across her face, uncontrived, devoid of anything slick or knowing—which makes her peril all the more fearfully harrowing to witness. Wonderful, too, are all the supporting characters: Ted Levine's shrieking, pathetic killer; Anthony Heald's officious, self-interested warden; and Brooke Smith's brilliantly gutsy survivor—who is no damsel in distress but warrior down a well.

All this craft, detail, and originality separated it from the pack and many of its subsequent imitators. It is an earnest film, serious not salacious. Hopkins meets the moment with a gargantuan performance that manages to pull off the film's more implausible moments, while Foster's truth keeps it rooted—a balance not achieved by subsequent films in the franchise. The FBI fully cooperated with the production, giving Demme and his crew access to buildings and research that lend it such realism and authenticity. They hoped it would serve as a recruiting tool for women, as there was a paucity of female personnel at the time. It worked, and applications surged—as did representations of female agents in TV and film. Rather than its ill-conceived sequels, I like to think of that as the legacy of this simply brilliant Best Picture.

WORST OF THE BEST: *AMERICAN BEAUTY*

Writer: Alan Ball
Director: Sam Mendes
Producer: Sam Bruce Cohen, Dan Jinks for DreamWorks
Cast: Kevin Spacey, Annette Bening, Thora Birch, Allison Janney, Mena Suvari, Wes Bentley, Chris Cooper, Peter Gallagher
Won: Best Picture, Best Director, Best Original Screenplay, Best Actor (Spacey), Best Cinematography (Conrad Hall)

Nominated: Best Actress (Bening), Best Original Score (Thomas Newman), Best Film Editing (Tariq Anwar, Christopher Greenbury)
Length: 122 minutes
Budget: $15 million
Box office: $356 million
Rotten Tomatoes: 87%

Tom Salinsky: Okay, this probably isn't the worst Best Picture winner of the decade. Certainly, *Braveheart* is significantly stupider in almost every way possible, and although *Forrest Gump* wasn't as bad as I expected it to be, I certainly didn't feel as if I'd missed out by not watching it the first time around. But we've chosen *American Beauty* to discuss here because it fails in a particularly interesting way. Barely two decades old, and it already seems horribly dated.

On its face, the idea of a film dating seems weird. Every film is a product of its time, but the film itself doesn't change. We don't expect the characters in *Bringing Up Baby* to be using iPhones or Twitter, and we don't see it as a failing of the film when they don't. But sometimes films that seem bitingly contemporary get left behind as society moves on. And sometimes, events outside the film color a modern reading of it in ways that are unavoidable.

American Beauty is definitely a film of its time. It has "twin scenes" in two other films released the same year—*Office Space* and *Fight Club*, both of which tackle the white male angst of working a meaningless desk job. And all three films indulge in wish-fulfillment fantasies, inviting us to imagine the cathartic power of genuinely being able to say, "Fuck you," to our intolerant overlords. *Office Space* is a goofy comedy, and its hero gets away scot-free. *Fight Club* is an unsettling and nightmarish drama, and its hero resolves his internal conflict by putting a Smith & Wesson in his mouth and pulling the trigger. *American Beauty*, poised between the two, awkwardly punishes its hero, but his comeuppance at the hands of a thinly-drawn homophobe-with-a-gun has no connection to any of his crimes. His fate is entirely in the hands of a supporting character.

So, on the one hand, Lester Burnham's midlife-crisis antics seem a little more stale, a little more overfamiliar than they did in 1999—and a little less daring even compared to other movies released the same year that cover the same ground. For that, writer Alan Ball and director Sam

Mendes (both making their movie debuts) should take a little flak. But we also have to contend with the fact that the rule-breaking, iconoclastic hero, whose "I'm taking my power" moments are meant to make us punch the air with glee, is played by Kevin Spacey, who in the wake of the #MeToo movement faced accusations of sexual misconduct from sixteen different individuals, mainly young men. And it's hard for a modern viewer to mentally put this to one side while watching a character played by Kevin Spacey do and say just whatever he wants. Yesterday's stick-it-to-the-man social warrior has become today's raging asshole.

Spacey aside, however, the cast is immaculate. While few of them made their debuts here, there were breakthrough performances from young up-and-comers, such as Mena Suvari, Wes Bentley, and Thora Birch, as well as more seasoned campaigners, like Chris Cooper. The rest of the cast is filled out with I'll-watch-them-in-anything players, like Allison Janney and Peter Gallagher. And while I'm not convinced that Annette Bening's performance is always in line with the tone that Mendes is going for, I'm aware that this is a minority view.

Alan Ball's script is also well constructed with some witty dialogue. He manages the tricky task of marshaling a sizeable cast of characters without losing focus, and all of them have some quirk, flaw, interiority, or contradiction, which enables the ensemble to do such fine work. Narrated by a dead man, the film can't help but have a slightly arch tone, which does distance the viewer, and Mendes leans into this. His stately camerawork and careful compositions call Kubrick to mind, but this (and the plinky-plonky music from Thomas Newman) ends up sucking some of the life out of the drama. So here as in *Barry Lyndon*. But *Barry Lyndon* has duels and costumes and wars and that amazing painterly cinematography. *American Beauty* is trying to wring some drama out of a man discovering that his life is boring.

Like that plastic bag that dances in the wind in front of Ricky's camcorder, Mendes's film contains some indelible images but is short on genuine passion and feeling. We stand wryly apart from Lester Burnham, smile at his put-downs, applaud (or are horrified by) his treatment of unsympathetic family and coworkers, and soberly consider the injustice of his execution, but it's hard to get emotionally involved. That shifts in social mores and the personal life of the leading man exacerbate these issues is nothing whatsoever to do with choices made by the filmmakers twenty years ago. But these problems were in the movie in 1999, and they haven't gone away.

DID THE ACADEMY GET IT RIGHT?

1990: *Dances with Wolves*

John Dorney: Sometimes you have to be objective. I don't tend to warm to gangster films, and *Goodfellas* is no exception. I just struggle to engage with the characters. But it is in a different cinematic league to everything else released this year. *Dances with Wolves* is more enjoyable than you might remember, but it really didn't deserve to beat Scorsese's masterwork. Despite my personal misgivings, I have little hesitation in voting for **Goodfellas**.

Jessica Regan: This is an impressive and unique film—not least as it's a directorial debut and Kevin Costner hasn't made it easy for himself. The director plays a man possessed by an almost-evangelical utilitarianism who would rather die in a mission than live unable to soldier. But at America's frontier, he finds himself through friendship. Costner's everyman works well on-screen (but not so well in the sound booth), and around him, Rodney A. Grant gives sterling support, as does Mary McDonnell, playing unknowable beats. Although I do enjoy the message of "A man will die or go mad without community," it's **Goodfellas**, hands down, all day, and twice on Sundays.

Tom Salinsky: *Dances with Wolves* feels inexpertly assembled from a variety of parts of differing quality. Some of the relationship stuff between Costner and Mary McDonnell threatens to elevate this to one of the all-time greats, but it's surrounded by much less interesting material on all sides. More than a quarter century after it was made, by contrast, **Goodfellas** still feels amazingly fresh, assured, and confident. Where Costner sometimes hesitates, Scorsese is always precise and surefooted.

1991: *The Silence of the Lambs*

John Dorney: The actual winner is a shamelessly entertaining horror thriller of the kind the Academy so rarely rewards. But it's up against

Beauty and the Beast, one of the most heartbreaking animated movies of all time, good enough to make it onto the main nomination list before Best Animated Feature was a thing. It is, simply, perfect.

Jessica Regan: Despite its grim subject matter and monstrous male lead, *The Silence of the Lambs* is so undeniable that it transcends the Academy's usual indifference to genre, rightly scooping up Best Picture and quite a few more besides. Our nerves may be rattled and our nails bitten down to the quick, but it still remains a treat—a chilling, visceral film that is deeply involving and, unlike quite a few winners this decade, has aged like a fine Chianti.

Tom Salinsky: An ideal Academy should celebrate movies in all genres and recognize quality wherever it finds it rather than just giving Best Picture to whichever biopic or war movie was the longest. *The Silence of the Lambs* is a thriller, sure. It won't tell you much about the human condition or get you to be less racist. But it's a hugely original thriller, built on a highly unusual structure, with a fascinating relationship at its core. I can't blame Demme's film for the lack of ambition of its various sequels and spin-offs. I can salute the Academy for paying it their highest honor.

1992: *Unforgiven*

John Dorney: It's not perfect and isn't particularly stirring—it's a film as cold as its director's eyes. But it's undeniably interesting and thought-provoking, and there's nothing else in the nomination list this year that really gives it a fight. The Academy got it right with *Unforgiven*.

Jessica Regan: Beautifully filmed, concisely plotted, extremely well acted—but I was left frustratingly unmoved. I appreciate it as a meditation on the national character—but Quentin Tarantino's debut ka-blammed its way onto our screens with audacity and ingenuity. Because of this film, I can pinpoint the precise moment I decided I wanted to become an actor—right as Tim Roth unleashed "The Commode Story." Perhaps my most personal of picks, it's *Reservoir Dogs*.

Tom Salinsky: A more complex, meditative film than I remembered, with a real humanity gleaming between the bullets and blood. Saul Rubinek's character, eagerly mythologizing the West before its time is up, provides a neat commentary that adds substance to the fairly linear story line. Only Hackman's resolutely modern performance lets it down in any way. It's rather less shocking and innovative than *Reservoir Dogs* and not as much fun as *The Player*, but **Unforgiven** really is the final word on Hollywood westerns, and that makes it a very worthy winner.

1993: Schindler's List

John Dorney: Any other year this would be nailed on for *Groundhog Day*, an evergreen, ever-rewatchable comedy classic. But Spielberg's remarkably accessible rendition of an appalling historical tragedy rendered in brutal detail and yet somehow still able to fill cinemas is a unique achievement. It has to be **Schindler's List**.

Jessica Regan: Spielberg wants you to look. He will lure you in with almost Wilder-esque dialogue, smooth cinematography, and no subtitles to contend with so that you stay with him through humanity's descent into all-out hell. Sir Ben Kingsley, Liam Neeson, and Ralph Fiennes give a triumvirate of unimpeachable performances, playing the unknowable, the unthinkable, and the unimaginable between them. Evil is here—diabolical, inescapable evil—but still you look; you bear witness. Historical facts take on form, shape, and faces before your horrified eyes. To put the Holocaust on film and make it possible to engage with in such a meaningful way, to make it watchable but unflinching, marks **Schindler's List** out as the single greatest achievement of filmmaking this year.

Tom Salinsky: Calling Spielberg's film simplistic or manipulative misses the point, which was to make a multiplex-friendly film that would tell the truth about the Holocaust. Given those as the ground rules, **Schindler's List** succeeds magnificently, and it was almost necessary to give it Best Picture for it to completely fulfill that project.

1994: Forrest Gump

John Dorney: *Forrest Gump* is dreadful, let's be honest. Almost any other nominee would be a perfectly legitimate winner of the trophy, with *The Lion King, Leon, Quiz Show*, and *Four Weddings and a Funeral* in particular all cracking movies and most obviously *Pulp Fiction* being iconic. But to go from borderline commercial disaster to beloved classic is an arc few movies have, and for the amount of people it moves to this day, I'm giving it to ***The Shawshank Redemption***.

Jessica Regan: Tom Hanks's likeability and towering talent are such that you are almost convinced you're having a good time. But he is constrained in a passive character who remains fundamentally unchanged by almost everything that happens to him. While the precise nature of his condition is ambiguous, the declaration of his child-level IQ makes his sexual relationship with Jenny—a survivor of sexual abuse herself—incredibly problematic, as is his mother having to trade sexual favors for his schooling. But it all gets wrapped in marzipan, baked in apple pie, and we are meant to gaily swallow it, despite it being a bit rotten. Pleasantly pointless at best and head-clutchingly tone deaf at other times, if it is satire, it doesn't set its stall out strongly enough. The Academy was not in the habit of rewarding upstarts, but ***Pulp Fiction*** made cinema cool again, defined the 1990s, and is far more nourishing than the hollow candies *Forrest Gump* serves up.

Tom Salinsky: Meandering and trivial, without Tom Hanks this would be less than nothing. As it is, it's less offensive than I had imagined but also less interesting. There are at least a half dozen all-time classics this year in various genres, including *Speed, Heavenly Creatures, True Lies,* and *The Shawshank Redemption,* but there's nothing else from this or any other year quite like ***Pulp Fiction***.

1995: Braveheart

John Dorney: *Braveheart* starts poorly and gets worse. This thumpingly stupid reimagining of history as badly put-together Hollywood action flick—a sort of *Medieval Weapon*—has a solid claim to being the worst winner of the Best Picture statuette, so it's a fairly obvious "no." In contrast, *12 Monkeys* is fun, *Il Postino* is sweet, *Heat* wasn't as good as I remembered, and *Se7en* is an impeccable thriller. But the winner for me is ***Toy Story***, a movie that even if we forget that it changed cinema, is still a masterpiece of characterization, structure, and plotting. You simply can't ask for a better piece of family entertainment.

Jessica Regan: *Braveheart* plays right into the worst impulses of the Academy—middle-aged macho vengeance packaged in period trappings, with John Toll photography and a James Horner score papering over the gaping fissures of inaccuracy and indulgence in plot and characterization. The long running time apes the epics of Best Picture winners past, but on closer scrutiny, it comes off as imitation David Lean. *Sense and Sensibility* is as far away from the winner as you could get, and that's a good thing. Packed with some of the best British acting of the century, Ang Lee directs it with grace and precision, and Emma Thompson's sensational adaptation shows the precarious position of women financially, physically, and emotionally in a society where they have no agency and men have no accountability. It's also terribly fun and bloody lovely to look at, whereas *Braveheart* is just bloody terrible.

Tom Salinsky: This one really is eye-wateringly bad. Wandering aimlessly from dumb plot point to even dumber one, Mel Gibson's William Wallace is bafflingly protean, becoming whatever the next silly scene or pointless set piece requires him to be, and nobody looks like they're having the least bit of fun, not even Patrick McGoohan. By the time Gibson has lovingly shot himself being crucified three times in a row, I'm almost ready to swap places with him and be nailed to a cross instead of having to watch this a moment longer. Almost anything would have been better, but *Toy Story* in particular was an ordeal to make, yet it sings with energy and has a lightness of touch that even the Disney golden age can't always achieve.

1996: *The English Patient*

John Dorney: There's a lot to admire and like about this film, even if it's a bit overblown and can veer a little Tesco-own-brand David Lean in direction. There's a solid story in there but probably one better suited to its original novelistic medium. It is a charge that can't be leveled against my pick, *Fargo*, which is a creature of pure cinema, an incredibly watchable and affecting piece that can make you laugh and make you cry—sometimes at the same moment.

Jessica Regan: The sweeping epic promise of the first half hour of this film is not fulfilled as time goes on (and on). There is phenomenal work to be savored from Kristin Scott Thomas, who raises Ralph Fiennes's game every time. The jagged, jarring urgency of their clandestine trysts rings very true with a moment of clumsiness from Scott Thomas at their final parting that embodies the painful, poignant absurdity of doomed, impossible love. But in Mike Leigh's *Secrets & Lies*, every single actor uncannily disappears into the world and the story that they helped create. It teems with humanity and demonstrates our great necessity for connection—always a knockout combination for me.

Tom Salinsky: Only patchily interesting and not nearly as well photographed as its reputation suggests or the material demands, *The English Patient* is a major disappointment, and I remain stubbornly unmoved by the fate of any of the characters, except possibly Juliette Binoche's winning Hana. It smells of the Academy rewarding a film that looks like a Best Picture winner but that isn't the best-made or most ambitious film of the year. *Fargo* from the Coen brothers, however, is a stone-cold masterpiece. Brilliantly plotted, highly original, blessed with marvelous performances all round, and expertly balancing a mordantly cynical outlook with trademark Minnesota optimism. It's a gem, and I could happily watch it twice a year.

1997: *Titanic*

John Dorney: My favorite film of this year is easily *LA Confidential.* It's a tautly plotted, brilliantly acted thriller, with one of the all-time great movie shocks. But it's shot in a relatively understated manner, which is something you can't say for *Titanic*. Yes, the dialogue is atrocious and the script simplistic, but the visuals are astonishing, and the scale is jaw-dropping. For a movie to connect with this many people, it has to be doing something right—and because of that. I think the Academy got something right, too.

Jessica Regan: A script full of clangers and a surfeit of Billy Zane, but my god . . . watching it twenty-odd years later, I was sobbing like a child. Winslet and DiCaprio together are a grandly romantic couple, which makes their cleaving by the tragedy all the more affecting. Cameron is no wordsmith, but the language of his camera cannot be assailed—Rose's dress fluttering through the engine room, everything being filmed at a tilt as the *Titanic* starts to go down, the momentum of the tracking matching the overwhelming of the ship—it all amounts to stupendous storytelling. In his final flourish, when the camera tracks up the grand staircase and all the cast beam and applaud, I am right there with them. It's *Titanic*.

Tom Salinsky: The framing sequence can go. Its only purpose is to generate a very uninteresting MacGuffin, and the film forgets that this is supposed to be Rose's personal recollections whenever it suits it. In fact, very little of the antics of the villainous Billy Zane and David Warner do much to raise the already-sky-high stakes. But in the middle of the film, the love story benefits from the measured pace, and the action sequences are world class, so I'm neither surprised nor annoyed that this film won. However, **LA Confidential** takes a fearsomely complicated novel and boils it down to its bare essentials without losing anything crucial—a near-miraculous feat. Not only that, it's beautifully photographed and fabulously well acted and will keep you guessing, both the first time you watch it and upon repeated viewings. Arguably the best American film of the 1990s. Come at me.

1998: Shakespeare in Love

John Dorney: It's a thoroughly pleasing film, probably unfairly maligned due to beating out the better-regarded *Saving Private Ryan*— and if anything, I probably prefer the doublets to the bullets. But it isn't the best of the year. So, what is? Certainly not the inane and simplistic bullshit of *American History X*. For me, it's a choice between the inventive beauty of *The Truman Show* and the most Coen brothers film the Coen brothers have ever made—**The Big Lebowski**. And I'm going for the latter for its lingering impact.

Jessica Regan: In something of a shoulder shrug of a year, this clever, sweet, and jovial film does stand out. The casting is spot on. Joseph Fiennes and Gwyneth Paltrow have fantastic chemistry, and the best of British populate much of the rest of the cast of characters, who prove the old maxim: there are no small parts. The screenwriters have such an ear for the music and majesty of Shakespeare's language. It not only punctuates the script, but also echoes of it flow through the speeches from other characters in such a seamless way, it really is to be commended. The Academy made a rare choice to reward a light touch, and **Shakespeare in Love** deserves its place in the pantheon.

Tom Salinsky: It's a delightful and well-made film, with perfectly judged performances and a satisfying plot. I know how difficult it is to make something as hard as this look as easy as this. *Saving Private Ryan* arguably has more to say, but I don't really like what it has to say. I don't think it's an antiwar film, as harrowing as that opening sequence is. I think it's the story of a man who has his faith in warfare tested and then reaffirmed. Ugh. **Shakespeare in Love** is a wonderful hymn to theater, poetry, and romance. I'm delighted that it won, and I would have voted the same way, given the chance.

1999: *American Beauty*

John Dorney: If you can get past its leading actor, *American Beauty* is an excellent film, probably the best contender in its category this year. But I've never quite managed to forget the haunting documentary **One Day in September** about the Munich massacre, which broke my heart in a way few fictional pieces do.

Jessica Regan: We are meant to empathize at least, if not identify, with Lester Burnham—who alternates between contempt and disregard for his wife and daughter and rapacious lust toward the latter's best friend. I am more interested in the vantage point of almost every character in this story other than our narrator, and that's a problem. Annette Bening is fantastic, and the kids are all right, by which I mean they are very good. But the Academy truly slept on **Magnolia**, when it should have been so proud of it—dazzling, granularly excellent, stuffed with performances from America's finest, made by a Los Angelean wunderkind, and unlike anything you've ever seen after a hundred-odd years of cinema.

Tom Salinsky: *The Matrix* is more influential but popcorn. *Magnolia* is a huge achievement. *Galaxy Quest*, *Office Space*, and *Mystery Men* are nailed-on nerd classics. *The Thomas Crown Affair* is a personal favorite. *The Blair Witch Project*, *Election*, and *Being John Malkovich* are breathtakingly original. *Boys Don't Cry* is incredibly moving and upsetting. But my pick is **The Iron Giant**—technically jaw-dropping, often very funny, beautifully constructed, terribly moving, and a film nobody wanted to make.

9

THE 2000s

THE OSCARS IN THE 2000s

This is the last decade that sees any film sweep the boards. The final installment of *The Lord of the Rings* got an eye-popping eleven nominations and won every single one of them, which didn't make for riveting television (halfway through the show, host Billy Crystal announced, "It's now official: There is nobody left in New Zealand to thank.") but was an incredible achievement. And then *Slumdog Millionaire* won eight of its

	Best Picture	Biggest Earner (worldwide)
2000	Gladiator	Mission: Impossible 2
2001	A Beautiful Mind	Harry Potter and the Sorcerer's Stone
2002	Chicago	The Lord of the Rings: The Two Towers
2003	The Lord of the Rings: The Return of the King	The Lord of the Rings: The Return of the King
2004	Million Dollar Baby	Shrek 2
2005	Crash	Harry Potter and the Goblet of Fire
2006	The Departed	Pirates of the Caribbean: Dead Man's Chest
2007	No Country for Old Men	Pirates of the Caribbean: At World's End
2008	Slumdog Millionaire	The Dark Knight
2009	The Hurt Locker	Avatar

ten nominations in 2008. No Best Picture winner after this has won more than six awards, and after 2011, none has won more than four.

But at the same time, the Academy started to broaden its horizons. The decade started off with ten nominations for *Crouching Tiger, Hidden Dragon*—by far the most nominations for any film not in the English language. It was the third film nominated for both Best Picture and Best Foreign Language Film in the same year (following *Life Is Beautiful* and *Z*), and it won Best Foreign Language Film and three other awards, tying *Fanny and Alexander* for the most Oscars for any film not in the English language.

Next year, the Oscars moved into a new home. The Kodak Theatre in Hollywood had only just opened and had been designed specifically with the Academy Awards in mind. Since 1969, the ceremony had been held at either the Shrine Auditorium or the Dorothy Chandler Pavilion, both in downtown LA, and before that, it had spent eight years at the Santa Monica Civic Auditorium, so you have to go back to 1959 and the Pantages Theatre to find the last Oscars actually taking place in Hollywood.

The Oscars' arrival at its current venue was also the first ceremony held following the attacks on the World Trade Center and the Pentagon on 11 September 2001. There was no production number to start the show. Instead, standing in front of a red velvet curtain, Tom Cruise quoted Billy Wilder and reassured the audience that it was not only okay but also necessary to celebrate the magic of the movies. Some time later (this was the longest ceremony to date, at four hours, twenty-three minutes), Woody Allen appeared at the Oscars for the first time ever. He was not nominated in any category, his film *The Curse of the Jade Scorpion* having sunk entirely without trace, but he did walk onstage and receive a standing ovation. "Thanks," he said, "that almost makes up for the strip search." He went on to introduce a short film assembled by Nora Ephron, showing clips of movies shot in New York.

And we reached another first this year, which was an even longer time coming. The first performer of color to win any Oscar at all was Hattie McDaniel, who won Best Supporting Actress in 1939. By 2001, this category only had one other Oscar winner, our host Whoopi Goldberg. The first Black winner of Best Actor was Sidney Poitier in 1963. In 1982, Louis Gossett Jr. had won Best Supporting Actor, but as of the 2001 awards, no performer of color had ever won Best Actress, despite nominations for Dorothy Dandridge, Diana Ross, Cicely Tyson, Diahann Carroll, and—once again—Whoopi Goldberg.

This year, it finally happened. Halle Berry received a standing ovation and clutched her face as she fought back tears. It's become one of the most celebrated speeches in Oscar history. She remains the only performer of color ever to have won in this category. Almost immediately afterward, Denzel Washington become the first African American performer to win two competitive Oscars. He had presented Sidney Poitier with an honorary award earlier in the evening, and now he told the audience, "Forty years I've been chasing Sidney. They finally give it to me, and what'd they do? They give it to him the same night."

In 2005, *Crash* won over *Brokeback Mountain* for Best Picture in what many see as one of the poorest decisions ever by Academy voters. *Crash* is an outlier in many ways. It was released in 2004 but didn't play for seven days in Los Angeles (as required by Academy rules) until 2005. It opened to mixed reviews and a scattering of awards, but 2005 marked the first time that a film won the Writers Guild Award, Directors Guild Award, Producers Guild Award, and then failed to win Best Picture—that film being *Brokeback Mountain*, directed by Ang Lee. *Crash* was also the second film ever to win Best Picture without winning a top Golden Globe (the first being *The Sting*).

However, it didn't come from nowhere. It was nominated for nine BAFTAs and won two, including for its screenplay. It earned six nominations at the Critics Choice Awards and won again for its screenplay. It got two Golden Globe nominations, won for its ensemble cast at the Screen Actors Guild, and so on. And that large cast probably helped it at the Oscars. By far the largest branch of the Academy is the actors, and almost everyone would have had a friend in the cast of *Crash*. We have our say on *Crash* below (spoiler: we didn't like it), and you can see that it currently holds a Rotten Tomatoes score of 74 percent. That sounds good, but it's pretty poor for a Best Picture winner. Only eight Best Picture winners have lower scores.

2006 was the arrival of the so-called Three Amigos—Alejandro González Iñárritu, Guillermo del Toro, and Alfonso Cuarón—who managed to rack up sixteen nominations between them for their films *Babel*, *Pan's Labyrinth*, and *Children of Men*. One of those nominations was for Best Director, making Iñárritu the first Mexican to be nominated in that category—but not the last. Cuarón was the first of the three to win the prize in 2013, followed by back-to-back wins for Iñárritu in 2014 and 2015, and finally del Toro in 2017. However, the 2006 Best Director fight was a rematch from 2004, when Scorsese and Eastwood had first gone head to head. That time, Eastwood's boxing drama *Million Dollar Baby* had knocked out Scorsese's biopic about movie mogul Howard Hughes, *The Aviator*—and films about Hollywood usually do well at the Academy Awards. But while *The Aviator* had been a $200 million hit, *The Departed* improved on that by another $100 million, and there's nothing the Academy likes more than success. *The Departed* duly picked up both Best Picture and Best Director—Scorsese finally winning, following five previous nominations, plus two writing nominations.

2007 was the year of the Coen brothers and *No Country for Old Men*. As producers, directors, and screenwriters of the movie, they had three chances to win Oscars, and *No Country for Old Men* also had a nomination for its editing, by one Roderick Jaynes. It didn't win in that category, but presumably if it had, then Joel and Ethan would have had to come clean and admit that that was them, too. The only other person to have previously had four nominations in different categories for the same film was Warren Beatty as writer, producer, director, and star of *Reds* in 1981. (Orson Welles fails on a technicality. Although he wrote, produced, directed, and starred in *Citizen Kane*, for the first twenty-three Academy Awards, Best Picture was given to the studio, not the producer, so Welles's name was not on the nomination certificate and would not have been inscribed on the statuette had justice prevailed.)

Beatty only won for his directing, but before the night was out, the Coens won three awards in total, starting with Best Adapted Screenplay. They then became the first directing team to win Best Director since Jerome Robbins and Robert Wise in 1961 (the only other dual nomination was for Buck Henry and Warren Beatty, who co-directed *Heaven Can Wait* in 1978), and almost as soon as they had finished accepting their second Oscar of the night from Martin Scorsese, they were back to accept Best Picture from Denzel Washington.

Another duo dominated the 2009 awards—previously married Kathryn Bigelow and James Cameron, whose movies led the way in nominations. Both *The Hurt Locker* and *Avatar* started with nine nominations, and *Avatar*—James Cameron's first film since *Titanic*—was on its way to becoming the highest-grossing movie of all time, whereas *The Hurt*

Locker ended up as the Best Picture winner with the worst ever performance at the North American box office. However, the night belonged to Bigelow, with Cameron's film picking up only Art Direction, Visual Effects, and Cinematography—the only category where it was up against *The Hurt Locker* and won. *The Hurt Locker*, however, won Best Original Screenplay, both Sound Editing and Sound Mixing, Best Editing, Best Picture, and Best Director, presented to Kathryn Bigelow by Barbra Streisand. Bigelow was only the fourth woman ever to be nominated in this category and the first winner. She won the Directors Guild award for *The Hurt Locker*, as well—again the first woman to do so.

2009 is also the year that the number of Best Picture nominees was increased from five to ten. This was presumably an attempt to reverse the falling ratings of the Oscars telecast by giving more films a shot at the big prize, but the hoped-for extra diversity didn't materialize—at least not this year. *Variety* quoted a veteran awards campaign consultant who told them, "This is not the solution, and they know it in their heart of hearts. The Academy is going to continue to nominate the kind of indie films that are now being attributed to the declining ratings."

And so it proved to be. No Best Picture nominations were forthcoming for popular films like *The Hangover*; the Liam Neeson thriller *Taken*; Guy Ritchie's take on *Sherlock Holmes*; J. J. Abrams's reboot of *Star Trek*; or the latest installments in long-running franchises like *Twilight*, *Harry Potter*, *Transformers*, and *X-Men*. Instead, the extra slots went to more of the same. The trend begun in the 1980s was reaching its apotheosis. Almost all the Oscar love was going to low-budget, quirky indies as box-office records continued to tumble. The last Best Picture winner to top the North American box office was *The Lord of the Rings: The Return of the King* in 2003.

THE MOVIES IN THE 2000s

The future was forged in this decade. The limitations of visual effects were shattered, franchises swelled box-office numbers like never before, and the internet went on to inexorably alter the dissemination and discourse of cinema. The "Decade of the Indie" was followed by the "Age of Adaptation." Seminal book series (*The Lord of the Rings*, *Harry Potter*, *Chronicles of Narnia*, *Twilight*); television shows (*Charlie's An-*

gels, Mission Impossible); computer games (*Tomb Raider, Resident Evil*); a Disneyland ride (*Pirates of the Caribbean*); and most ubiquitously comic books (*X-Men, Spider-Man, Batman, Superman*) all provided source material for a huge proportion of Hollywood's output. This trend did not fade but actually calcified as Marvel unleashed its universe in the subsequent decade. But it is in the first decade of the 2000s that we see how the juggernaut cranked up and became unstoppable.

Documentaries enjoyed more popularity than ever before. *The Corporation, March of the Penguins, Enron: The Smartest Guys in the Room, Man on Wire,* and *An Inconvenient Truth,* far from being relegated to the confines of the art-house cinemas, found their way to the multiplexes and the masses. Flushed with success from his record-breaking documentary *Bowling for Columbine* in 2003, Michael Moore surpassed himself as *Fahrenheit 9/11* won the Palme d'Or at the Cannes Film Festival in 2004, the first US documentary to win the award. It also broke the record for the highest opening weekend earnings in the United States for a documentary and was the first ever to cross the $100 million mark domestically.

Kill Bill was Tarantino's first film in six years. He was facing a backlash over his decision to divide this fervently anticipated film into two parts, but I believe everyone was ready to stagger into the daylight at the end of part one—which concludes with one of cinema's best bombshells. *The Guardian*'s Peter Bradshaw wrote at the time, "It's a martial-arts movie universe where the normal laws of economics, police work, physiology and gravity do not apply: a world composed of a brilliantly allusive tissue of spaghetti western and Asian martial-arts genres, on which the director's own, instantly identifiable presence is mounted as a superstructure."

It is striking that this review could apply to the *Matrix* movies. Cinema of this period is so much about creation and simulation, as filmmakers were using technology to bend filmmaking to their worlds, not the other way round. ESC Entertainment was set up by Warner Bros. purely to develop technologies for *The Matrix Reloaded*. This team created Universal Capture, which was essentially virtual cinematography. Every scene component, from performers to location and beyond, could be created digitally and viewed through virtual cameras. I find it very pleasing that a film about an encoded simulated world created its own to execute its vision of that world.

Over in New Zealand, visual effects company WETA used artificial intelligence to develop Multiple Agent Simulation System in Virtual Environment, or MASSIVE, for the colossal battle sequences in the *Lord of the Rings* trilogy. Far from being a monolith of computer clones, the technology allowed for the digitally rendered armies to be individualized into orcs, goblins, elves, and so on, with each figure moving independently of the others.

The effects innovation of the time spawned a new subgenre: that of the "digital backlot" film, where everything except the main characters could be computer generated. *Sky Captain and the World of Tomorrow*, starring Jude Law and Angelina Jolie, was the first big-budget release to do this, followed by *Immortel ad vitam*, which combines CGI sets with physical ones, and perhaps most successfully *Sin City* in 2004. *The Polar Express*, also released this year, goes even further and was the first "all-digital-capture" film. The actors' movements were digitally recorded and then translated into computer animation. However, audiences were put off by the "uncanny valley" nature of this new, synthetic-seeming cinema, and further refinement was needed to integrate and utilize these technologies effectively.

Franchises continued to hold strong, and in 2007, Hollywood had its first ever $4 billion summer. But there were also stumbles: *Superman Returns* was oddly dreary, and while it made $200 million domestically, it had cost a staggering $270 million to make, meaning it was unlikely to make a profit for the studio, even when overseas sales were included. *Mission: Impossible III* performed well but not well enough for Paramount, based on its early projections of its opening weekend. Tom Cruise's erratic behavior at the time was considered the culprit, and he was dropped by Paramount after fourteen years of collaboration. *The Golden Compass*, adapted from the book series by Philip Pullman, cost New Line $180 million, but the box office was disappointing, so plans to make a trilogy based on Pullman's novels were shelved in short order.

Rather more successfully, veteran franchise James Bond enjoyed a glorious reinvention rather than mere resuscitation. In *Casino Royale*, Daniel Craig gives us a haunted Bond for a complex age and a seminal spy-on-the-beach moment for the ages. It is hard to believe that his casting was so controversial at the time ("Bond can't be blond!" spluttered the internet), but his buff, annealed super-spy silenced the naysayers and revitalized the film series.

Franchises were not the only fruit. Early indie successes of the first decade of the 2000s included *My Big Fat Greek Wedding*. It started life as a one-woman show, and with a little help from Tom Hanks and Rita Wilson—who happened to catch Nia Vardalos performing it one fated LA evening—it went on to be one of the most profitable films of all time. It is the highest-grossing film that was never number one at the box office. Across the pond, *Bend It Like Beckham* was directed by Gurinder Chadha and starred Keira Knightley and Parminder Nagra. It was made for £6 million and went on to gross £104 million.

As computer animation replaced traditional animation, Dream-Works dominated the field with megahits *Shrek*, *Kung-Fu Panda*, and *Madagascar*, followed closely by Pixar (*Monsters Inc.*, *The Incredibles*, *Finding Nemo*). But alongside this, hand-drawn anime films gained more exposure outside Japan with the release of *Spirited Away*, while stop-motion animated films enjoyed a resurgence with the release of *Chicken Run*, *Wallace and Gromit: The Curse of the Were-Rabbit*, and *Coraline*.

Our old friends the MPAA, formed in 1922 to regulate censorship in film, became subject to new practices and greater transparency. Possibly prompted by Kirby Dick's documentary *This Film Is Not Yet Rated* in 2006 (which showed how hard it was to learn who served on the MPAA board and how it made ratings decisions), changes were made that included making ratings rules and regulations public, describing the standards for each rating and the appeals process, revealing more about the board's members, and allowing filmmakers to cite scenes in other films when appealing a harsh rating.

By the early 2000s, revenues from DVD rentals and sales had become more lucrative than box-office returns. VHS was going quietly into the night as major studios stopped releasing or were phasing out VHS versions of their films, and major retail stores stopped selling VHS altogether. But even bigger shake-ups were to come.

In 2005, director Steven Soderbergh's film *Bubble* was the first film to be released in cinemas and on pay-per-view cable channel HDNet at the same time and on DVD just four days later. The first film to be released in cinemas and then become legally available via broadband within two weeks of its theatrical debut was *10 Items or Less*. The mode of these films' release was not massively heralded at the time, but they signaled an irreversible shift in how we viewed our movies. In 2007—

the year that Netflix announced the mailing of its billionth DVD—
Apple TV was launched. This was a set-top box microconsole that allowed viewers to watch live TV, movies, and videos on their HD TVs.
The first broadband movie ever distributed by a major studio—Paramount's *Jackass 2.5*—was made available for online viewing in the United States in late December of the same year.

One of the consequences of these new technologies was a strike by
the Writers Guild after a breakdown in negotiations occurred with the
studios. The Guild wanted increased rates for film and TV writers for
DVD residuals and for these "new media" methods of distribution.
When the three-month strike ended in mid-February 2008, it was estimated that it had resulted in a total loss to the industry of $2.5 billion.

As we entered the latter part of the first decade of the 2000s, the
internet could be felt guiding proceedings in an unprecedented manner. Hollywood studios started using such social networking sites as
Facebook and Twitter to market films for children (Spike Jonze's
Where the Wild Things Are had a huge Facebook following before it
debuted), teens (*The Twilight Saga: New Moon* was an early adopter of
having a Twitter presence), and grown-ups (the first screening of Tarantino's *Inglourious Basterds* was attended by people who won admis-
sion via Twitter). Writer-director Oren Peli's *Paranormal Activity* was a
prime example of how the internet and its viral fan-fueled marketing—
"Tweet your Scream!"—could make a very low-budget film do eye-
watering business thanks to social media word of mouth.

The last year of the decade was a milestone year for women in
film—not just at the Oscars but also at the box office. Betty Thomas was
the most successful woman director ever in the United States at the
time for *Alvin and the Chipmunks: The Squeakquel*, which made more
than $200 million domestically and more than $400 million worldwide.
Director Anne Fletcher's *The Proposal* earned $164 million. *It's Com-
plicated*, directed and written by Nancy Meyers and starring Meryl
Streep, made $112 million at the box office. Nora Ephron's *Julie &
Julia*, also starring Streep, made $94 million in the United States alone.

Appropriately enough, we close out with a box-office bang: James
Cameron's *Avatar*, a synecdoche of the decade itself, with its simulated
world, mo-cap characters, and record-shattering box office. It became
only the fifth film in movie history to exceed $1 billion in worldwide
grosses, and it did so in less than three weeks—soon surpassing *The*

Dark Knight to become the top-grossing domestic film of the entire decade. It went on to become the highest-grossing film of all time until *Avengers: Endgame* ten years later and was the first film to gross $2 billion worldwide. It was the highest-grossing domestic film of 2009 by a massive margin, taking in $749.8 million.

The first decade of the 2000s in film is a strange hotchpotch of a decade, transitional rather than timeless. Cinema was getting more extreme in every sense. Anything imagined could be digitally rendered. The lack of constraints in terms of content and capability meant quality varied wildly. Audiences flocked consistently to franchises, but the runaway box-office success of both Moore's documentaries and Mel Gibson's *The Passion of the Christ* could be interpreted as anticipating the political schism that was to engulf America. With fault lines being drawn in every area of discourse, the internet would soon shape our engagement with cinema as much as facilitate it.

THE MAKING OF *THE LORD OF THE RINGS: THE RETURN OF THE KING*

Writers: Fran Walsh, Philippa Boyens, Peter Jackson; based on the novel by J. R. R. Tolkien

Director: Peter Jackson

Producers: Barrie M. Osborne, Peter Jackson, Fran Walsh for Wingnut Films/New Line

Cast: Elijah Wood, Ian McKellen, Liv Tyler, Viggo Mortensen, Sean Astin, Cate Blanchett, John Rhys-Davies, Bernard Hill, Billy Boyd, Dominic Monaghan, Orlando Bloom, Hugo Weaving, Miranda Otto, David Wenham, Karl Urban, John Noble, Andy Serkis, Ian Holm

Won: Best Picture, Best Director, Best Adapted Screenplay, Best Art Direction (Dan Hennah, Alan Lee, Grant Major), Best Costume Design (Ngila Dickson, Richard Taylor), Best Makeup (Peter King, Richard Taylor), Best Original Score (Howard Shore), Best Original Song—"Into the West" (Walsh, Howard Shore, Annie Lennox), Best Sound Mixing (Christopher Boyes, Michael Semanick, Michael Hedges, Hammond Peek), Best Film Editing

(Jamie Selkirk), Best Visual Effects (Jim Rygiel, Joe Letteri, Randall William Cook, Alex Funke)
Length: 201 minutes
Budget: $94 million
Box office: $1.142 billion
Rotten Tomatoes: 93%

Very few books have been read more than *The Lord of the Rings*. In fact, in the twentieth century, it was only beaten by the Bible. So, of course people had been considering adapting it for the cinema. In fact, people had been attempting to make a movie version for years—not least because Tolkien had sold the rights for a pittance, believing it was impossible to film. And for a while he was proved right—all the people who tried to make it as a movie had failed. The rights moved about for decades, with every director you can think of being considered at one time or another. It even got close to being completed once, when the first of two animated movies made by Ralph Bakshi was actually released in 1978—but it wasn't profitable enough for the second one to get the go-ahead. One of the few people to see the animated film, however, was a teenager called Peter Jackson. He'd never read the book, but he enjoyed the film—at least to start with. Toward the end, he found he'd got a bit lost, and so he started reading the book to figure out what had actually happened.

By 1997, Jackson was an established filmmaker who had created a number of successful movies with his partner, Fran Walsh. He began his career making low-budget splatter-horror films with a tongue-in-cheek tone, but he had recently moved into the mainstream with *Heavenly Creatures* and *The Frighteners*. Jackson and Walsh were considering a fantasy film as their next project—mainly to employ the effects house they'd developed for *The Frighteners*—but they couldn't think of an idea that didn't feel like it was ripping off Tolkien. So, they decided to look into who had the rights to the Tolkien books. And that was Saul Zaentz.

At the time, Jackson was under contract to the Weinsteins and Miramax. Unsure if he had to go to them first, he spoke to Harvey and Bob—both as a courtesy and because he knew they'd worked with Zaentz on *The English Patient*. Working with them on *The Lord of the Rings* turned out to be a very unpleasant, if short-lived, experience.

Jackson had wanted to make a movie trilogy but not the one we're now familiar with. He intended to make a single film of *The Hobbit*, to be followed by a two-part version of *The Lord of the Rings*—shooting both parts back to back, if the first film was successful. But the *Hobbit* rights were much more complex to negotiate, and so they decided to save that story, possibly as a later prequel. Meanwhile, Miramax weren't keen on the risk implicit in making three films back-to-back, but they did agree to make two *Lord of the Rings* films. With that agreement in place, Jackson and Walsh—alongside writer Stephen Sinclair—got to work on the script. Sinclair had written with Jackson before, but he eventually dropped out due to obligations to theater work. Some of his contributions do survive—to the degree that he does get on-screen credit for the second film of the eventual trilogy, *The Two Towers*. His partner, a massive Tolkien fan called Philippa Boyens, essentially took over, and the scripts took thirteen or so months to complete.

Despite pushing for Daniel Day-Lewis to play Aragorn, Miramax was in general quite keen to Americanize the material, suggesting actors like Morgan Freeman for Gandalf. Harvey Weinstein did, however, steer Jackson away from actors like Ashley Judd and Mira Sorvino, for reasons that would become clear when the #MeToo movement gathered steam in 2018. By this time, the budget was rising, closing in on $150 million, which was far beyond Miramax's capabilities. They approached Disney for further funding, but Michael Eisner turned them down. At the time, he had been cutting spending across the board, but he later said that his main reason for declining the partnership was that he wasn't allowed a detailed look at the project by the Weinsteins.

Miramax suggested making it into a single film, even preparing a shortened treatment. Jackson said he'd consider it if it was four hours, but he felt there was no possible way to do justice to the complex material in a single two-hour film. Now, after months of work, it felt like the whole project was falling apart. Miramax's view was that if Jackson couldn't deliver a two-hour *Lord of the Rings* film, they'd find a director who could, suggesting possible replacements like John Madden or Quentin Tarantino. But Jackson held firm, so Miramax eventually agreed to let him shop the project around to try to set it up somewhere else. But he was only given four weeks to find Tolkien's Middle Earth a new home.

After a frantic round of hastily arranged meetings, it seemed as if none of the other studios were interested. But Jackson pretended to be a hot property in order to get into a room with the CEO of New Line, Robert Shaye—who Jackson knew was a fan of the books. Shaye was unsure—the Weinsteins were demanding a big cut—but New Line did need a new franchise. After Jackson's presentation to him, there was a big pause. Shaye said, "Why would anyone in their right mind make two films?" Jackson's heart sank. "This," Shaye continued, "is three films."

And they were on. Preproduction began in 1997, and filming started in New Zealand in October 1999 for an initial 438 days. Casting took place across multiple countries—the United Kingdom, the United States, Australia, and New Zealand. Jackson, Walsh, and Boyens had put together an initial casting wish list, which included the eventually cast Cate Blanchett as Galadriel and Ian Holm as Bilbo—although there were backup options: Lucy Lawless and Nicole Kidman were alternative Galadriels; Anthony Hopkins and Sylvester McCoy were standby Bilbos.

After initially only wanting to consider UK actors, the team was eventually persuaded to consider Americans for the hobbits. Eighteen-year-old Elijah Wood had sent in a tape, reading from the book, and was the first to be cast out of 150 actors in consideration. Sean Astin, a recent father, was cast as Sam and developed a very similar bond with Wood as his character has with Frodo, looking after the younger man on set.

New Line suggested Christopher Plummer or Sean Connery for Gandalf, though both said no (the latter claiming not to understand the script). Others considered included Tom Baker, Tom Wilkinson, Sam Neill, Bernard Hill, Sir Nigel Hawthorne, Peter O'Toole, and Patrick Stewart—but when looking at Stewart's tape, they instead opted for the actor he was performing with, Sir Ian McKellen. McKellen had a clash with the *X-Men* films, so he needed to rearrange his schedule, but he happily came onboard, basing his vocal performance on Tolkien himself.

Options for the evil Saruman included Paul Scofield, Jeremy Irons, Malcolm McDowell, and Tim Curry, but the role ended up going to a man who'd inquired after Gandalf but had been considered too old—Christopher Lee (who was a massive fan of the book, reading it once a year, almost religiously). In fact, it was something of a pattern that not everyone was cast in the role they auditioned for—Dominic Monaghan had auditioned for Frodo and ended up playing another hobbit, Merry; John Rhys-Davies was up for Denethor and was cast as the dwarf Gimli; and Orlando Bloom was considered for Faramir before landing the role of the elf Legolas.

Stuart Townsend was initially cast as Aragorn, but with the start of principal photography only weeks away, Jackson's team realized he was too young and hurriedly substituted Viggo Mortensen (with a rejected Boromir, Russell Crowe, as a backup). Mortensen had no time at all to make up his mind and agreed to play the part mainly because of the enthusiasm of his son for the books. (Other non-Boromirs included Daniel Craig, who auditioned; Liam Neeson, who declined; and Nicolas Cage, whom the filmmakers declined.) Mortensen got so into character that during a conversation, Peter Jackson referred to him as Aragorn for more than a half hour without Mortensen even realizing.

The script continued to develop throughout the filming process, with Fran Walsh comparing it to frantically laying track ahead of themselves with the train already in motion. Each film had a different editor, as they were shooting more or less simultaneously, and it would have been too much for one person. For the finale, Jackson went with his long-time collaborator Jamie Selkirk. *The Return of the King* was the script that Jackson felt was the easiest to write—it didn't have to introduce everyone like the first one, and it didn't have to interweave the stories without the benefit of a beginning or end like the second one. Though because the story isn't entirely linear in the original novel, several chapters of the book of *The Two Towers* end up in the film version of *The Return of the King*.

They filmed broadly in chronological order, starting with the four hobbits to help them bond. This meant that *The Return of the King* was mainly shot from May to December 2000, although some shots for the third film were suddenly brought forward into 1999 when Queenstown floods disrupted the filming of the first film, *The Fellowship of the Ring*. With planned locations all rained off, the crew erected sets in the squash court of the hotel they were staying in. They only had space for one set, and only a few actors were available, so the only material they could shoot was a huge emotional scene between Frodo and Sam near the end of the last film. The actors protested—they had only just started to get to grips with their characters—but there was no easy alternative.

This tough acting challenge began with angles on Sean Astin, whose work was made even harder because he had to play his side of the action without Andy Serkis—who hadn't even been cast at this stage of production. With Astin's material in the can, the intention was to pick up Elijah Wood's side of the interaction next day. But, in the morning, the sun was shining again, so they left the set standing on the squash court, assuming they would come back to it later in the week or whenever location work was next rained off. In fact, the rest of the sequence wasn't filmed until a year later.

Each of the cast members was given a gift on their last day of shooting, usually a significant prop—most notably, Wood and Serkis (the two ring bearers) getting rings. John Rhys-Davies's present was unusual— having hated his dwarf makeup, he was offered the opportunity to burn his final mask, which he joyously did. These gifts weren't the only souvenirs for some of the cast—horses owned by the production company were placed up for auction after shooting, and Viggo Mortensen purchased two: the one he rode for most of the movie and one for Liv Tyler's riding double.

A lot of the material was tweaked in two months of pickups filmed in the Wellington studio parking lot in 2003. One of the bigger alterations was the Mouth of Sauron sequence, where the heroes are falsely told Frodo is dead (which didn't work well in its restructured context, as the audience knew he wasn't). Likewise, a big finale sword fight between Aragorn and Sauron was dropped, although a lot of the footage was repurposed, replacing Sauron with a CGI troll. Other reworked sections included Aragorn's coronation, which they felt had been a bit rushed on the initial filming, and more material for Legolas, who'd gotten good reactions in the previous films. And he wasn't the only one—future Oscar winner Bret McKenzie's silent cameo as an elf in *Fellowship* had gotten such positive feedback from female fans that he came back as Arwen's escort and got two lines of dialogue. Andy Serkis's last day of work on the film was only a few weeks before the theatrical release, lying on the floor of Peter Jackson's house, where he was filmed as Gollum reacting to the news that Frodo intends to destroy the ring.

The destruction of the ring itself proved a big headache. In the book, a jubilant Gollum slips and falls into the fires of Mount Doom while celebrating his victory, and he takes the ring with him. Jackson wanted

Frodo to be more active in the finale, and so a sequence was devised in which the hobbit pushes Gollum over the edge, but this made the story's hero seem like a stone-cold murderer. So, on Elijah Wood's second-to-last day in New Zealand, they gave it one final go, creating the more ambiguous sequence you can see in the finished film.

Pickups ended on 27 June 2003, and postproduction on the final reel of the movie was completed only five days before the world premiere in Wellington, New Zealand. It was still wet from developing because there was no time to dry it. That premiere was the first time that director Peter Jackson saw the completed movie from beginning to end.

However, that wasn't quite the end. Extended editions of all three films were released on DVD and Blu-ray, and as well as restoring cut footage, Peter Jackson shot new material for these new versions of the films. Shooting was still taking place for the extended edition of *The Return of the King* as late as March 2004—making Jackson the only director ever to shoot scenes for a film *after* it had won Best Picture at the Oscars.

BEST OF THE BEST: *THE HURT LOCKER*

Writer: Mark Boal
Director: Kathryn Bigelow
Producers: Kathryn Bigelow, Mark Boal, Nicolas Chartier, Greg
    Shapiro for Summit Entertainment
Cast: Jeremy Renner, Anthony Mackie, Brian Geraghty, Evangeline
    Lilly, Ralph Fiennes, David Morse, Guy Pearce
Won: Best Picture, Best Director, Best Original Screenplay, Best
    Film Editing (Chris Innis, Bob Murawski), Best Sound Mixing
    (Paul N. J. Ottosson, Ray Beckett), Best Sound Editing (Paul N.
    J. Ottosson)
Nominated: Best Actor (Renner), Best Cinematography (Barry
    Ackroyd), Best Original Score (Marco Beltrami, Buck Sanders)
Length: 131 minutes
Budget: $15 million
Box office: $49.2 million
Rotten Tomatoes: 97%

Tom Salinsky: Kathryn Bigelow's place in Oscar history is assured. In an industry, and within a part of that industry, that has a fairly shocking record for rewarding and recognizing women, she was the first female Academy Award Best Director winner following an unbroken procession of eighty-one men. What's possibly not so surprising is that the movie has an effectively all-male cast, was written by a man, and is about that most manly of pursuits—war. However, much as I might wish that Sofia Coppola or Jane Campion or Greta Gerwig had gained more recognition, none of this alters the fact that *The Hurt Locker* is an artistic triumph.

The focus of Mark Boal's script on a bomb-disposal team sweeps away the political side of the Iraq War, which in this instance is a strength rather than a weakness. We are able to focus fully on the ordeal of these men, the psychological terror they face every day, how they deal with it, and what it does to them. Although the structure is very episodic, the slowly growing respect that Sanborn (Anthony Mackie) has for James (Jeremy Renner) provides a strong enough narrative thread, avoiding the issue of "These scenes could come in any order, and now we've filled two hours, the film is over," which bedevils other movies. Indeed, when things take a brief turn for the more melodramatic and Renner becomes a more traditional hero, the movie just loses credibility slightly and becomes lesser, not greater.

Neither Sanborn nor James is especially likeable. We maybe side more with Sanborn early on, struggling to deal with a new loose-cannon squad leader following the death of Guy Pearce's Thompson, but it's Renner's story, and he rises to the occasion. Two years before Hawkeye (and five years before Falcon), Renner was pretty much an unknown, and he's arguably never been better then here as walled-off, risk-taking William James. Even the male bonding rituals that he and Sanborn engage in seem horrifying to this hand-wringing, North London liberal.

Bigelow shoots all this amazingly, deploying every trick in her very considerable arsenal, from playing with sound to speed ramping to bleached-out photography to unexpected music cues to nervy camerawork. But this never feels "cool" or a thrill ride. Watching *The Hurt Locker* is always a profoundly unsettling experience, even when we aren't watching Renner excavate a corpse in search of hidden explosives. And then, in a beat familiar to Oscar watchers from *All Quiet on the Western Front*, Boal and Bigelow detonate their most deadly charge. The terrifying life of a bomb-disposal expert in Iraq has re-shaped and reformed William James so that he no longer fits into do-mestic American life. His return to service for another—year-long!—rotation is the only happy ending he can get, but he's a happy man in purgatory, celebrating his return to the one place on earth capable of feeding his adrenaline habit.

My personal taste in films leans toward strong stories with rich char-acters and away from war films and westerns, with their emphasis on self-actualization through superior firepower. I can easily get frustrated by films that refuse to acknowledge the primacy of basic cause and effect in storytelling. I generally don't see such films as boldly tearing up the rule book but instead as avoiding the complicated issue of having to arrange a sequence of events artfully yet organically and opting for the far easier (and less satisfying) just-one-thing-after-another ap-proach. But cause-and-effect storytelling can be done obviously and clumsily, where every setup sticks out a mile and half, the audience sees the payoffs coming twenty minutes out, which is why sometimes even well-constructed stories can feel simplistic or just inauthentic. Finding that sweet spot is genuinely tough, which is why so few films manage it.

Some, like *The Godfather* or *The Apartment* do it by so artfully concealing the plot points and creating such rich characters that every-thing flows along and there's no hint of the scaffolding that the film-makers once needed to erect to hold the edifice together. Others, like *The Hurt Locker*, pare the cause-and-effect storytelling to the bone and trust that the set pieces, the conviction of the actors, the intrinsic high stakes, and the detail in the world will be enough.

It's a risky strategy. One of the reasons that *Zero Dark Thirty*—from the same writer-director team—is less impressive is that it takes a sim-ple story with a built-in beginning, middle, and end and then keeps throwing new unrelated subplots at it, not all of which come off. Here the balance works beautifully, and although this is a very hard movie to love and not one I would want to watch terribly often, it's a huge achievement and I think one of the very, very finest Best Picture win-ners for at least ten years either side.

WORST OF THE BEST: *CRASH*

Writers: Paul Haggis, Bobby Moresco
Director: Paul Haggis
Producers: Don Cheadle, Paul Haggis, Mark R. Harris, Bobby Moresco for Lionsgate Films
Cast: Sandra Bullock, Don Cheadle, Matt Dillon, Jennifer Esposito, Brendan Fraser, Terrence Howard, Chris "Ludacris" Bridges, Thandiwe Newton, Ryan Phillippe, Michael Peña, Larenz Tate
Won: Best Picture, Best Original Screenplay, Best Film Editing (Hughes Winborne)
Nominated: Best Director, Best Supporting Actor (Dillon), Best Original Song ("In the Deep")
Length: 112 minutes
Budget: $6.5 million
Box office: $101 million
Rotten Tomatoes: 74%

John Dorney: At the very least, it's appropriate that a movie that is a bit of a car crash . . . is based around a car crash. This isn't a spoiler. Because one of this movie's biggest flaws is its determination to explain, as early and as laboriously as possible, the metaphor at its heart—literally opening with an awkward Don Cheadle monologue that does just that. This is a film with no subtlety—unwilling to let the audience gradually tease out its ideas and secrets, it accelerates them at you head first, and the results are fairly predictable.

To say this feels slightly mean, as the film has become a sort of shorthand for unworthy Oscar winners, often touted as the weakest ever, and that feels over the top. At the very least, it's far shorter than a lot of the other bottom-of-the-barrel entries, it has some good performances, and it is trying to say something relevant and true, albeit in a heavy-handed way. Certainly, people can heap opprobrium on things that don't entirely deserve the hate purely because they find them over-praised, as *Crash* certainly was.

But the truth is that this is an incredibly cloth-eared piece, relying on multiple ludicrous (or Ludacris) coincidences to drive the plot, and is filled with many scenes where characters fail to react to their situations in a remotely believable way. The vast, sprawling city of Los Angeles is seemingly populated by no more than about twelve people, who all know each other in some way, and the whole piece comes over as little more than a pound-shop version of *Magnolia*—although *Magnolia* at least acknowledged its own contrivances from the get-go. *Crash* doesn't seem to even realize that everything about it feels artificial.

As the film continues, people stop being characters and become simply mouthpieces for opinions. They're ciphers, not human beings. We want to see people change, but we're never allowed to build sympathy for the protagonists and therefore feel for them when things collapse because they're always starting from eleven out of ten. There's practically nobody to like or admire or root for, and that's before we even get to the movie's clunky handling of its central theme—racism.

For the first hour or so, the film's characters can't stop talking about race, bringing it up randomly in unrelated situations and signaling the movie's themes as hard as they can, so even the most distracted of viewers can understand what it's about—but leaving everyone else weary by the heavy-handed repetition. When it eases off the pedal about halfway through and allows the movie itself to do the talking, it's already lost a good chunk of its audience.

Which is a pity because there is at least an interesting point to be made here. For a long time now, Hollywood has often used racism as a lazy shorthand to identify characters as wrong'uns, where we can easily dismiss them as evil without much thought. This film tries to suggest that it isn't, ironically, always that black and white. Unfortunately, it goes about this without the nuance and complexity that such a delicate notion really requires, instead preferring to reiterate its points over and over again. It thinks it's switching hats, changing its characters from good to bad and back again . . . but really, this is no more than a device, and they all still feel like wrong'uns by the end of the film, regardless of any good deeds they may have done in the interim.

It doesn't help that the film's soundtrack and visuals do so little to improve the experience, with endless shots of people looking moody in cars feeling just as repetitive and a pretentious score relentlessly trying to tell us what to feel. But it's those coarse and ham-fisted attempts at depth that are ultimately the main problem with the film. The musical *Avenue Q* once said, "Everyone's a Little Bit Racist," in a five-and-a-half-minute comedy song. And it says a great deal about *Crash*'s failure that it takes more than a hundred minutes more to say considerably less.

DID THE ACADEMY GET IT RIGHT?

2000: *Gladiator*

John Dorney: A film that is nowhere near as important or worthy as it thinks it is, *Gladiator* is one of the more misguided choices for the big prize, an overlong spectacle of style over content. This is not an accusation that can be leveled against my pick, **The Emperor's New Groove**, a joyous, fast-paced romp that crosses classic Disney with Looney Tunes hijinks and is shamelessly enjoyable viewing every single time.

Jessica Regan: Thudding rather than bone crunching, this is an oddly sterile film, considering it deals in mortal combat. With a protagonist whose decisions undermine his actions at every turn, a baddie whose charisma knocks the film off its axis, and a love interest given lingering looks rather than actual lines, it is as circular as the gladiatorial arena it depicts, doubling back on itself without delivering on promises. It is punctuated by ersatz profundity, overdeployed postproduction slo-mo, and Three. Good. Lines. I would give it to another epic, one with oodles more charm and engagement. **Crouching Tiger, Hidden Dragon** is sensual and splendid, refreshingly female driven, and original in its action sequences, and unlike the unworthy winner that is *Gladiator*, it is never boring.

Tom Salinsky: Although Ridley Scott flings everything he's got at the screen, the result is fatally muddled and incoherent—everyone is acting in a different film. Joaquin Phoenix is most able to find the right tone, but no one has given any thought to the protagonist's character development and how that affects the plot, so it's just a series of scenes rather than a story. In a not very strong year, I'll go for Steven Soderbergh's **Traffic**, a rich and intricate set of interlocking narratives that isn't afraid of complexity and will take the necessary time to guide the viewer through it.

2001: *A Beautiful Mind*

John Dorney: There are several great movies up against this at the Oscars, so why on earth did the Academy feel the urge to give the Best Picture statuette to such a dreary and borderline-offensive production that takes a real man's tragedy and tries to turn it into an action thriller?

What would I have had win instead? Literally any other film nominated this year in any category.

Jessica Regan: Occasionally the Academy's choice can feel like a dumb person's idea of a smart film, and this is one such instance. A work of utter fiction masquerading as a serious biopic that bears little resemblance to the events that occurred and are well documented. A little liberty is understandable, and a lot might be forgiven if it was in the service of a good story. Instead, we endure a lengthy trudge through poorly structured, opaque storytelling and some merciful bits of Paul Bettany doing his best when nobody else is, except perhaps James Horner. I am agog the Academy didn't reward **The Lord of the Rings: The Fellowship of the Ring**. I am aware plaudits pile on subsequently, particularly for the final installment, but the world-building is so sublime, the craft and care so impeccable. The whole film is essentially setup for a journey that barely begins, but it is as plenteous an experience as one could have in a cinema.

Tom Salinsky: Oh dear. It's a fascinating story told in a novel way, but my chief experience of watching this movie is that nobody brought their A game. The screenplay imagines that one arresting element will do all the heavy lifting (no matter how early they give the game away); director Ron Howard shoots fantasy, reality, tragedy, and comedy all with identical setups; Jennifer Connelly is going through the motions; and Russell Crowe is only occasionally watchable. Worst of all, it doesn't even hint at what made its hero, John Nash, so brilliant. Vastly better is the intricate and humane Australian drama **Lantana**, written by Andrew Bovell, adapting his own play; directed by Ray Lawrence; and starring Anthony LaPaglia. If you only know him from *Frasier* (he's Daphne's brother), you should check this one out.

2002: *Chicago*

John Dorney: This feels like a good year to me, with *Spirited Away*, *Confessions of a Dangerous Mind*, and *Adaptation* all worth flagging up. But **Chicago** manages to reinvent a form that was long thought dead, with the tiniest amount of resources possible, and I'm perfectly happy to award it the top prize.

Jessica Regan: *Chicago* is a firework of a film with excellent performances, Fosse choreography at its finest, and iconic numbers that sizzle on celluloid as much as they do onstage. I give huge credit to director Rob Marshall for creating a fully realized world of razzle-dazzle that uses the form expertly to overcome rather than accede to the limitations of adapting a stage show to film. But this study of superficiality, this satire of media, and the monsters it makes or breaks, remains a feast for my eyes and ears but not for my heart, I'm afraid. I give it to *The Hours* instead, a lonely film that made me feel less alone, that gently warned me of the complications that were coming as I stared down the barrel of adulthood. It seeded the belief in me that melancholy, depression, and alienation were all survivable and part of the human condition, often afflicting the most sensitive and loving of us.

Tom Salinsky: Sometimes, in answering this question, we're forced to choose between an ambitious film that doesn't quite succeed in fulfilling all its potential and a more modest film that doesn't screw anything up. Here, the dilemma does not arise. *Chicago* is vaultingly ambitious—a genuinely new way to present a musical theater show on film—and it doesn't put a perfectly choreographed foot wrong.

2003: *The Lord of the Rings: The Return of the King*

John Dorney: It's not the best film of the trilogy, and it's notoriously overextended at the end(s). But it's the finale of an enormously ambitious project that paid off remarkably, connecting with audiences around the globe and providing the cinematic world with the only real contender to *Star Wars'* blockbuster trilogy crown. *The Lord of the Rings: The Return of the King* is, in every way, an amazing achievement, and it would seem ridiculous to give the award to anything else.

Jessica Regan: Is there any doubt? You can't please all people all the time, but Peter Jackson and his incredible collaborators come pretty damn close as this seminal adaptation comes to an emotional finale. The film beautifully balances the epic with the intimate, while the achievements of *every* department are so staggering that they cannot be absorbed on one viewing alone. I am so delighted the Academy rewarded *The Lord of the Rings: The Return of the King* (and ultimately the whole trilogy) for all the smiles, gasps, tears, and sighs it gave us and the extraordinary places it took us to.

Tom Salinsky: The achievement of putting Middle Earth on film is undeniable, and this clearly is an award for the trilogy rather than an attempt to elevate the last chapter above the other two. But as immense and impressive an accomplishment as this is and as engaging as the saga is to sit and watch with a bucket of popcorn, it isn't perfect, and nor is this film my personal favorite of 2003. I would have cast my vote for another visually stunning story with an antipodean flavor about an unassuming hero who goes on a mighty journey, meeting new friends and allies along the way, including traditional enemies, and who eventually makes it home, his perspective on the world changed forever—Pixar's masterpiece *Finding Nemo*.

2004: *Million Dollar Baby*

John Dorney: *Million Dollar Baby* is only interested in making you cry, and as a result, it resolutely fails to do so. There's nothing wrong with a film having a downbeat ending, but this one is utterly contrived and mean spirited and, most importantly, is utterly untrue to its own characters. *Sideways* is slight but always pretty enjoyable, with a bittersweet edge that reflects the wine it takes as its subject and a quartet of marvelous performances. It takes the victory for me, while *Million Dollar Baby* is out for the count.

   Jessica Regan: Unfortunately veering into misery porn as catastrophic misfortunes pile on, the overall effect is of two movies of the week—plucky-underdog-rises-in-the-world-of-boxing-overseen-by-grouchy-reluctant-mentor sports film and paraplegic-euthanasia drama—smash-cut together. The script needed further drafts, the scenes needed more takes, and the fight direction needed a complete overhaul. In a photo finish of my favorites this year, Charlie Kaufman's deliriously original *Eternal Sunshine of the Spotless Mind* nudges past Mike Leigh's *Vera Drake* to take my top spot.

   Tom Salinsky: Whereas *Rocky* wallows in the working-class roots of boxing, *Million Dollar Baby* looks for something noble, but the architecture needed to support a true tragedy isn't there, so this just becomes monotonously gloomy, as a young woman who sought self-actualization by hitting people in the face gets paralyzed and euthanized because that's what it takes to make Clint Eastwood misty eyed. Now, that's rather a tough reading of what's often an elegantly shot and powerfully acted film, but Oliver Hirschbiegel's *Downfall*, depicting the last days of Adolf Hitler, retains real potency and shock value—even after all those parodies! It feels real and earned in ways that Paul Haggis and Clint Eastwood's film never does.

2005: *Crash*

John Dorney: *Crash* has always had a reputation as being one of the worst of the Best Picture winners, and it's hard not to feel this reputation is deserved. It is, if anything, worse than you remember. I could be tempted to offer the main prize to Shane Black's dazzling *Kiss Kiss Bang Bang* but will instead opt for another favorite from this year— Nick Park's **Curse of the Were-Rabbit**, a movie that shows sometimes even plasticine people can have the biggest hearts.

Jessica Regan: Have they ever got it *more* wrong? It is tin eared and trite and misfires on every level because it doesn't know what story it's telling. I am aware the road to movie hell is paved with good intentions. I think people meant well when they made this film, and Academy members meant well when they voted for it. But paying lip service to race relations isn't the same as dealing with them head on in any kind of meaningful way. This is a mealy-mouthed conscience salve and a waste of everyone's considerable talents. The rightful winner is **Brokeback Mountain**, with its hopeless, yearning heart; tender truth; and melancholic beauty filling every frame. Ang Lee's direction is sublime, and Heath Ledger and Jake Gyllenhaal make for an unforgettable pairing.

Tom Salinsky: *Crash* isn't simply misjudged; it's shockingly bad in almost all departments, and the handfuls of glimmers of quality don't in any way make up for how crass, clumsy, and badly executed the rest of it is. I could throw a dart and find a more worthy winner of Best Picture. I'm not as big a fan of *Brokeback Mountain* as some, although clearly it should have won over *Crash*. I think the film that feels most like a Best Picture winner that got overlooked is George Clooney's **Goodnight and Good Luck**, with its smooth-as-silk storytelling, beautiful cinematography, and important message delivered without sanctimony or lack of nuance. A black-and-white film with lots of shades of gray.

2006: *The Departed*

John Dorney: Martin Scorsese's consolation prize is pretty average by his standards and certainly pales in comparison to the film it's remade from, *Infernal Affairs*, spoiling at least one character arc. It's by no means bad, but it's just not special. My pick would be the indie-as-hell road movie **Little Miss Sunshine**, which isn't quite as saccharine as it might at first appear and is filled with great acting and some fantastic surprises.

Jessica Regan: *The Departed* is a heady, delirious few hours stuffed with compelling, complex performances, cracking camerawork, a plot as breathless as it is demented, some proper belly-laugh-inducing dialogue—rare in a Best Picture winner—and some pretty moral messages under all that violence. I originally thought it was a return to form, but I realize now it was a step in Scorsese's evolution. A messy, imperfect step but a necessary one, and for that, I can forgive its fumbles and cul-de-sacs and celebrate with the Academy the sheer bloody cinema of it all.

Tom Salinsky: It's a very strong year, with a lot of filmmakers trying new things. Giving Scorsese a Best Director win as a lifetime achievement award I can sort of understand, but giving this chaotic mess of a film Best Picture is totally unwarranted. On the podcast, I was torn between *Children of Men* and *The Lives of Others*, two films that I watched for the first time in the week before recording. On the day, I plumped for the cinematic ambition of *Children of Men*, but it's the quiet isolation of **The Lives of Others** that has stayed with me.

2007: *No Country for Old Men*

John Dorney: The other strong contender this year is Paul Thomas Anderson's rich and meaty *There Will Be Blood*. Both eschew narrative convention to tell darker stories without easy answers. I'm by no means pleased about having to pick between them, and while I've opted for **No Country for Old Men**—just for the faint sense that it's a little more in control of its own story than its rival—it really is a hair's breadth between them and could easily go the other way another day.

Jessica Regan: An impromptu caper where no hijinks ensue, only bloody, terrible mayhem that ultimately distills into a meditation on the soul of America through the musings of an old man . . . *Fargo* it ain't. There's no Mike Yanagita moment to give respite from the nasty dread that builds to an uncomfortable, almost-nauseating pitch. I salute the Academy for this unexpected and deeply sophisticated choice, but I don't echo it. I give it instead to **There Will Be Blood**—a thoroughly rambunctious, almost-outré offering from Paul Thomas Anderson that deals in similar themes but is the more cinematic and satisfying of the two.

Tom Salinsky: History records this year as a two-horse race—are you a Coen brothers fan who's happy with the way in which the action-adventure tale of Cormac McCarthy's book gives way to a nihilistic conversation about fate and destiny? Or do you favor the hugely exciting yet wildly undisciplined explosion of oil, guts, and moustaches from Paul Thomas Anderson's *There Will Be Blood*? To be honest, I find I lose patience with both by the end, and I don't think it's an especially strong field. My pick probably isn't extraordinary enough to win in any other year, but it leaves me far more satisfied and stirred than either of the other two. I'm not altogether happy with this, but I'm choosing Tony Gilroy's legal thriller **Michael Clayton**.

2008: *Slumdog Millionaire*

John Dorney: For showing us new places and faces while still managing to tell an entertaining and touching story that doesn't shy away from going to some very dark areas—well, I have to give it to **Slumdog Millionaire**. It's a brilliantly directed tour de force that still seems unique more than a decade after it was released.

Jessica Regan: Danny Boyle gleefully unleashes a riot of color and kinetic energy as we follow the progress of one brother and the descent of another against the backdrop of Mumbai at its most vivid, among other color-saturated locations. When the story focuses more on the romance, it struggles a bit because there is a dearth of characterization in Freida Pinto's role—reduced to mere ornamentation as the film progresses—and that is regrettable. But it's not enough to make me disagree with the Academy's choice. **Slumdog Millionaire** broke them out of a dreary, "worthy" rut by being boldly original and redefined what a Best Picture winner can look like.

Tom Salinsky: There are problems with this, to be sure. The plot doesn't really make sense. The moments of violence and child exploitation are glossed over so as not to upset the tone. The female characters exist to be killed or to be rescued. And it's clear they're having to cut around a very inexperienced Freida Pinto. But Danny Boyle flings everything he's got at the screen to make it work, and taken on its own merits, as a wild, colorful fantasy; a Bollywood-infused fairy tale; a feel-good fable for a cynical age, it's so uplifting, so life affirming, and just so much fun that I can't help but applaud the Academy for choosing *Slumdog Millionaire*.

2009: *The Hurt Locker*

John Dorney: There's a real sense that ***The Hurt Locker***, the lowest-grossing Best Picture winner at the time, is quite the outlier in Academy history, feeling more art house than even *Moonlight*, leading with no famous stars and an almost-documentary sense to its material. Yet it still manages to display some utterly beautiful camerawork and tension that wouldn't seem out of place in a thriller. It might not be my favorite film of the year, but it is the best one.

Jessica Regan: I do not like this film. I did not enjoy this film. I walked out of this film. But I returned and watched it until the end, so I feel qualified to say that yes, the Academy got it right. I can see past the hot tears of anger to witness an almost flawlessly executed war film that felt visceral, immediate, and as horrific as it ought to. Bigelow made $15 million look like $50 million and marshaled her cast impeccably. Without hesitation, it's ***The Hurt Locker***.

Tom Salinsky: For once, an episodic structure helps rather than hurts. The plot unfolds with brutal simplicity, and the performances are outstanding, from Jeremy Renner down. It stings a bit that the first Best Picture winner directed by a woman is a male story from a male writer about men doing man things, but that doesn't mean it didn't deserve to win because ***The Hurt Locker*** might be my favorite Best Picture winner of the decade.

10

THE 2010s

THE OSCARS IN THE 2010s

In this most recent decade, many things were tried to make the Oscars relevant again in the face of falling ratings and the declining box-office performance of Oscar-nominated films. For the 2010 awards, producers looking for new hosts mysteriously landed on Anne Hathaway and James Franco. Hathaway doesn't look back on the event with fondness. When 2014 Oscars host Neil Patrick Harris asked her for advice, she just told him, "Do the opposite of what I did."

	Best Picture	Biggest Earner (worldwide)
2010	The King's Speech	Toy Story 3
2011	The Artist	Harry Potter and the Deathly Hallows: Part 2
2012	Argo	The Avengers
2013	12 Years a Slave	Frozen
2014	Birdman or (The Unexpected Virtue of Innocence)	Transformers: Age of Extinction
2015	Spotlight	Star Wars: Episode VII—The Force Awakens
2016	Moonlight	Captain America: Civil War
2017	The Shape of Water	Star Wars: Episode VIII—The Last Jedi
2018	Green Book	Avengers: Infinity War
2019	Parasite	Avengers: Endgame

This year also marks the first audible F-bomb at the Oscars. Accepting her award for Best Supporting Actress, Melissa Leo looked genuinely overcome and told the audience, "When I watched Kate two years ago it looked so fucking easy," before realizing what she'd said and covering her mouth in shock.

Franco and Hathaway got lousy reviews, and a new producer was sought who would bring a fresh, youthful, "edgy" energy to proceedings. In August 2011, the Academy announced that the architect of the next awards would be producer and director Brett Ratner, and in September 2011, it was confirmed that Eddie Murphy would be hosting the show. Murphy was quoted as saying, "I am enormously honored to join the great list of past Academy Award hosts, from Hope and Carson to Crystal, Martin, and Goldberg, among others."

And then . . . At a Q and A following a screening of his film *Tower Heist*, when someone asked Ratner about rehearsing, he responded, "Rehearsing is for fags." Two days later, Ratner resigned from the job of producing the Oscars, followed the next day by Eddie Murphy. Only a day after that, the Academy confirmed that the job was going to Brian Grazer, Ron Howard's producing partner. Later that same day, Billy Crystal tweeted, "Am doing the Oscars so the young woman in the pharmacy will stop asking my name when I pick up my prescriptions. Looking forward to the show." It was his ninth and last time hosting the awards.

The desire to find a host with "edge" reached its nadir in 2012, when Seth MacFarlane opened proceedings with a song entitled "We Saw Your Boobs" about women who have appeared topless in movies. The next day, the press crucified MacFarlane. Writing for *Vulture*, Margaret Lyons said, "MacFarlane's opening musical number might as well have been a siren blaring, 'This isn't for you.' Actual gender equality is a ways away, but I'd settle for one four-hour ceremony where women aren't being actively degraded."

Expanding the number of movies nominated for Best Picture finally started to pay off in the form of greater variety among those competing for the top award. The 2013 nominees included a couple of blockbusters, as well as the usual 2010s crop of earnest-issue films and quirky indies. Alfonso Cuarón's 3D space-travaganza *Gravity* took more than $700 million worldwide, and Martin Scorsese's *The Wolf of Wall Street* took almost $400 million. It's still Scorsese's best box-office performer ever. *Gravity* won seven awards from its ten nominations, more than any other film this year and including Best Director for Alfonso Cuarón, but *12 Years a Slave* won Best Picture. Only *Cabaret* has won more Oscars without winning Best Picture.

Diversity of another kind was also on the agenda. 2013 saw nominations for eight Black filmmakers, with wins for Steve McQueen (as producer), Lupita Nyong'o, and screenwriter John Ridley. And 2014 had seen the release of *Selma*, starring David Oyelowo as Martin Luther King Jr., directed by Ava DuVernay, and shot by Bradford Young; *Beyond the Lights*, starring Gugu Mbatha-Raw and directed by Gina Prince-Bythewood; and *Get On Up*, starring Chadwick Boseman as James Brown.

But on 15 January 2015, what jumped out at many viewers was the fact that—for only the second time in twenty years—every single one of the acting nominees was white. In fact, the only non-white nominees were Common and John Legend, jointly nominated for the song "Glory," which featured in *Selma*, itself nominated as Best Picture (with Oprah Winfrey among its producers) but whose director and star had both been overlooked. Additionally, all the nominated directors, screenwriters, and cinematographers were men—for the first time since 1999.

Academy president Cheryl Boone Isaacs said that when she saw the nominations, her heart sank. She knew what was coming, in general, if not in detail. At 1:56 p.m., a writer in Washington, DC, named April Reign tweeted, "#OscarsSoWhite they asked to touch my hair." The hashtag went viral. More jokes piled up: "#OscarsSoWhite they wear Birkenstocks in the wintertime." "#OscarsSoWhite they have a perfect credit score." And so on. Activist Al Sharpton proposed a demonstration at the ceremony, but *Selma* director Ava DuVernay talked him out of it, suggesting a direct dialogue with the Academy instead.

By this stage, of course, the Academy's hands were tied. Neil Patrick Harris had been announced as the host of the awards back in October, so the producing team just tried to maintain business as usual. Harris had hosted the Tonys four times to rave reviews, but his Oscars hosting stint was less well received, with a laborious magic trick in which he appeared to have predicted the outcome, adding nothing except length to an already-lavish running time—the longest since 2006, when *The Departed* won Best Picture. His best joke was probably his opener— "Tonight we honor Hollywood's best and whitest—sorry brightest."

In the year that followed, the Academy considered what it could do to better reflect the diversity of people making films and with stories to tell. And in that time, they achieved . . . nothing. For the second year running, there were twenty white people nominated in the acting categories, and once again, Twitter was in flames. Five white men were nominated as Best Director, and of the twenty-one people nominated for writing screenplays, four were white women, one was a Filipino man, and all the rest were white men. The white screenwriters of *Straight Outta Compton* were nominated, but the cast was completely ignored. Idris Elba had been widely expected to receive a nomination for his work on *Beasts of No Nation*, as had Will Smith in *Concussion* and the writer-director of *Creed*, Ryan Coogler, and its star, Michael B. Jordan, but all of them were omitted.

Jada Pinkett Smith, Al Sharpton, and Spike Lee announced that they were not attending and called for a boycott of the ceremony. Both 50 Cent and Tyrese Gibson pressured Chris Rock to stand down as Oscars host. And other no-shows included Will Smith, Ryan Coogler, and Ava DuVernay. Following the nominations, the Academy did announce various rule changes, including removing automatic Oscar voting privileges from people who were no longer active in the movie industry, which was probably a step in the right direction, but one screenwriter who lost her voting rights commented, "Replacing racism with ageism is not the answer."

Best Song this year went to Sam Smith for "Writing's on the Wall," which is upsetting for a number of reasons. First, it's a terrible song that Smith said took as long to write as it does to play. Second, Smith told the audience. "I read an article a few months ago by Sir Ian McKellen, and he said that no openly gay man had ever won an Oscar. And if this is the case, even if it isn't the case, I want to dedicate this to the LGBT community all around the world." McKellen had been specifically talking about Best Actor, and Smith was forced to apologize to Best Adapted Screenplay winner Dustin Lance Black, who wrote *Milk*; Best Original Song winners Stephen Sondheim and Elton John; and writer-director Pedro Almodóvar, to name a few. A reporter from *Entertainment Tonight* informed Smith that, among others, Howard Ashman had won Best Original Song, as well. Smith responded cheerfully, "I should know him. We should date." Howard Ashman died of AIDS in 1991.

But if it's mistakes you want, there's one that will long live in infamy. At the 2016 awards, shortly before the end of what had been quite a long show, Faye Dunaway announced that *La La Land* had won Best Picture. Two and a half minutes of speeches, congratulations, and celebrations later, *La La Land* producer Jordan Horowitz corrected the error and held up the card reading, "*Moonlight.*"

Mistakes have happened before at the Oscars, of course. In 1963, Sammy Davis Jr. read out the winner of Best *Original* Score having gone through the nominees for Best *Adapted* Score. And in 1984, Laurence Olivier went ahead and declared that *Amadeus* had won Best Picture without reading out the nominees, causing some speculation that he'd just read out the first name that he'd seen on the alphabetical list in front of him. But nothing like this had ever happened before.

It eventually transpired that one of the PwC accountants (who are the only ones who know the outcome of the voting) had been distracted taking selfies backstage and had handed Faye Dunaway's fellow presenter Warren Beatty a duplicate Best Actress envelope instead of the one for Best Picture. Dunaway saw "*La La Land*" (in much bigger type than "Emma Stone") and read out the words she had been expecting to say. PwC swiftly apologized, moved the accountant in question to a different role, and managed to keep their biggest and most glamorous client. But Americans failed to tune in the following year to see if the gaffe would be repeated (or even referred to). The 2017 show, when *The Shape of Water* won Best Picture, recorded viewing figures of 26.5 million—the lowest to date. Something had to be done. And the Academy had plenty of ideas.

On 7 August 2018, the Academy Board of Governors met and voted on a proposal to add a new category to the Academy Awards—the first since Best Animated Feature in 2001. Best Popular Film was designed to reward the kind of blockbusters that had been getting more and more critical appeal but rarely if ever breaking through at the Oscars, except in technical categories. At the time, the Academy was very vague about what would and would not be eligible in this new category. In the same message, they announced that they had agreed to limit the Oscars telecast to three hours and that this would be achieved by giving out certain awards during commercial breaks, highlights of which could be shown later in the broadcast.

Almost immediately, they were deluged with criticism for both innovations. Barely a month after the announcement, on 6 September, the Academy confirmed that no award for Best Popular Film would be presented at the ninety-first Oscars. Currently, the official position of the Academy is that the award may still be given at a future ceremony, but they've been awfully quiet about it lately (to be fair, they've had other things to worry about).

Next, the Academy's thoughts turned to a host, and their first pick was Hollywood's highest-paid actor, Dwayne "The Rock" Johnson, who was paid $124 million for his film roles in 2018. Johnson was keen to participate, but filming commitments made it impossible. So, on 4 December 2018, the Academy announced that Kevin Hart would host the show. This appointment lasted around forty-eight hours, which was the time it took for his homophobic Tweets to be discovered and for him to step down for fear of being a distraction. Three days after that, the Academy confirmed that there would be no host, for the first time since the ill-fated sixty-first Oscars, with Snow White and Rob Lowe.

With less than two weeks to go before the ceremony, the Academy reiterated what they had already announced in August—that four categories would not be presented live—and yet again, there was uproar and another climb-down. On 15 February, the Academy issued a statement saying, "All Academy Awards will be presented without edits, in our traditional format." The show aired nine days later.

Black Panther, the movie that was instrumental in the Best Popular Film debate, was nominated in seven categories but was shut out of Screenplay, Director, and the acting categories. It managed to win for its score, costumes, and production design—partly thanks to the work of an Oscar strategist hired by Disney and a much bigger campaign budget than for any previous Marvel film.

Green Book won Best Picture, Best Supporting Actor for Mahershala Ali, and Best Original Screenplay. It was also nominated for its editing and Viggo Mortensen for Best Actor. But Peter Farrelly wasn't even nominated as Best Director—only the fifth time that this has happened to the Best Picture winner. One of those times was 1989, which is when Spike Lee's Do the Right Thing was theoretically in contention with actual Best Picture winner Driving Miss Daisy. And Lee—whose film BlacKkKlansman was nominated for Best Picture and five other awards—wasn't the only person in the Dolby Theater to be acutely aware of just how much history was repeating itself.

At the most recent awards, for the best films of 2019, Best Foreign Language Film was renamed Best International Feature. Given that *Parasite* had received a total of six nominations, its win in this category was never in any doubt. But because no film in a language other than English had ever won Best Picture (or even Best Director), plenty of people watching the ceremony—me included—assumed that the top awards were still wide open, even though *Parasite* had already nabbed Best Original Screenplay.

That thinking started to change when Spike Lee announced that—from a field that included Sam Mendes, Martin Scorsese, and Quentin Tarantino—the winner of Best Director was Bong Joon Ho for *Parasite*. Bong seemed overcome, telling the audience through his interpreter, "After winning Best International Feature, I thought I was done for the day and was ready to relax."

But minutes later, *Parasite* won Best Picture, as well, and Bong Joon Ho became the eighth filmmaker to win Oscars for writing, producing, and directing the same film. By now, Bong was happy to let his producing partner, Kwak Sin Ae, and his executive producer, Miky Lee, do most of the talking, but a few weeks earlier at the Golden Globes, he'd addressed an American audience not used to non-English-language content, telling them, "Once you overcome the one-inch-tall barrier of subtitles, you will be introduced to so many more amazing films."

As part of an attempt to arrest falling ratings and tackle awards-season fatigue, these Oscars were held on the earliest date ever, 9 February—but viewing figures continued to slide. Another rethink was clearly needed. For the next awards, however, the Academy would have far bigger problems to worry about.

THE MOVIES IN THE 2010s

On the eve of this decade, 29 December 2009, Disney bought Marvel for $4.24 billion. In the years that followed, this studio continued swallowing up companies and acquiring intellectual properties at such a ravenous rate that the true extent of its holdings is actually now indeterminate. The age of Disney was underway. In 2010, Disney paid $115 million for the worldwide distribution rights to *The Avengers* and *Iron Man 3*, and in 2013, Disney also purchased the rights to previously released films from the franchise. The previous October, Disney had officially announced its deal to purchase Lucasfilm. For a cool $4.05 billion (half in shares), Disney now owned *Star Wars*; *Indiana Jones*; Lucasfilm's operating businesses in live-action film production; and all associated consumer products, video games, animation, visual effects, and audio postproduction.

Disney was also steadily remaking its back catalogue, reimagining its greatest hits (*Cinderella*, *Aladdin*, *The Lion King*) as live-action films and centering new films around previously peripheral characters, such as *Maleficent*. Having acquired Pixar the previous decade, their complete domination of output meant that almost all the annual highest-grossing films of the decade were Disney joints, be they Marvel (four), *Star Wars* (two), Pixar (one), or an actual Disney original—*Frozen*.

The US cinema industry made more than $11 billion in domestic box-office revenue in 2010, putting it in first place. Second was Japan, with $2.5 billion, and India third, with $2.2 billion. But according to Guinness World Records, 2010 was the most expensive year in Hollywood (to date). The fifty biggest blockbusters released by major Hollywood studios in 2010 cost a combined total of $5.2 billion—the highest total in one year in US cinematic history.

Animation enjoyed its best decade yet, and *Toy Story 3* was the first animated film to gross $1 billion. But cinema attendance was down from the previous year, based on a 5.4 percent decline in ticket sales. It was the largest year-to-year drop since 2005. Filmgoing in 2010 was the second lowest of the entire decade. The following year, audiences were down 20 percent in eight years. Rising ticket prices offset much of this fall, so bottom lines still looked impressive, but consumer fatigue at the glut of remakes and sequels had set in. The $15–$20 million character-driven films that had thrived in the 1990s were squeezed out in favor of content that would be already familiar to audiences. But this familiarity was breeding contempt—twenty-seven sequels were released in 2011 alone—and the golden age of television kept people binge-watching box sets rather than flocking to the movies.

In 2013, the visual effects industry was in crisis, as many of the visual effects houses closed or struggled to survive. A surfeit of visual effects houses, small profit margins, non-unionized workers, and the threat from cheaper labor overseas all contributed to this sharp slump. At the same time, 3D ticket sales were seriously declining. Consistently, shares of 3D grosses were below 40 percent of total grosses. It seemed audiences were not enamored with substandard 3D products and unnecessary postconversions of films to 3D. Despite these troubling numbers, Hollywood remained committed to at least five dozen 3D movies during 2016.

In a major shake-up to movie theaters reminiscent of the adaptations that had to be made when sound came in, Paramount Pictures was the first major studio to stop releasing movies on celluloid in the United States. In a somewhat-ignominious swan song, *Anchorman 2: The Legend Continues* was their last production released on 35mm film. Their first major all-digital release was Martin Scorsese's *The Wolf of Wall Street*. By this stage, 92 percent of the more than 40,000 screens in the United States had converted to digital, according to the National Association of Theatre Owners. Paramount vowed to help exhibitors by either replacing film projectors with digital systems (at a cost of $70,000 each) or to install satellite systems to receive digitally beamed movies. Paramount calculated that it would recoup the cost in the long run by no longer having to strike new prints and ship them to movie theaters.

A new method emerged to help with financing for new films, particularly indies and passion projects—crowdfunding. Rather than try to raise the necessary capital from a small number of professional investors, this model asks fans to prepurchase products in order to generate the cash needed to create them. Among various competing systems, the website Kickstarter became the world's largest funding platform for creative projects.

An early success for this model in feature films was the Rob Thomas TV series *Veronica Mars*, which had ended (temporarily, it turns out) in 2007. In 2014, it came back as a feature film due to record-breaking funding with Kickstarter. It was the all-time highest-funded project in Kickstarter's "Film and Video" category, raising $5.7 million and the movie was such a hit that the series was reinstated on the streaming service Hulu. And Charlie Kaufman's stop-motion film *Anomalisa* received six thousand donations, raising $400,000, more than double its original goal.

In late November 2014, in a plot twist worthy of a 1990s cyberthriller, a skeleton popped up on thousands of Sony computer screens with the message "We've obtained all your internal data, including your secrets." According to the FBI, it was the work of North Korea—possibly in response to the impending release of the Seth Rogen/James Franco vehicle *The Interview*. The data dumps that followed revealed damning e-mail exchanges (including one where producer Scott Rudin refers to Angelina Jolie as a "minimally talented spoiled brat"), sensitive trade secrets, and plans for various upcoming projects—but most apparent from the e-mails was Hollywood's problem with race. In one exchange, Sony executive Amy Pascal and producer Scott Rudin go through a list of films they think President Obama has enjoyed, joking that they were likely Lee Daniels's *The Butler*, *Django Unchained*, and *Ride Along*. The culture in an organization comes from the top down, and Al Sharpton released a statement saying, "What is most troubling about these statements is that they reflect a continued lack of diversity in positions of power in major Hollywood studios. The statements clearly show how comfortable major studio powers are with racial language and marginalization."

More than eighty people have died in fifty-three fatal accidents while filming in the United States, but until very recently, there had been no successful prosecutions. This finally changed in 2015, when American film director Randall Miller became the first filmmaker to go to prison on the charge of involuntary manslaughter for a film-related death. While filming the Gregg Allman biopic *Midnight Rider*, twenty-seven-year-old camera assistant Sarah Jones was killed during a reckless attempt to shoot footage on a working train track. The first production-related death was in 1914 when sixteen-year-old actress Grace McHugh drowned, and cameraman Owen Carter died trying to rescue her while filming a scene for the western short *Across the Border*. It would be a century before a custodial sentence was finally handed down to the responsible party.

In 2014, the top-grossing actor for the year was Jennifer Lawrence, with her two films, *The Hunger Games: Mockingjay—Part 1* and *X-Men: Days of Future Past*, grossing a combined $1.5 billion at the worldwide box office. In 2015, Sam Taylor-Johnson's adaptation of *Fifty Shades of Grey* made $166 million domestically. Director Elizabeth Banks's *Pitch Perfect 2* became the best-performing movie directed by a woman, with a domestic gross of $184.3 million. Female-fronted films, such as *Spy* and *Trainwreck*, outperformed expectations. But despite all this, the Center for the Study of Women in Television and Film at San Diego State University reported that of the top one hundred highest-grossing (domestic) feature films released in 2016, women were the protagonists in only 29 percent of them. Women played only 37 percent of those films' major characters and had only 32 percent of all speaking roles. These facts reflected the reality that women only produced 19 percent of those films and were writers on one in ten.

In 2016, we lost so many luminaries: the incomparable Alan Rickman; the Star-Man and Goblin King, David Bowie; screenwriter of *LA Confidential* and *8 Mile* Curtis Hanson; the one and only Willy Wonka, Gene Wilder; and Alexis Arquette, one of the first visible trans actresses. And, in a bitterly cruel and heartbreaking finale to all this loss, Carrie Fisher died on 27 December, and her mother, Debbie Reynolds, died the very next day.

On 5 October 2017, after years of rumors that had become so commonplace it had become an industry in-joke, Harvey Weinstein was accused of sexual harassment by a number of actresses, including Ashley Judd. They were joined on the record by former Weinstein Company employees in a shocking exposé by Jodi Kantor and Meghan Twohey for the *New York Times*. Within five days of the article's publication, more than one hundred women came forward with more allegations. Weinstein was fired from his production company, and a *New Yorker* article by Ronan Farrow itemized the sexual harassment or assault of thirteen more women by Weinstein. In a follow-up story, Farrow detailed how Weinstein allegedly used ex-Mossad agents to spy on women in a campaign of fear and intimidation. More than ten years after it was created by activist Tarana Burke, the #MeToo movement was adopted on Twitter by Alyssa Milano in the wake of these industry-quaking revelations to encourage people to share their stories of sexual abuse and harassment to illustrate their prevalence.

Hollywood was far from the only industry revealed to be riven with abuses—but because we had watched the faces of many of the victims flicker on our screens and through ticket sales helped line the pockets of their abusers, the revelations felt personal and immediate. Story after story emerged of rape and violation, of careers thwarted, reputations impugned, and the enabling that had to occur at every level to keep these stories in the shadows and the public largely in the dark. People asked the question, if wealthy, successful movie stars were locking themselves in bathrooms (Gwyneth Paltrow) or barricading themselves in hotel rooms (Daryl Hannah) to avoid their predator, what on earth could be befalling those who had no power? Who was enabling these situations—either by their silence or their compliance? This was not the oft-invoked "few bad apples." The Dream Factory was unmasked to be a whole industry of harm, of compliance and enablement that protected abusers and sought to discredit such survivors as Rose McGowan, who spoke out against their "monster."

Universal canceled the upcoming release of its satirical thriller *The Hunt*, due for late September 2019, because of pressure from Fox News and President Donald Trump in the wake of the El Paso shootings. The subject matter (rich, liberal elites hunt and kill MAGA-hat "deplorables") was condemned—despite not being a particularly new story; franchise smash *The Hunger Games* and even the Schwarzenegger starrer *The Running Man* cover similar territory.

Ten years after purchasing Marvel, the Walt Disney Company completed its acquisition of the assets of 21st Century Fox, which includes 20th Century Fox and its subsidiaries. Disney's appetite for takeover shows no sign of abating, but one wonders how it can be sustained. The landscape of the industry has permanently changed at every level, from power structures to the vocabulary used around workplace harassment. Hollywood was forced to reckon with itself and the behaviors it not only tolerated but also tacitly supported. The dearth of women in key roles and the ubiquity of harassment are not mutually exclusive. Improve the former, and the latter will struggle to thrive. We have so far to go, but I cannot help but feel encouraged by *Parasite*'s Best Picture win in 2019 and the host of female directors and people of color across different categories nominated in 2020. After a sluggish decade in terms of representation, the 2020s have hit the ground running. Perhaps after the bow being drawn back for so long, the arrow pointed toward progress has finally taken flight.

THE MAKING OF *ARGO*

Writer: Chris Terrio; based on *The Master of Disguise* by Antonio J. Mendez and "The Great Escape" by Joshuah Bearman
Director: Ben Affleck

Producers: Ben Affleck, George Clooney, Grant Heslov for Smokehouse Pictures/Warner Bros.

Cast: Ben Affleck, Bryan Cranston, Alan Arkin, John Goodman,
Tate Donovan, Clea DuVall, Christopher Denham, Scoot
McNairy, Kerry Bishé, Rory Cochrane, Victor Garber

Won: Best Picture, Best Adapted Screenplay, Best Film Editing
(William Goldenberg)

Nominated: Best Supporting Actor (Arkin), Best Sound Editing
(Erik Aadahl, Ethan Van der Ryn), Best Sound Mixing (John
Reitz, Gregg Rudloff, Jose Antonio Garcia), Best Original Score
(Alexandre Desplat)

Length: 120 minutes

Budget: $44.5 million

Box office: $232 million

Rotten Tomatoes: 96%

The "Canadian Caper," as it came to be known, was a joint rescue
operation of six trapped American diplomats performed by the Canadian government and the CIA in Iran on 4 November 1979. Although it
was kept secret for nearly three decades, an article about the operation
was eventually written by Joshuah Bearman and published under the
name "The Great Escape" in *Wired* in 2007. The story was one of those
that's almost too good to be true. The CIA created a fake science-fiction
movie, including placing ads in Hollywood trade papers, and assigned
the diplomats new identities as Canadian filmmakers scouting locations
as part of the nonexistent film's preproduction.

It was a tale with obvious cinematic possibilities and was swiftly
snapped up by Smokehouse Pictures' Grant Heslov and George Clooney, with development executive Nina Wolarsky suggesting the relatively green screenwriter Chris Terrio to develop the screenplay, also basing it on *The Master of Disguise*, the book written by operation leader
Tony Mendez. Everyone was very happy with Terrio's work, but neither
Heslov nor Clooney (whom Terrio had visualized in the Mendez role)
had the time to make it, both being extremely busy with other projects.

So the script sat at Warner Bros. for several years, until in 2010, it
found its way to actor Ben Affleck, who was looking to follow up his
sophomore film as a director, *The Town*. He was immediately taken
with the script, saying that he'd usually read material in twenty-page
bursts but was instantly tuned in to this new piece. He called Clooney

and Heslov to pitch for the directing gig, telling them that he wanted to shift the story from its current semicomedic tone into something more serious—which was completely in line with Clooney and Heslov's own ideas. He was given the job—and was so eager to get going that he'd started prepping the film before the Smokehouse team had finished their previous film, *The Ides of March*.

Filming began in Los Angeles in August 2011, with Turkey selected to double for Iran and additional filming taking place in Washington and Istanbul. The scene of Affleck approaching the CIA building was filmed at the old CIA building in Virginia, and this commitment to authenticity was typical of the production. Affleck had researched the events scrupulously, speaking to the diplomats and Mendez and reading everything he could get his hands on. The costumes were precise, as Mendez had kept some of his clothing from the period, and while the crew didn't feel they could use the actual items, they were able to recreate them perfectly, alongside such equally fastidious reproductions as matching up eyeglasses with the passport photographs of the diplomats.

To further make the film feel truthful, Affleck asked the actors playing the diplomats to live together for a week in a house dressed authentically to the period, with no cell phones, internet, or computers—and only items from the time to keep them occupied. And extras playing demonstrators in the early stages of the film were given 8mm cameras and told to shoot what they liked. This handheld footage was later incorporated into the final cut—which uses almost no real contemporary footage although appears to be cutting between newsreels and modern recreations of events.

Affleck's use of Led Zeppelin's song "When the Levee Breaks" did create a minor problem. Being a huge fan of the band, he'd pursued them for the rights, and they agreed, but they noted that when the piece was played in the film as part of the action, the needle was placed at the start of the record—despite the song being the last track on the second side. Affleck admired the attention to detail, and so he agreed to a reshoot. But such authenticity comes at a cost—and *Argo* only had a comparatively small construction budget of $1.5 million. This meant very few sets could be built from scratch, so a lot of the interiors of the embassy and airport had to be decorated and altered digitally.

It was all, however, undeniably effective—to such a degree that after the film was released, an incensed Iran hired a radical French lawyer to sue the film, claiming it was designed to build anger against them and pave the way for US military attacks. A claim was filed accusing Affleck of war crimes, but the French judge immediately dismissed the case. The Oscar voters took a rather different stance—failing to even nominate Affleck in the Best Director category. Affleck had already won eight awards for directing this film, including from the Directors Guild of America, but with him out of the race, the way was open for Ang Lee to take the prize for *Life of Pi*, which made that film the evening's overall champ, as it also won for its cinematography, music and visual effects—four awards to *Argo*'s three.

Another group who was upset at the way the film handled events was the Canadian government. Any film based on a true story (as so many Best Picture winners are) will necessarily have to make cuts, streamline events, invent new material to paper over the joints, and so on. So the fact that the fake movie in *Argo* was actually called *Lord of Light* or that the tension in the climactic airport sequence has been massively ramped up or that Alan Arkin's character is a fictional composite of various people who helped Mendez out should dismay no one and surprise hardly anyone.

But what's tricky about *Argo* is that it wasn't possible for the CIA to acknowledge its role in the operation in any way—as the film accurately depicts. The Canadian government, who had prepared the documents and arranged safe passage for the escapees, took all the credit, and the CIA kept its involvement classified for almost twenty years. So when the movie was first released, a lot of Canadians were pretty pissed off that the America-centric version of the story effectively reduced the Canadian activity to little more than Canadian ambassador Ken Taylor (played in the movie by Victor Garber) acting as butler for six houseguests. The film's final caption ironically mentions the citations that Ken Taylor received while suggesting that he didn't really deserve any of them. In fact, it was Taylor, his staff, and the Canadian government who produced the needed passports and plane tickets, scouted the airport, sent people in and out of Iran to establish regular travel patterns between the two countries, and worked with the houseguests on their Canadian accents and backstories.

When he saw the film, an understandably pissed-off Taylor told the press, "In reality, Canada was responsible for the six houseguests, and the CIA was a junior partner." He also said that he thought the house-guests having Canadian passports was the crucial factor and that the Hollywood backstory was basically irrelevant. After hearing from Taylor, a suitably embarrassed Ben Affleck told him that, no matter the extra cost, he could change the final caption to anything he wanted. The new caption describes the operation as an "enduring model of international co-operation between governments."

BEST OF THE BEST: *MOONLIGHT*

Writer: Barry Jenkins; based on the play by Tarell Alvin McCraney
Director: Barry Jenkins
Producers: Adele Romanski, Dede Gardner, Jeremy Kleiner for A24
Cast: Trevante Rhodes, André Holland, Janelle Monáe, Ashton Sanders, Jharrel Jerome, Naomie Harris, Mahershala Ali, Alex Hibbert
Won: Best Picture, Best Original Screenplay, Best Supporting Actor (Ali)
Nominated: Best Director, Best Supporting Actress (Harris), Best Original Score (Nicholas Britell), Best Cinematography (James Laxton), Best Film Editing (Joi McMillon, Nat Sanders)
Length: 111 minutes
Budget: $4 million
Box office: $65 million
Rotten Tomatoes: 98%

Jessica Regan: The only winner in the history of the Academy Awards that can claim to have been robbed, *Moonlight* is unique and special for many reasons that have nothing to do with the complacency and incompetence that stole their moment. It's the very rare kind of care and consideration taken by Barry Jenkins with his precious material and cast that make this small film so finely wrought and sublimely rendered.

Adapted from *In Moonlight Black Boys Look Blue*, a Tarell Alvin McCraney play that was never produced, *Moonlight* charts the progress of Chiron from boy to young man through three substantial vignettes taken from his childhood, teenage years, and adulthood. Although three actors shared the role of Chiron, they never met before or during filming. Director Barry Jenkins was less concerned about resemblance or impersonation than he was about the performers sharing a kind of "essence." This is magnificently achieved, with each actor playing Chiron bringing a soulful sadness to the part and a yearning for connection to their mother, another boy, and another man. Opposite them, Naomie Harris is tremendous. I understand her initial reluctance at playing a crack-addicted mother, but she is no cliché, creating a fully fleshed-out character in the few days' filming she was able to squeeze in while in the United States doing promotion for *Spectre*.

The youngest Chiron (or "Little") is played touchingly and truthfully by Alex Hibbert. At the behest of Jenkins, he gives an almost silent film performance, seeing more than a young boy ever should and absorbing every stroke and slap—both the verbal and the physical kind. Mahershala Ali is typically excellent as father figure Juan, and Janelle Monáe as his girlfriend Teresa provides welcome levity as they give complicated sanctuary to Little.

Ashton Saunders as the teen Chiron carries the fire and is deeply affecting as Chiron's sexual identity marks him out for scorn from his peers and his mother. There are no safe spaces for him, except for a few fleeting moments on a moonlit beach, in the arms of Kevin (played to perfection here by Jharrel Jerome and in the third act by André Holland).

The breadth of the action shrinks in the third act, and yet it is here that perhaps the most profound shifts happen, in the spaces between where no one speaks and the soul can live and breathe and be. Trevante Rhodes's grown-up "Black" takes Chiron from a secondary character in the lives of others to becoming his own person at the center of his story by finally going to the edge of his wants and desires—and it is nothing short of heroic when he does. The risk of walking into that diner. The risk of telling someone they were the only one who ever touched you, after all these years. It is almost unbearably tender and sad and beautiful.

It looks gorgeous, too—not prettified but shot with a palette of bleach and blue that is always telling a story about the emotional landscape Chiron is negotiating. In twenty-five days, Jenkins and his crew conjured the most incredible sense of time and place—contemporary and immediate yet reminiscent of such old masters and influences as Edward Hopper and Tennessee Williams. A film this stylish can lack substance but not here. It is so whole, despite being composed of incomplete fragments. Its lulling, disquieting quality is aided by rhythmic editing and an aching score, which creates something of the feeling one has after a melancholy dream. But don't be put off; it is no misery fest or trauma porn. It is a film about light, and it opens up like a flower.

As well as being a true work of art, the impact of a gay story line with Black protagonists in an internationally-released film cannot be underestimated. As actor and friend of the pod Syrus Lowe told us, "Had I seen *Moonlight* when I was fourteen, it would have been life changing." Representation matters. It matters for underrepresented people to see their story on-screen so as not to feel alone in this world or that the role they play will always be a peripheral one. It matters for overrepresented groups to see stories that aren't about them, as it increases empathy and understanding, and that makes life better for everyone, truly, not least for children like Chiron.

WORST OF THE BEST: *GREEN BOOK*

> **Writers:** Nick Vallelonga, Brian Hayes Currie, Peter Farrelly
> **Director:** Peter Farrelly
> **Producers:** Jim Burke, Brian Hayes Currie, Peter Farrelly, Nick Vallelonga, Charles B. Wessler for Universal Pictures
> **Cast:** Viggo Mortensen, Mahershala Ali, Linda Cardellini, Dimiter D. Marinov, Mike Hatton
> **Won:** Best Picture, Best Adapted Screenplay, Best Supporting Actor (Ali)
> **Nominated:** Best Actor (Mortensen), Best Film Editing (Patrick J. Don Vito)
> **Length:** 130 minutes
> **Budget:** $23 million
> **Box office:** $330 million
> **Rotten Tomatoes:** 78%

John Dorney: Mahershala Ali's second Best Supporting Actor win comes from a film that couldn't be more of a contrast to his first. When *Moonlight* won the Best Picture Oscar in 2016, it felt like something of

a sea-change, particularly given the awkward circumstances of its announcement, with the belated rejection of the far more typical Academy fare presented by *La La Land*.

So, it's disappointing that, only two years later, *Green Book* feels like
such a retrograde piece, symptomatic of the Academy learning nothing.
As other people have pointed out, when the Black actor in your movie
about racism is up for Best Supporting Actor rather than in the lead
role, you're doing something wrong.

The setup is a relatively simple one. Concert pianist Don Shirley
(Mahershala Ali) needs a driver to get him from venue to venue on his
tour of the southern states of America. The only problem is that this is
the segregated South of 1962, and Don Shirley is Black. The "Green
Book" of the title was a guidebook for African American travelers com-
piled by Victor Hugo Green that listed hotels, restaurants, campsites,
and the like where Black patrons would be welcome. Frank Vallelonga
(a.k.a., Tony Lip; Viggo Mortensen) is just the kind of capable "fixer"
who not only can get Shirley where he needs to be but also can deal
with any issues that might arise on the journey.

The sadness is that there probably is a half-decent story in there. It's
just not the one we end up seeing. The film itself is likeable enough on
its own terms, but it never really crosses the line into anything special.
On a purely aesthetic level, it fails to engage with us cinematically—
underwhelming camera setups and a trite incidental score lend the
whole piece the air of a Lifetime TV movie that's somehow bagged a
couple of Hollywood stars rather than the prestige piece it clearly wants
to be. For a piece that is nominally a travelogue of America, it never
actually feels inclined to show any of the beautiful landscapes so richly
teased in Mortensen's letters home.

The storytelling is also muddled—and in some senses hampered by
its status as a true story. The film can only present itself from the point
of view of Viggo Mortensen's Tony Lip, as it's this character's real-life
son who has written the screenplay. But this means we only see Don
Shirley through Tony's eyes, which removes the chance to properly
understand and explore this far more complex figure in quite as much
depth. His sexuality, for example, is reduced to the merest footnote,
which is surely a missed opportunity. If you can keep up an equal billing
in *Hobbs and Shaw*, you can manage it in *Green Book*.

Here we end up leaning into a white-savior narrative, more concerned with the redemption of a racist than the person of color at its heart. And that redemption seems borderline instantaneous. A man so racist that he puts glasses used by Black men in the garbage is suddenly best friends with another without any obvious trigger. There's a definite sense of a son not wanting to say anything too egregious about his late father, with Lip pretty much a stand-up guy from that point on, without even the faintest flicker of a reaction when he realizes he's about to be employed by a Black man—which does rather remove the sense of a journey. Even when the protagonists are literally on a journey. Lip almost seems to have been redeemed before he even meets Shirley.

That's not to say the film is without merit. Mortensen's performance is great, and Ali's is even better, beautifully exploring his character's layers without anywhere near enough detail in the material he's working with. And the structure of the storytelling, with every setup paid off and every beat in place, is very satisfying. It's easy to be moved by Don Shirley ending up behind the wheel of the car toward the end of the film, and the final reunion, because the way the movie has been put together is undeniably slick and effective.

But this leads to a slightly uncomfortable sense that it feels like its fixed racism somehow—as if problems are solved simply because they're acknowledged. When it actually tries to engage with the racist politics of its time (such as in an awkward sequence where the heroes are locking eyes with a group of literally cotton-picking slaves), it doesn't really have a clue what to do. It's a movie that makes white people feel better about racism but is ultimately a bit of a fantasy—which is profoundly odd for a true story.

DID THE ACADEMY GET IT RIGHT?

2010: *The King's Speech*

John Dorney: Look, it's a perfectly entertaining film, probably more so than you remember, a fun and funny afternoon. But Best Picture? Nope. For me, there are only two serious contenders for the top prize—the first is *Toy Story 3*, which is one of the all-time great sequels. But for coming from a standing start and for sheer relevance, I'm going with **The Social Network**. Aaron Sorkin and David Fincher are variable filmmakers, but their collaboration allows them to fill in each other's gaps and deliver a terrific of-its-time thriller about nerds.

Jessica Regan: A very fine film mischaracterized as pure Oscar bait when really it has so much heart and kindness at its core. Colin Firth and Geoffrey Rush are exceedingly good, the script is deft and sometimes surprising, and the exploration of both men's vulnerability and the friendship that heals them is very affecting. But **Toy Story** 3 nearly had me on the floor. Its technical achievement is more than matched by its vocal performances and superlative storytelling. I, along with the other adults in the cinema, sobbed harder than any of the younger attendees as I watched Andy put away childish things and a rag-tag bunch of toys face almost certain death with dignity, grace, and care for each other.

Tom Salinsky: Do you know what? Yes. **The King's Speech** deservedly won Best Picture. All right, I concede you have to be in a bit of an indulgent mood to reach this conclusion. This is never going to shatter any preconceptions, and its vague nods in the direction of Big Important Themes about Identity and Leadership only serve to make it even more comforting and even less confrontational. But those Big Important Themes *are* present, and it is genuinely fascinating to observe the collision between the divine right to rule endowed by God and the fragility of the earthly instrument upon which that bequest lands. Both leads do exceptional work, and at its heart, this is a love story, delicately layered with class and status. What could possibly be the matter with that?

2011: *The Artist*

John Dorney: Is *The Artist* slight? Yes. But I like what it's doing. It's trying to be something different, and it manages that with style. It might not have the depth or complexity of many other films this year, but it has heart, and it leaves me smiling. What more can you ask? I'd vote for **The Artist**.

Jessica Regan: When *The Artist* does something well, it does it again in short order. Beats are repeated as the film winks at us and then itself. It feels as if the material for a stylish and dazzling short is stretched to a feature, and as appealing a curiosity as it is, it gives the impression of it being a little too self-aware, prettified, and pleased with itself to be a pure period piece. I would have voted instead for a film about as far from cute as you can get. **We Need to Talk about Kevin** is wincingly brave, adapted from a novel that felt unfilmable, and yet it is faithfully rendered in all its ugly, unbearable truth. Lynne Ramsay moors the film beautifully, balancing trauma and intensity so that we never look away, even when we want to.

Tom Salinsky: Even at one hundred minutes, *The Artist* manages to outstay its welcome. Despite some electrifying moments, the gimmick can't sustain it once the story peters out. Keeping me absolutely gripped from start to finish was the Iranian film **A Separation**, which won Best Foreign Language Film. It's a heartrending tale of flawed but decent people trying their best in very trying circumstances, told with economy and clarity by a humane and compassionate filmmaker.

2012: *Argo*

John Dorney: I like but don't love *Argo*, a solidly constructed thriller but not one I can ever quite buy. This is something I can't say about *The Pirates! Band of Misfits*, which is Aardman at the top of their game, or *The Avengers*, which manages to achieve the impossible for the first time in the Marvel Cinematic Universe and does so with style. They're all three, however, bags of fun and well worth watching. But none of them is **Amour**, Michael Haneke's heartbreaking tale of love and loss that—in contrast to *Argo*—never feels anything other than brutally and unflinchingly true.

Jessica Regan: Affleck does deliver a very slick piece of cinema, populated by a splendid roster of national treasures, including brief but perfect turns from Richard Kind and Philip Baker Hall. It is technically very accomplished but also emotionally distant. I believe Paul Thomas Anderson's Scientology-in-disguise venality tale **The Master** to be a superior work. Joaquin Phoenix's chaotic talent is anchored beautifully by Philip Seymour Hoffman's eerie paterfamilias. Resolutely original and not fitting neatly into any familiar genre, it is the more challenging watch of the two but I believe the more resonant and rewarding.

Tom Salinsky: Smooth, funny, suspenseful, satirical, political, and beautifully acted, **Argo** succeeds on every level. While it doesn't have as much to say as *Lincoln* or as much depth of human misery as the bleakly brilliant *Amour* and it won't make you laugh as much as *The Pirates! Band of Misfits*, it is nevertheless an expertly crafted piece of cinema and a thoroughly deserving winner, particularly next to the rather flimsy *Silver Linings Playbook* and the charming but twee *Life of Pi*.

2013: *12 Years a Slave*

John Dorney: This is an incredibly hard watch, but that's exactly how it should be. Shots linger on, forcing you to bear witness to the atrocities within. The story is, perhaps, a little wanting, but this is compensated for by beautiful camerawork and scoring and some amazing acting, particularly from Chiwetel Ejiofor and Lupita Nyong'o. You won't want to watch it regularly, but you really do have to see **12 Years a Slave** at least once.

Jessica Regan: What a beautifully filmed, brilliantly acted, complete and utter ordeal this is to watch—but watch it you must, if only once. At times it plays like a horror film, as unspeakable depravity fills the frame, or its effects linger in a corner of it. We do not get relief in cutaways or reaction shots, as the sole camera the film was shot with is trained unflinchingly on the action. We do get some respite in the bursts of humanity that break through, connecting us to our own. A tale told in sorrow rather than anger, **12 Years a Slave** is the rightful winner this year, not because of its subject matter, but because of director Steve McQueen's astonishing execution of it.

Tom Salinsky: This film is more of an ordeal than I felt it needed to be. After a very smooth-running first half, the structure collapses when we exchange Benedict Cumberbatch's benevolent master for Michael Fassbender's psychopath, and it starts to feel as if the episodes could come in any order, which prevents them from gaining power from each other as they build. Still, maybe, when the images presented are this strong, that isn't necessary. And maybe a film about slavery should feel like an ordeal for the comfortable, middle-class white audience, judging the film over a bucket of popcorn. Ryan Coogler's remarkable debut *Fruitvale Station* tells a simple story with great control, and Martin Scorsese's amazing *The Wolf of Wall Street* is his most entertaining film in years. But the Academy probably did get it right by giving Best Picture to **12 Years a Slave**.

2014: *Birdman or (The Unexpected Virtue of Innocence)*

John Dorney: As a technical achievement, *Birdman* is hard to beat. The conceit of seemingly shooting an entire feature film in one shot—once attempted by Alfred Hitchcock with mixed results—here looks absolutely seamless. And the whole thing is rooted by an astonishing performance from the robbed-of-a-trophy Michael Keaton. But it has its issues, particularly regarding the treatment of women, and it might just be a bit too pleased with itself. So, I'm going to give Best Picture to a simpler, sweeter film that flies effortlessly—the magnificent **Paddington**.

Jessica Regan: Devices such as that employed by *Birdman* are meant to enhance storytelling, not replace story altogether. Once my admiration for the shiny technical triumphs had dissipated, I found myself not caring about Riggan Thompson's miserable existence or Mike Shiner's egregious behavior in the name of art—in the same way this film doesn't care about the interior life of any of its female characters. Women in this film, apart from Lindsay Duncan's pleasingly acerbic theater critic, are there to fuck you or forgive you. Ambiguity can add layers of meaning, or it can render something a meaningless fever dream, and *Birdman* for me falls squarely in the latter category. Give me instead the full-throttle, emotional Pollock painting that is the Argentinian film **Wild Tales**, a sixth of which has more guts and grace than the whole of *Birdman*.

Tom Salinsky: What seemed so dazzling and inventive a half-dozen years ago now sometimes seems indulgent and male-gaze-y. Post #MeToo, it's difficult to see such obnoxious characters get critiqued so little. And it's not exactly a thin year once you look outside the Best Picture nominees and the top ten list, with the amazing *Force Majeure*, the terrifying *Nightcrawler*, the effervescent *Paddington*, and the blackly funny *Calvary*. But the biggest tragedy of this year's Oscars is the overlooking of Ava DuVernay and David Oyelowo, director and star of **Selma**, a biopic that effortlessly balances the demands of plot, history, politics, and character and even makes writing new speeches for Martin Luther King Jr. to say (they couldn't get the rights) look easy.

2015: *Spotlight*

John Dorney: It's a solid, unshowy piece with a lot to commend it and vital, weighty subject matter that is certainly deserving of its place on the short list. But it's a compromise win, really, and the statuette should have gone to *Mad Max: Fury Road*, which is a remarkable, bravura piece of filmmaking, as thrilling to watch as it must have been insane to make. There is quite simply not another film like it.

Jessica Regan: I really appreciate the intent behind the somber telling of this sad and terrible story. They could have thrown in more bells and whistles, but the filmmakers and performers kept it simple in a manner that honors the survivors of sexual abuse at the hands of the clergy rather than exploits the shocking, scandalous elements of it. But my admiration doesn't amount to immersion, and it is a respectable choice but at the cost of a thrill ride that doesn't put a foot wrong. *Mad Max: Fury Road* is densely packed, with brilliantly physical performances—most notably from Charlize Theron and Nicholas Hoult—plus the production design of the decade and action sequences that catch your breath and blow your hair back.

Tom Salinsky: *Spotlight*'s decision to tell its story cleanly and without affect is to be commended, and it's certain that a more hysterical rendering of the facts would have been in no way an improvement. However, there are far more ambitious films being made this year, possibly none more so than George Miller's absolutely extraordinary *Mad Max: Fury Road*. The film that stuck with me the longest though, was Lenny Abrahamson's adaptation of Emma Donoghue's book *Room* (Donoghue also wrote the screenplay). At first, a thrilling tale of two tiny Davids facing an all-powerful Goliath, it becomes a meditation on how to return to normality after years of confinement and trauma. No wonder it resonated with me so strongly, watching it again in 2021.

2016: *Moonlight*

John Dorney: There are several good entries this year, but *Moonlight* is a cut above. A film that gets richer with every successive viewing, that manages to take a story from a niche world and render it universal, staying with you long after the credits roll. This movie is simply beautiful in every way and the only possible choice for the award. In fact, it's a strong contender for the best Best Picture of all.

Jessica Regan: The Academy got it right unquestionably, voting for the small film that could make a big difference to hearts and minds of all kinds, which makes the shambolic manner of its Best Picture bestowing so wrenching, the fumbling of this watershed moment such a gut punch. But *Moonlight*'s power speaks for itself. It was, is, and always will be the rightful winner.

Tom Salinsky: What at first struck me as lacking the traditional catharsis I was looking for turns out on a second viewing to be rich almost beyond measure, beautifully photographed and acted with clarity and simplicity. *Moonlight* is a remarkable film and a thoroughly deserving winner.

2017: *The Shape of Water*

John Dorney: Cards on the table—I adore ***The Shape of Water***. A richly told fairy tale feast for the eyes, there really is nothing else like it in cinema. The obvious beauty of the direction and cinematography is matched by a plot that deepens like water the further you go in. It's a solid year, with many other serious contenders for the crown, but in this case, I feel the Academy got it right.

Jessica Regan: I don't deny that *The Shape of Water* is a beguiling, grown-up fairy tale that can certainly claim to be original and full of artistry. Sally Hawkins inhabits the character and Guillermo del Toro's world with a charming conviction. But French film ***Heal the Living*** was the standout cinematic offering for me from 2017. It looks at the fragility and force of our being, and I don't know why more people weren't hailing this as the film of the year. It has the magic of a fairy tale, if that's what you're after, but using medical science as the diving board into the extraordinary. Sure, a sexy fish-man is cool—but have you ever considered that someone could potentially put their hands into your chest cavity and massage your heart to keep you alive?

Tom Salinsky: There's much to savor in *The Shape of Water*, and I love that the Academy is willing to give its highest honor to something so authored, individual, and strange. But as soon as the thought entered my head—hang on, isn't all of this a bit silly?—the edifice started to crumble, and some of the social commentary is a bit on the nose.

Among a slew of other interesting films this year, including the delightful *Lady Bird* and the innovative *Dunkirk*, it was Jordan Peele's debut **Get Out** that knocked me sideways. An Academy that voted for *The Shape of Water* could have voted for *Get Out*, and I'm disappointed that they didn't.

2018: *Green Book*

John Dorney: *Green Book* never really wanted all this attention. Is it a great film? No. But it's perfectly tolerable for a movie about intolerance and would probably evoke very little feeling either way without Oscar success as a weight around its neck. Truth be told, of the nominees this year, very few hit the highest tiers, with *Roma* the only one that's truly outstanding, even though *BlacKkKlansman* and *The Favourite* come close. But for being a beautiful, pure, little diamond that was somehow overlooked, I'm going to give the Oscar to **Eighth Grade**, which is a tiny treat.

    Jessica Regan: Look, I'm not going to kick a corpse. *Green Book*'s moment in the sun was brief and outlived by the ignominy it suffered upon closer analysis, and with no disrespect to the good but misplaced intentions of those who made it, I think that is fair. Painfully and poignantly, Spike Lee's **BlacKkKlansman** is terrific! Fabulously filmed, brilliantly acted, edifying, and entertaining, it's everything you could want from a Best Picture winner! Redemption for the Academy over the *Driving Miss Daisy* debacle of 1989 was there for the taking, they had a shot at being the hero in their own story, but maddeningly they doubled down.

    Tom Salinsky: *Green Book* is pretty thin gruel, even by the standards of crowd-pleasing Oscar bait of the twenty-first century. Wonderful films like *Can You Ever Forgive Me*, *If Beale Street Could Talk*, *Three Identical Strangers*, *Eighth Grade*, and *Sorry to Bother You* all found themselves largely or completely shut out of the list. But I can't be too grumpy because as well as the defiantly quirky *The Favourite* getting ten nominations, Alfonso Cuarón's miraculous **Roma** won three awards, including Best Foreign Language Film and Best Director. This delicate, confronting, authentic, stylized, colorful, monochrome masterpiece might be my favorite film of the last ten years. There's nothing else quite like it.

2019: *Parasite*

John Dorney: Historical significance aside, *Parasite* is still a magnificent film and a truly deserving winner of the Best Picture Oscar. A complex, dark film that's often funnier than you remember and is always keen to surprise, flitting back and forth between genres with an ease other films can only dream of. Its victory at the Academy Awards was its final twist, but as with the best movie endings, it was utterly the right and correct thing to happen.

Jessica Regan: After the ridiculous comes the sublime. Not only is this the best film of the year, but I also believe it to be the number one Best Picture winner of the twenty-first century. *Parasite* is a satire, a soap opera, an indie family drama, a state-of-the-world story, a thriller, and a gothic fairy tale. The poorer the character, the closer to the ground they go, with the wealthy Park family gliding past—or sometimes literally walking over—their employees, who always seem to be squatting, stooping, or crawling. Utilizing distinctive kinetic, spatial, and aural vocabularies to conduct our attention so precisely but not obviously, it is little wonder Bong Joon Ho's work transcended any potential limitations of subtitling to become a welcome and longed-for part of Oscar history.

Tom Salinsky: At the time, Sam Mendes's *1917* was my personal favorite of the Best Picture nominees—using the one-shot constraint to achieve precisely the opposite effect of *Birdman*. But over the following year, it was Bong Joon Ho's film that stuck in my head—and rewatching it in 2021, I can see why. Told with miraculous economy by a stellar cast, it expertly threads the needle of its ever-shifting tone and genre without ever feeling forced or uneven. Thrilling, funny, satirical, terrifying, poignant, and wonderfully observed, *Parasite* is clearly the film of the year.

AFTERWORD

We ended up writing this book during very strange times. While the ninety-second Academy Awards was occupying the familiar stage of the Dolby Theater and *Parasite* was breaking all sorts of records, there had already been confirmed cases of a novel coronavirus in various countries, including America, Australia, Malaysia, Canada, and Nepal. In fact, the World Health Organization declared a state of emergency on 31 January—not that anyone paid any attention.

But in mid-March 2020, suddenly, everybody appreciated the dire situation we were in. Urgent action was needed, and it was taken. Lockdown orders swept the globe, and the three of us found ourselves struggling to complete our podcast marathon via Zoom, Netflix, and other devices. Webcams sold out on Amazon. In some parts of the world, supermarket shelves were almost bare. We were unable to see our families and friends. We were working from home and staying indoors.

It would all be over by the summer. It would all be over by the autumn. It would all be over by Christmas. Blockbuster movies had their release dates pushed back. *Tenet* tempted a few people out to the cinemas but not enough. Disney+ released *Hamilton* years earlier than its creators ever intended. HBO Max brought us *Zack Snyder's Justice League*. The James Bond film scheduled for April 2020 was delayed and at the time of writing still has not been released. The dividing line between TV and cinema was blurred yet further. Even the Oscars relaxed its rules about films needing to debut in cinemas in LA County to be eligible.

When the ninety-third Academy Awards finally happened, more than two months later than planned, and as we were putting the finishing touches to this book, they were unlike any we ever remembered watching. Leading a team of producers, Steven Soderbergh picked LA's Union Station as the central "hub," forbade any Zoom speeches from winners' homes, and put the focus on personal stories about who the nominees were. The stripped-down running order with no silly set pieces (or almost none), no performances of nominated songs, and no honorary awards to give out meant that there was no time limit on speeches, which the three of us appreciated, even if some winners ended up rambling just a little.

It looks like Soderbergh and company bet everything on the late Chadwick Boseman winning for his performance in *Ma Rainey's Black Bottom*—to the extent that they rearranged the running order and had Best Picture (which had traditionally been the last award of the night since 1948) followed by Best Actress and Best Actor. When the actual winner was an absent Anthony Hopkins, asleep at home in Wales, the event finished with a whimper rather than a roar.

But what was obvious just from the nominations is that more variety of styles, approaches, stories, and backgrounds had been given prominence at this event than ever before. From hymns to old Hollywood to quiet family dramas to fizzing feminist fantasies to powerful slices of human rights history to desperate stories of loss and isolation—there was a breadth and a scope to this crop of films that felt genuinely new.

Not to mention that the all-white quota of acting nominees and the all-male quota of directing nominees, which had been in place for so many years, had apparently been lifted at last. *Nomadland* became the ninety-third winner of Best Picture and Chloé Zhao, one of two—yes two!—female directors to be nominated, won Best Director. In fact, David Fincher was the only white American man nominated in this category, and although his film *Mank* had a big lead in nominations, it won only for its cinematography and its production design.

To be clear, rewarding filmmakers who don't look or sound like David Fincher is not an end in itself. But reviewing ninety-plus years of cinema oriented around Hollywood, it becomes clear that for decades, a great many stories and a great many points of view have been systematically shut out of the industry's biggest night. It's just possible that this might be changing, and that's exciting.

Of course, we've been here before. Halle Berry's win in 2001 was thought to be the beginning of something new, but twenty years later, she remains the only woman of color ever to win Best Actress. As Spike Lee (whose film *Da 5 Bloods* was almost completely overlooked this year) told the *New York Times* after the seventy-fourth Oscars,

> It's easy for Hollywood to pat itself on the back and to say, "Oh, that should satisfy them, that should keep them quiet for a while." But the same jubilation that people feel now, people were also probably feeling nearly 40 years ago in the aftermath of Sidney Poitier winning the first lead Oscar for a Black actor. I'm optimistic, but let's hope there's not another 40-year drought.

Whatever the next year holds, one thing is for certain: We will still be watching. Pass the popcorn.

ACKNOWLEDGMENTS

Our podcast has been a labor of love, and we're hugely grateful to any number of people who came on the journey with us. First must be Deborah Frances-White, who suffered her flat becoming a radio studio and screening room, as well as three-plus years of having the television monopolized by films of a bygone era. Her unswerving support and promotion of the podcast is also something we're deeply grateful for. Likewise, Natasha Jenkins and Flavia Fraser-Cannon put up with seemingly endless remote recording sessions during 2020 and beyond.

Others who helped make the podcast what it is include Jon Monkhouse, whose graphics adorned every episode; Chris Sharp and Grundy Le Zimbra, who advised us on what gear we would need; our amazing Patreon supporters, notably Jonquil Coy and James Murray; and our favorite fan on Twitter, @GurneySlade, whose film-of-the-year choices were always enlightening and never predictable.

We were delighted to welcome some marvelous guests on the podcast, all of whom brightened their episodes with their insight, charm, and good humor. Warm thanks go to Julian Simpson, David K. Barnes, Nat Luurtsema, Yasmine Akram, Garrett Millerick, Joy Wilkinson, Tish Potter, Kiri Pritchard-McLean, Sarah Bennetto, Kobi Omenaka, Felicity Ward, Phill Jupitus, Syrus Lowe, Natalie Bochenski, Dan Beeston, Helen O'Hara, Sam Bain, Matheus Carvalho, Ned Sedgwick, and Thom Tuck—who set our fiendishly hard annual Christmas Quizzes.

And although these were curtailed by the 2020 coronavirus pandemic, we were able to stage some live recordings, so thanks to Kings Place, the Cinema Museum, and the Curzon Victoria for all their help with those and to Ben Blacker, who arranged a virtual victory lap for us.

This book would not have happened without the tireless efforts of our amazing literary agent, Victoria Hobbs, at A. M. Heath and the fantastic team at Rowman & Littlefield, who were a joy to work with. Thanks to James Harkin for his eleventh-hour fact-finding. And extra thanks to Joy Wilkinson, who not only guested on the podcast but also was instrumental in helping us to figure out the structure of the book version.

Last, if you downloaded the podcast, told a friend about it, sent us an e-mail, or posted on our Facebook group, thank you for coming on this journey with us. And see you at the next Oscars.

As well as the Academy, Jessica would like to thank: Sisters Claire and Jenny, who support me in all I do. Ailish, Fiona, Rachel, Maeve, Sarah, and Aideen—our lifelong friendship is the great prize of my life. My four pillars, Siobhán, Simon, Maggie, and Maeve H. Actual angels Aileen and Aoibheann. My London sisters, Jeany, Lu, Milly, and Laura. My captains, Bobby, Polly, and Catrin. My honorary brother, Michael Benz. And Deborah Frances-White, who believes in her friends with a fierceness that carries us.

APPENDIX

Our Cinematic Journey

As noted, for the podcast, we watched these films in a completely random order. Here's how ninety-two years of film history worked out for us.

1928: *Wings* (episode 69, 9 September 2020)

1929: *The Broadway Melody* (episode 25, 2 January 2019)

1930: *All Quiet on the Western Front* (episode 2, 7 February 2018)

1931: *Cimarron* (episode 24, 19 December 2018)

1932: *Grand Hotel* (episode 14, 1 August 2018)

1933: *Cavalcade* (episode 56, 11 March 2020)

1934: *It Happened One Night* (episode 20, with special guest Nat Luurtsema, 24 October 2018)

1935: *Mutiny on the Bounty* (episode 75, 2 December 2020)

1936: *The Great Ziegfeld* (episode 27, 30 January 2019)

1937: *The Life of Emile Zola* (episode 64, 1 July 2020)

1938: *You Can't Take It with You* (episode 81, with special guest Sam Bain, 24 February 2021)

1939: *Gone with the Wind* (episode 29, 6 March 2019)

1940: *Rebecca* (episode 45, live from the London Podcast Festival, 9 October 2019)

1941: *How Green Was My Valley* (episode 60, 6 May 2020)

1942: *Mrs. Miniver* (episode 78, with special guest Helen O'Hara, 13 January 2021)

1943: *Casablanca* (episode 28, live from the Cinema Museum with special guest Deborah Frances-White, 13 February 2019)

1944: *Going My Way* (episode 66, 29 July 2020)

1945: *The Lost Weekend* (episode 37, 19 June 2019)

1946: *The Best Years of Our Lives* (episode 43, 11 September 2019)

1947: *Gentleman's Agreement* (episode 67, 12 August 2020)

1948: *Hamlet* (episode 52, 15 January 2020)

1949: *All the King's Men* (episode 54, 12 February 2020)

1950: *All about Eve* (episode 26, with special guest Yasmine Akram, 16 January 2019)

1951: *An American in Paris* (episode 83, with special guest Matheus Carvalho, 24 March 2021)

1952: *The Greatest Show on Earth* (episode 48, 20 November 2019)

1953: *From Here to Eternity* (episode 4, 14 March 2018)

1954: *On the Waterfront* (episode 23, 5 December 2018)

1955: *Marty* (episode 84, 7 April 2021)

1956: *Around the World in 80 Days* (episode 17, with special guest David K. Barnes, 12 September 2018)

1957: *The Bridge on the River Kwai* (episode 85, with special guest Ned Sedgwick, 21 April 2021)

1958: *Gigi* (episode 47, with special guest Kiri Pritchard-McLean, 6 November 2019)

1959: *Ben-Hur* (episode 6, 11 April 2018)

1960: *The Apartment* (episode 57, 25 March 2020)

1961: *West Side Story* (episode 10, 6 June 2018)

1962: *Lawrence of Arabia* (episode 9, 23 May 2018)

1963: *Tom Jones* (episode 65, with special guest patron James Murray, 15 July 2020)

1964: *My Fair Lady* (episode 71, 7 October 2020)

1965: *The Sound of Music* (episode 19, 10 October 2018)

1966: *A Man for All Seasons* (episode 32, with special guest Garrett Millerick, 10 April 2019)

1967: *In the Heat of the Night* (episode 16, 29 August 2018)

1968: *Oliver!* (episode 59, 22 April 2020)

1969: *Midnight Cowboy* (episode 44, 25 September 2019)

1970: *Patton* (episode 15, 15 August 2018)

1971: *The French Connection* (episode 39, 17 July 2019)

1972: *The Godfather* (episode 22, 22 November 2018)

1973: *The Sting* (episode 1, 24 January 2018)

1974: *The Godfather Part II* (episode 73, with special guest Phill Jupitus, 4 November 2020)

1975: *One Flew over the Cuckoo's Nest* (episode 50, 18 December 2019)

1976: *Rocky* (episode 72, 21 October 2020)

1977: *Annie Hall* (episode 18, live from the London Podcast Festival, 26 September 2018)

1978: *The Deer Hunter* (episode 61, 20 May 2020)

1979: *Kramer vs. Kramer* (episode 21, 7 November 2018)

1980: *Ordinary People* (episode 46, 23 October 2019)

1981: *Chariots of Fire* (episode 36, with special guest Deborah Frances-White, 5 June 2019)

1982: *Gandhi* (episode 88, 2 June 2021)

1983: *Terms of Endearment* (episode 8, 9 May 2018)

1984: *Amadeus* (episode 62, 3 June 2020)

1985: *Out of Africa* (episode 63, with special guest Deborah Frances-White, 17 June 2020)

1986: *Platoon* (episode 35, 22 May 2019)

1987: *The Last Emperor* (episode 51, 1 January 2020)

1988: *Rain Man* (episode 41, 14 August 2019)

1989: *Driving Miss Daisy* (episode 68, 26 August 2020)

1990: *Dances with Wolves* (episode 33, 24 April 2019)

1991: *The Silence of the Lambs* (episode 11, 20 June 2018)

1992: *Unforgiven* (episode 31, 3 April 2019)

1993: *Schindler's List* (episode 13, with special guest Julian Simpson, 18 July 2018)

1994: *Forrest Gump* (episode 34, with special guest Joy Wilkinson, 8 May 2019)

1995: *Braveheart* (episode 49, 4 December 2019)

1996: *The English Patient* (episode 30, 20 March 2019)

1997: *Titanic* (episode 77, with special guests Natalie Bochenski and Dan Beeston, 30 December 2020)

1998: *Shakespeare in Love* (episode 42, with special guest Tish Potter, 28 August 2019)

1999: *American Beauty* (episode 5, with special guest Deborah Frances-White, 28 March 2018)

2000: *Gladiator* (episode 3, 21 February 2018)

2001: *A Beautiful Mind* (episode 89, with special guest Thom Tuck,
16 June 2021)

2002: *Chicago* (episode 38, 3 July 2019)

2003: *The Lord of the Rings: The Return of the King* (episode 70,
with special guest Felicity Ward, 23 September 2020)

2004: *Million Dollar Baby* (episode 80, 10 February 2021)

2005: *Crash* (episode 12, 4 July 2018)

2006: *The Departed* (episode 7, 25 April 2018)

2007: *No Country for Old Men* (episode 87, 19 May 2021)

2008: *Slumdog Millionaire* (episode 91, 14 July 2021)

2009: *The Hurt Locker* (episode 76, 16 December 2020)

2010: *The King's Speech* (episode 92, 28 July 2021)

2011: *The Artist* (episode 40, 31 July 2019)

2012: *Argo* (episode 55, 26 February 2020)

2013: *12 Years a Slave* (episode 82, 10 March 2021)

2014: *Birdman or (The Unexpected Virtue of Ignorance)* (episode 79,
27 January 2021)

2015: *Spotlight* (episode 90, 30 June 2021)

2016: *Moonlight* (episode 74, 18 November 2020)

2017: *The Shape of Water* (episode 53, with special guest Sarah
Bennetto, 29 January 2020)

2018: *Green Book* (episode 58, with special guest Kobe Omenaka, 8
April 2020)

2019: *Parasite* (episode 86, 5 May 2021)

BIBLIOGRAPHY

AFI Catalog. *"Amadeus* (1984)." Accessed 8 August 2021. https://catalog.afi.com/Film/ 56996-AMADEUS.

———. *"The French Connection* (1971)." Accessed 8 August 2021. https://catalog.afi.com/ Film/53919-THE-FRENCHCONNECTION.

———. *"The Lord of the Rings: The Return of the King* (2003)." Accessed 8 August 2021. https://catalog.afi.com/Film/54279-THE-LORDOFTHERINGSTHERETURN OFTHEKING.

———. *"On the Waterfront* (1954)." Accessed 8 August 2021. https://catalog.afi.com/ Catalog/moviedetails/51286.

———. *"Rebecca* (1940)." Accessed 8 August 2021. https://catalog.afi.com/Catalog/ moviedetails/5132.

———. *"The Sound of Music* (1965)." Accessed 8 August 2021. https://catalog.afi.com/Film/ 22305-THE-SOUNDOFMUSIC.

Associated Press. "John M. Saunders Suicide in Florida." *New York Times*, 12 March 1940.

Barber, Nicholas. "Film in the 2010s: The Decade That Changed Cinema Forever." BBC Culture. 6 December 2019. https://www.bbc.com/culture/article/20191205-film-in-the-2010s-the-decade-that-changed-cinema-forever.

Bearman, Joshua. "How the CIA Used a Fake Sci-Fi Flick to Rescue Americans from Tehran." *Wired*, 24 April 2007.

Be Kind Rewind. "How Barbra Streisand and Katharine Hepburn Tied for Best Actress." 27 October 2018. Video, 15:21. https://www.youtube.com/watch?v=r5ly_iAmEOE.

Benson, Michael. *Space Odyssey: Stanley Kubrick, Arthur C. Clarke, and the Making of a Masterpiece*. Simon & Schuster, 2018.

Bona, Damien. *Inside Oscar 2*. Ballantine Books, 2002.

Borshukov, George, Dan Piponi, Oystein Larsen, J. P. Lewis, and Christina Tempelaar-Lietz. "Universal Capture: Image-Based Facial Animation for 'The Matrix Reloaded.'" *ACM Digital Library* (July 2006).

Broverman, Neal. "Violent Gay Protests at the Oscars: Could It Happen Again?" *Advocate*, 27 February 2016. https://www.advocate.com/arts-entertainment/2016/2/27/violent-gay-protests-oscars-could-it-happen-again.

Brown, Garrett. Garrett Brown: Filmmaker and Inventor. Accessed 9 August 2021. https:// www.garrettcam.com.

Brown, Peter H., and Jim Pinkston. *Oscar Dearest: Six Decades of Scandal, Politics, and Greed behind Hollywood's Academy Awards*. HarperCollins, 1988.

Brownlow, Kevin, and David Gill, dirs. *Buster Keaton: A Hard Act to Follow*. Thames Television, 1987.

Bryson, Bill. *One Summer: America 1927*. Black Swan, 2014.

Byrge, Duane, and Robert Milton Miller. *The Screwball Comedy Films: A History and Filmography, 1934–1942*. McFarland, 2001.

Callow, Simon. *Orson Welles*. Vol. 1, *The Road to Xanadu*. Jonathan Cape, 1995.

Capra, Frank. *The Name above the Title: An Autobiography*. Da Capo Press, 1971.

Child, Ben. "Spike Lee to Boycott the 2016 Oscars over Lack of Nominee Diversity." *Guardian*, 18 January 2016. https://www.theguardian.com/film/2016/jan/18/spike-lee-boycott-2016-oscars-nominations-academy-awards-lack-of-diversity.

Ciccotello, Len, ed. *Argo: Absolute Authenticity*. Warner Home Video, 2013.

Clubb, Issa, prod. *I'm Standin' over Here Now*. Criterion Collection, 2013.

Cork, John, dir. *The Making of Rebecca*. Cloverland Productions, 2008.

Crosby, Gary, and Ross Firestone. *Going My Own Way*. Doubleday, 1983.

Crowe, Cameron. *Conversations with Wilder*. Faber & Faber, 2000.

Dawn, Randee. "Frankly, My Dear, I Don't Give a Straw: The Secret History of 'Gone with the Wind's' Curse." *Today*. 15 December 2014. https://www.today.com/popculture/frankly-my-dear-i-dont-give-straw-gone-winds-secret-1D80341776.

Doherty, Thomas. *Hollywood's Censor: Joseph I. Breen and the Production Code Administration*. Columbia University Press, 2007.

Edwards, Colin. "Wings or—The Ecstasy of Flight?" Medium. 26 January 2021. https://colinedwards.medium.com/wings-or-the-ecstasy-of-flight-92c61da15981.

Evans, Guy, dir. *Secret Voices of Hollywood*. RDF Television, BBC Four, 2013.

Eyman, Scott. *The Speed of Sound: Hollywood and the Talkie Revolution, 1926–1930*. Simon & Schuster, 1997.

Farrow, Ronan. *Catch and Kill: Lies, Spies, and a Conspiracy to Protect Predators*. Fleet, 2019.

Feinberg, Scott. "'They Got the Wrong Envelope!': The Oral History of Oscar's Epic Best Picture Fiasco." *Hollywood Reporter*. 29 February 2018. https://www.hollywoodreporter.com/movies/movie-features/they-got-wrong-envelope-oral-history-oscars-epic-best-picture-fiasco-1087829/.

Finler, Joel W. *The Hollywood Story: Everything You Always Wanted to Know about the American Movie Business but Didn't Know Where to Look*. 3rd ed. Wallflower Press, 2003.

Fisher, David. "The British Film Import Duty 1947–48." Terra Media. 8 June 2004. https://www.terramedia.co.uk/reference/law/british_film_import_duty.htm.

Flinn, Caryl. *The Sound of Music*. British Film Institute, 2015.

Fonseca, Mariana. "Maria Schneider Already Called the *Last Tango in Paris* Scene Rape—Why Did We Only Listen When Bernardo Bertolucci Admitted It?" Independent. 4 December 2016. https://www.independent.co.uk/voices/last-tango-paris-maria-schneider-marlon-brando-bertolucci-director-butter-anal-rape-scene-male-director-a7455166.html.

Fretts, Bruce. "Oscar Rewind: The Acceptance Speech That Spawned Another Movie." *New York Times*, 8 February 2019.

Geldzahler, Henry. "Marnie/One Potato, Two Potato." *Vogue*, 15 August 1964.

Gill, David, and Kevin Brownlow, dirs. *Harold Lloyd: The Third Genius*. Thames Television, 1989.

Greene, Naomi. *The French New Wave—A New Look*. Wallflower Press, 2007.

Harmetz, Aljean. *The Making of Casablanca: Bogart, Bergman, and World War II*. Hyperion, 2002.

———. *On the Road to Tara: The Making of Gone with the Wind*. Harry N. Abrams, 1996.

Haver, Ronald. *David O. Selznick's Hollywood*. Outlet, 1985.

Hawks, Howard, and Joseph McBride, eds. *Hawks on Hawks*. University of California Press, 1982.

Higgins, Bill. "The Odd Hollywood History behind Ben Affleck's *Argo*.'" *Hollywood Reporter*, 26 September 2012.

Hillier, Jim, ed. *Cahiers Du Cinema: New Wave, New Cinema, Re-evaluating Hollywood*. Harvard University Press, 1992.

Hinton, David, dir. *The Making of a Legend: Gone with the Wind*. MGM/UA Home Entertainment, 1988.

Hirsch, Julia Antopol. *The Sound of Music: The Making of America's Favorite Movie*. Chicago Review Press, 2018.

Hofler, Robert. "The Worst Oscars Ever." *Los Angeles Magazine*, 1 March 2020. https://www.lamag.com/longform/snow-job/.

Holden, Anthony. *Behind the Oscar*. Simon & Schuster, 1993.

Holpuch, Amanda. "Sony Email Hack: What We've Learned about Greed, Racism, and Sexism." *Guardian*, 15 December 2014.

Jackson, Peter, dir. *The Lord of the Rings: The Appendices*. Wingnut Films, 2004.

Jakab, Peter. "The First Significant Anti-War Movie." Smithsonian Air and Space Museum. 23 May 2017. https://airandspace.si.edu/stories/editorial/first-significant-anti-war-movie.

Jersey, Bill, dir. *The Making of Amadeus*. Quest Productions, 2002.

Johnson, Keith, writer. *Making the Connection: Untold Stories of 'The French Connection.'* Fox Movie Channel, 2001.

Jones, Owen. "Sam Smith's Oscar Faux Pas Shows LGBT People Must Learn Their History." *Guardian*, 1 March 2016.

Kael, Pauline. *1001 Nights at the Movies*. Marion Boyars, 1993.

———. *Raising Kane*. Marion Boyars, 1996.

Kantor, Loren. "The Making of *The French Connection*." Medium. 8 October 2020. https://medium.com/picture-palace/the-making-of-the-french-connection-7425206a75b1.

Karney, Robyn, ed. *Chronicle of the Cinema*. Dorling Kindersley, 1996.

Kermode, Mark, writer. *The Poughkeepsie Shuffle: Tracing 'The French Connection.'* BBC, 2000.

King, Tim, dir. *Wings: Grandeur in the Sky*. King Media Services, 2012.

Kinn, Gail. *The Academy Awards: The Complete Unofficial History*. Black Dog & Leventhal, 2014.

Knelman, Martin. "Ben Affleck Changes *Argo* postscript for Ken Taylor." *Toronto Star*, 19 September 2012. https://www.thestar.com/entertainment/2012/09/19/ben_affleck_changes_argo_postscript_for_ken_taylor.html.

Koch, Hawk, and Molly Jordan. *Magic Time: My Life in Hollywood*. Post Hill Press, 2019.

Koppes, Clayton R., Gregory D Black. *Hollywood Goes to War: How Politics, Profits and Propaganda Shaped World War Two*. Barbara Ward, 1988.

Lambert, Gavin. "The Making of *Gone with the Wind* (Part I)." *Atlantic*, February 1973.

Landau, Jon, prod. *Titanic's Production: Behind the Scenes*. Fox Home Video, 2004.

Lebowitz, Shana. "The Way Walt Disney Inspired His Team to Make *Snow White* Reveals His Creative Genius—and Insane Perfectionism." *Business Insider Australia*, 2015.

Leff, Leonard J. *Hitchcock and Selznick: The Rich and Strange Collaboration of Alfred Hitchcock and David O. Selznick in Hollywood*. Grove Press, 1987.

Levy, Emanuel. *All about Oscar: The History and Politics of the Academy Awards*. Continuum, 2003.

Lew, Julie. "Gay Groups Protest a Film Script." *New York Times*, 4 May 1991.

Lyman, Rick. "Hollywood Questions the Meaning of Its Historic Oscar Night." *New York Times*, 26 March 2002. https://www.nytimes.com/2002/03/26/us/hollywood-questions-the-meaning-of-its-historic-oscar-night.html.

Lyons, Margaret. "Why Seth MacFarlane's Misogyny Matters." *Vulture*, 25 February 2013. https://www.vulture.com/2013/02/why-seth-macfarlanes-misogyny-matters.html.

Macavinia, Courteney. "Digital Actors in Rings Can Think." *Wired*, December 2002.

Matessino, Michael, dir. *The Sound of Music: From Fact to Phenomenon*. Fox Video, 1994.

Mogensen, Jackie Flynn. "The Incredible True Story of the Oscar Everyone Thought Had Literally Been Stolen." *Mother Jones*, 2 March 2018. https://www.motherjones.com/media/2018/03/the-incredible-true-story-of-the-oscar-everyone-thought-had-literally-been-stolen/.

Mooring, William H. *Kinematograph Weekly*, 10 January 1946.

Morton, Ray. *Music on Film: Amadeus*. Limelight, 2011.

Nash Information Services. "Highest Grossing Stars of 2018 at the Domestic Box Office." *The Numbers*. Accessed 2 September 2021. https://www.the-numbers.com/box-office-star-records/domestic/yearly-acting/highest-grossing-2018-stars.

Nathan, Sara, and Liz Thomas. "'I Had a Crush on Captain von Trapp,' Admits the Actress Who Played His Daughter Liesl as *The Sound of Music* Cast Reunite on *Oprah*." Mail Online. 29 October 2010. https://www.dailymail.co.uk/tvshowbiz/article-1324749/Sound-Of-Music-reunion-Liesl-tells-Oprah-I-crush-Captain-von-Trapp.html.

Oulahan, Richard. "Low Budget Realism, Warts and All." *Life*, 24 April 1964.

Parisi, Paula. *Titanic and the Making of James Cameron*. Newmarket, 1998.

Peary, Danny. *Alternate Oscars*. Simon & Schuster, 1993.

Perry, Kevin E. G. "Tracing France's History in the Heroin Trade." Vice. 28 May 2015. https://www.vice.com/en/article/vdxegj/french-connection-kevin-perry-marseille.

Rich, Katey. "Titanic's Greatest Unsolved Mystery Involves a Conga Line, PCP, and an Unidentified Chowder." *Vanity Fair*, 19 December 2017. https://www.vanityfair.com/hollywood/2017/12/titanic-pcp-chowder.

Richards, John, prod. *Rescued from Tehran: We Were There*. Warner Home Video, 2013.

Robinson, David. *World Cinema 1895–1980*. Metheun Eyre, 1981.

Robinson, Tasha. "Milos Forman." AV Club. 24 April 2002. https://www.avclub.com/milos-forman-1798208216.

Rutigliano, Olivia. "On the Trail of Hollywood's Stolen Oscars." Politics/Letters. 24 April 2016. http://quarterly.politicsslashletters.org/stolen-oscars/.

Safire, William. "On Language: The Bloopie Awards." *New York Times Magazine*, 6 November 1994.

Severo, Richard. "Anthony Devincenzo, a Boss on Docks Portrayed in Novel." *New York Times*, 23 November 1983.

Shone, Tom. *Tarantino: A Retrospective*. Grund, 2017.

Sibley, Brian. *Peter Jackson: A Film-maker's Journey*. HarperCollins, 2006.

Sims, David. "The Magic of Titanic's Ending, 20 Years Later." *Atlantic*, 2017.

Smith, Adam. "Second Chance for Fallen Maverick." *Guardian*, 23 July 2000. https://www.theguardian.com/film/2000/jul/23/features.

Spoto, Donald. *The Dark Side of Genius: The Life of Alfred Hitchcock*. Little, Brown, 1983.

Stenn, David. *Clara Bow: Runnin' Wild*. Cooper Square Press, 2000.

Sweet, Matthew. "Milos Forman: The Envy and the Ecstasy." *Independent*, 24 January 2014.

———. *Shepperton Babylon*. Faber & Faber, 2006.

Thomas, Frank, and Ollie Johnston. *The Illusion of Life: Disney Animation*. Hyperion, 1997.

Thomson, David. *The Big Screen: The Story of the Movies and What They Did to Us*. Allen Lane, 2012.

———. *Have You Seen . . . ?* Penguin, 2010.

Tresgot, Annie, dir. *Elia Kazan: An Outsider*. Argos Films, 1982.

Truffaut, Francois. *Hitchcock*. Gallimard, 1993.

Turner, George E., and Orville Goldner. *The Making of* King Kong. Ballantine Books, 1975.

Turner Classic Movies. *Gone with the Wind*. https://web.archive.org/web/20110917212714/http://www.tcm.com/tcmdb/title/414427/Gone-With-the-Wind/notes.html.

Ugwu, Reggie. "The Hashtag That Changed the Oscars: An Oral History." *New York Times*, 6 February 2020.

Vieira, Mark A. *Irving Thalberg: Boy Wonder to Producer Prince*. University of California Press, 2009.

Vizzard, Jack. *See No Evil: Life inside a Hollywood Censor*. Simon & Schuster, 1970.

Wakelin Michael. *J. Arthur Rank: The Man behind the Gong*. Lion Books, 1996.

Wakeman, Gregory. "*The Philadelphia Story*: How an 80-Year-Old Comedy Resonates." BBC Culture. 20 January 2021. https://www.bbc.com/culture/article/20210120-the-philadelphia-story-how-an-80-year-old-comedy-resonates.

Weinraub, Bernard. "A Day to Demonstrate Affection for the Stars and Some Dismay." *New York Times*, 31 March 1992.

———. "Play a Hooker and Win an Oscar." *New York Times*, 20 February 1996.

Wellman, William A. *A Short Time for Insanity*. Hawthorn, 1974.

Whipp, Glen. "Critics Fear Effects of 10 Best Pic Noms." *Variety*, 30 October 2009. https://variety.com/2009/film/awards/critics-fear-effects-of-10-best-pic-noms-1118010642/.

————. "Led Zeppelin Loosens Its Grip on Using Its Music in Films." *Los Angeles Times*, 3 December 2012.

Wiley, Mason, and Damien Bona. *Inside Oscar: The Unofficial History of the Academy Awards*. 10th anniversary ed. Edited by Gail MacColl. Ballantine Books, 1996.

INDEX

ABOUT THE AUTHORS

John Dorney is an actor and a writer. He's acted at the National Theatre, had a script on at the Royal Court Theatre, and won the BBC's Sketch Factor and Show Me the Funny talent searches. He's also written more than one hundred audio dramas for Big Finish Productions, for which he's won two Scribe Awards, an Audie, and a BBC Audio Drama Awards. He sometimes takes a weekend off.

Jessica Regan is an Irish actor and writer based in London, where she can be usually found in the cinema on her own. She has performed at the National Theatre and in the West End and appeared in multiple television shows, mostly for the BBC. She is a prolific audio artist and likes using her voice to help people find theirs. She appeared on *Celebrity Mastermind* answering questions on the films of Quentin Tarantino. She did not win, but she did get a podcast and this book out of it so who's the real winner here?

Tom Salinsky is a writer, podcaster, communications coach, and improviser. As a founder member of London-based improvisation company the Spontaneity Shop, he cowrote *The Improv Handbook* (2008). As well as *Best Pick*, he is the producer of the award-winning podcast *The Guilty Feminist*. With Robert Khan, he is the author of five plays and several audio dramas for Big Finish. He's a cat person.